It's Off To The Match I Go
My Journey With The 'Gers

– DUNCAN WHITELAW –

An environmentally friendly book printed and bound in England by
www.printondemand-worldwide.com

Mixed Sources
Product group from well-managed
forests, and other controlled sources
www.fsc.org Cert no. TT-COC-002641
© 1996 Forest Stewardship Council
FSC

PEFC Certified
This product is
from sustainably
managed forests
and controlled
sources
PEFC
PEFC/16-33-415   www.pefc.org

This book is made entirely of chain-of-custody materials

www.fast-print.net/store.php

It's Off To The Match I Go
My Journey With The 'Gers

ISBN 978-178035-048-6

First published 2011 by
FASTPRINT PUBLISHING
Peterborough, England.

Scottish War Blinded

Scottish War Blinded is one of the key veterans' charities. Their aim is to provide assistance to members of the armed forces who have a significant visual impairment. In 2010 the charity took a big step forward by building the new Linburn Centre.

The new Linburn Centre accommodates up to thirty-five members daily and offers its services free of charge. There are a wide range of leisure, social and educational activities available, including arts, crafts, daily living skills, IT, physical fitness and of course a canteen where members can relax and socialise over a hot meal. The original facility was opened 1944, to provide retraining and vocational skills for service men and women blinded in the Second World War. Today Scottish War Blinded is supporting older people experiencing progressive blindness as well as giving support to those who have lost their sight in the Iraq and Afghanistan conflicts.

The Linburn Centre is situated in the West Lothian village of Wilkieston, on the A71, between Livingston and Edinburgh, and a place I pass every day going to and from my work. Having the germ of an idea about donating some of my book proceeds to charity, I decided to drop in, to see what the centre was all about. What I discovered was a group of people determined to improve their own quality of life, to gain as much independence as possible. The staff at the centre equally determined to help them towards that goal.

The men and women of the armed forces gave so much in the defence of our country, to protect, and maintain, our freedom and way of life. The least that we can do is to help them, in their hour of need. I'm pleased to say that I'll donate twenty percent of any proceeds from this book to the Scottish War Blinded and their Linburn Centre.

Acknowledgements

This book is respectfully dedicated to some people very important and close to me.

To my dad, the man who introduced me to the Rangers.

To my mother who put up with me for so many years.

To my wife, Jacqui, and sons, Graeme and Dale – for suffering all my tantrums and mood swings when my football team lose.

To Peter Dollan, John Niven and Gary Lynch; Good friends and true blue Rangers' men, who were taken far too young.

I'd also like to acknowledge the help of everyone at the Mitchell Library, a truly wonderful place that should be treasured by all in Glasgow.

Invaluable for checking facts and figures were following:

The magnificent Rangers results spreadsheet, produced and published online by "a Man called Horse".

The quite wonderful book, Rangers: The Complete Record, by Bob Ferrier and Robert McElroy.

Thanks also to Buddy Whitman, The World of Wonder, for the cover photograph.

Introduction

Football supporters, over the years, have garnered a pretty poor reputation, often regarded as anti-social yobs, or foul-mouthed hoodlums – and at times that reputation has been well deserved. Some supporters though, fare worse than others, and fans of Rangers Football Club seem to be particularly vilified, very often castigated en masse as nothing more than Neanderthal, knuckle-dragging, bigoted thugs. Well, I'm a Rangers fan and I'm none of the above! And neither, for that matter, are any of my friends or associates. It's true that we have a few rogues amongst our support, but show me a football club that doesn't! By and large Rangers' fans are good, honest, hard working people who love their team, nothing more and nothing less. We enjoy our own personal achievements, triumphs and relationships, just as we suffer pain, tragedy and disappointment – normal people, living normal lives.

In the following pages, I hope to show how I've grown as a person, and grown as football fan – the two sides of my life forever intertwining. I've tried, to the best of my ability, to ensure all the facts and figures quoted here are correct; everything else though comes from my own memory. My recollections may differ from others, but that's the beauty of football. Fifty thousand people can go to a game and all of them will see an incident differently. Was it a penalty? Was it a dive? Their opinion, of course, is often dependant on the colour of scarf being worn.

My scarf is red, white and blue, and this is my story – my journey with the 'Gers.

Chapter 1:
First Steps

Every other Saturdays my half day off,
And it's off to the match I go,
Happily we wander down the Copland Road,
Me and my wee pal Joe,
We love to see the lassies with their blue scarves on,
We love to hear the boys all roar,
But I don't have to tell you that the best of all,
We love to see the Rangers score.

L ike so many Rangers supporters, I was born that way. My dad was a Rangers man, so I suppose it was only natural that I should follow in his footsteps. In 1963 he took me to Ibrox for the first time, to see 'the Rangers'. I was five years old and remember absolutely nothing of the game. It must have been good though, because nearly fifty years later I'm still going.

My dad was a production manager with Singer, the sewing machine people, who had at the time a huge factory in my home town of Clydebank. He was successful at his job, and after a couple of promotions was given the opportunity to work abroad. It was an opportunity he enthusiastically grasped, working initially in Italy, before moving further afield. The result was financial stability for his family, but, on the down side, it meant that he was away for months, sometimes years on end. Because of that, my visits to Ibrox were few and far between.

In 1967 the family followed him abroad, when he took up the offer of a job in Singapore. We spent a couple of years there before moving to the Thai capital city, Bangkok. During these years I became a follower from afar, relying on the monthly bundle of newspapers we received from relatives back home in Scotland. I'd eagerly await the delivery of the Sunday Post and Sunday Mail, to find out the latest scores, to read the match reports and then, much to the annoyance of my parents, to immediately chop up those papers to fill the scrap books that I religiously maintained.

As time passed, the demands of education meant that once again my family were to be split up. My dad had been given a new job in Pakistan, and with no suitable schools in that country, I had to move back to Scotland with my mother and sisters. In 1970 I returned to Clydebank, my life as a Rangers supporter was about to take off.

I started at my new school, Clydebank High, but found it very difficult to settle. Having been abroad for over three years, everything seemed so strange, so different. Most days I'd come home from school and mope about the house, bored, complaining that I'd nothing to do. My mother was heartily sick of it, and arranged for me to visit an old primary school friend, David Ross. Anything, I think, to get me away from under her feet. I wasn't over-keen, but was persuaded when I found out that David went to see the Rangers, and with a home game due, I could go to Ibrox with him. That sounded good to me! So, on a fine October morning I made the thirty minute bus ride down to Yoker, little knowing that this short trip would be the start of a lifetime journey, following the fortunes of The Rangers.

Down at David's house I was introduced to what would become a well worn routine. His Mum made us beans on toast whilst we settled down in front of the old black and white television, to watch the football preview shows – The BBC's *Football Focus* and ITV's *On the Ball*. Both programmes lasted a half hour and both, irritatingly, were on at exactly the same time. With no remote control in those days we sat a couple of feet from the TV, switching backwards and forwards, from one channel to the other, cutting out the chat and watching the goals. Waiting for the final few minutes when they had the token Scottish feature. If we were lucky there would be a Rangers goal to cheer, perhaps even an interview with one of our players. The start of the horse racing then signalled our departure for the football.

David, already an Ibrox veteran was looking forward to the game but more important to him was getting a ticket for the following weeks League Cup Final, a keenly anticipated Old Firm match, and an opportunity for Rangers to lift their first trophy in nearly five years. I just wanted to get to a game; any Rangers game would do for me.

A bus journey took us to Merkland Street subway station, where I got my first whiff of the Glasgow Underground; a dank and musty aroma, not exactly pleasant, but strangely intoxicating. We were rattled and rocked under the River Clyde on a rickety old train carriage before emerging into the sunlight of Copland Road. A short walk then saw us, at last, at Ibrox Stadium. Rangers played Aberdeen that day – the attendance was 39,763 – and I was one of them!

A Colin Jackson own goal (how many of them was I to suffer in the coming years?) and a further strike from dumpy forward Joe Harper gave Aberdeen a 2–0 victory. It was a defeat, but I didn't mind too much. I'd loved the experience from start to finish, and wanted more. If the truth be told though, I didn't actually hear the final whistle as we had left the ground ten minutes early. Heavens sake, one game in and I was already a member of the Subway Loyal ... not really. Tickets for the aforementioned League Cup Final went on sale outside Ibrox at 5pm, and David wanted to ensure getting one. So along with thousands of others, we left early to queue up. David got his ticket. Was I jealous? You bet I was!

Seven days later the Old Firm squared up in the League Cup Final, David was on the Hampden terraces and I waited at home, nervously tuned into the radio, listening for news. These were the days before live televised games; even radio coverage was limited, the football authorities only allowing the second half to be broadcast. When I eventually got news from Hampden I was jumping for joy – Derek Johnstone, a sixteen year old boy, in only his third game for the club had scored and given Rangers a first half lead. I listened to the second half, with my stomach in knots, hoping for another goal, but mostly praying for the final whistle to sound. After a long forty five minutes, which felt like an eternity, it did, to signal victory!

I hadn't been at Hampden, but I was at Ibrox the following week to see Rangers play Airdrie. In a nice touch the visitors sportingly applauded the home team onto the park, and in return were given a sound thrashing! It was an enjoyable day's football: the 5–0 victory was great, and the fact that I got to see the League Cup as it was paraded round the ground just topped it all off perfectly.

I was hooked on the Ibrox experience, and in the following months I learned how to dodge my fare on the trains and buses, and how to double up going through the turnstiles. On a good day we could get over to Ibrox, into the game, and home again, without spending a penny. The only expense was a programme and copies of the Evening Times and Citizen; not for the news, but for the full colour poster that surrounded said paper. Those posters soon adorned my bedroom wall, gradually filling every available space. They were also the perfect size to cover my school books, giving me the opportunity to show off, to brag to all my school mates about how, I went to the games.

As Christmas approached, the New Year Old Firm game loomed ever closer. I really wanted to go, but I knew that it was a contentious fixture, and the chances of me being allowed to attend were somewhat remote. My mother had already made it crystal clear; she didn't want me going to ... that game. Resigned to missing out, my joy was therefore unconfined when I opened an envelope on Christmas day and two tickets for the New Year game fell out. My dad was home for the festive period and he wanted to go as well. He'd got a ticket for himself and, very kindly, one for me as well. Best Christmas present ever!

Saturday 2nd January 1971 was a very cold, misty, grey day. My dad and I set off for Ibrox, not really sure if the game would be on, such were the poor conditions. To my great relief the turnstiles were open and we made our way in, our tickets, significantly, for the East Enclosure and not the terracing where I would normally have stood. At my insistence we stood next to the trackside wall, it wasn't the best position for my dad to view the game, but it meant that I could see the whole ground, and I didn't want to miss an instant.

Ninety minutes came and went, with the game heading for a 0–0 draw, then Celtic's Jimmy Johnstone, the smallest man on the park, scored with a header. It was a devastating moment and the noise from the Celtic end that accompanied the goal was deafening, like nothing I had ever heard before. Through the mist I watched as their supporters celebrated and felt stunned, but, within a minute, that Celtic roar was eclipsed. Colin Stein equalised and it was the Rangers fans making all the noise. Despair to ecstasy in the space of sixty seconds; it was football drama at its very best.

Considering the timing of the goals it was a most satisfying 1–1 draw, and we left Ibrox happy. Our journey home took us into Renfrew, and across the Clyde on the ferry. A somewhat convoluted route and not one I would personally have chosen, but my dad had paid for the tickets, and was paying for the travel, so I wasn't about to complain. It meant however that we were very late in getting home, and it must have been about eight o'clock.

On arrival, I was surprised to find my house full of relatives, friends and neighbours, all waiting for our return. My mum seemed very angry and shouted at my dad, lashing out at him. She sobbed and demanded to know where we had been. I didn't understand. I was confused. Why was she so angry? What had we done wrong? Of course as a parent now, I fully understand. She was scared witless, and anger was her only outlet.

We were updated with some devastating news. There had been an accident at Ibrox. Supporters were injured, supporters were dead. We gathered in the living room and listened to the news on the TV and radio, as rumours of the death toll mounted. The underlying thought, unsaid by all was: What if our tickets had been for the terracing instead of the Enclosure? What if?

As the evening drew on my uncles and aunties told stories of 'the good old days' and we had, what kind of passed off as a New Year party, though it was anything but a celebration. We were just a family, happy to still be together.

Sunday dawned, and the full enormity of the disaster emerged. Sixty-six people were dead, with scores more injured. The night before I hadn't really understood, or even appreciated what had occurred. In fact, I'd been a bit annoyed that the football highlights hadn't been on the television. I wanted to relive the game, to see Colin Stein score that last gasp equaliser. However, as the days followed, I started to read the names of the supporters who died and their ages.

Five young boys, thirteen, fourteen and fifteen years old from Markinch in Fife, a man from my own home town of Clydebank, a nine year old boy from Liverpool ... the list seemed heartbreakingly endless. I felt then, and still feel to this day, deeply ashamed of those Saturday night thoughts. Bill Shankly, the famous Liverpool manager, was once quoted as saying:

"Some people believe football is a matter of life and death, I am very disappointed with that attitude. I can assure you it is much, much more important than that."

Well, Shankly was a great man, and a great football manager, but as a human being, he could not have been more wrong.

Sport took a back seat for the next week or so as the funerals of those supporters took place, players attending when, and where possible. Inevitably, football did return to Ibrox, a mere two weeks after the disaster, with Dundee United the visitors.

The day started off as normal. The subway was busy, full of the chatter of supporters ready for their day's entertainment. We emerged from Copland Road station, and made our way round to the ground. On turning the corner towards Ibrox the chatter stopped, and an eerie silence fell upon us. There in full view was the twisted metal of the handrails on Stairway 13, where the disaster had occurred, where so many people had lost their lives. After that the game was incidental, a cloud hung heavy over the stadium.

At this stage I was a home game only supporter, though that was soon to change. Rangers were away at Motherwell, and feeling a little bored, David and I thought we'd head over to Ibrox to watch the corresponding reserve team fixture. We did just that, and watched them win 3–1. It was so strange standing in an empty stadium. We could hear for the first time the players shouting to each other, smell the liniment they rubbed on their legs, even hear the sound of the ball as it was kicked. The highlight of the day, for me, was standing next to the player's tunnel. I got a chance to pat some of the players on the back as they emerged. Derek Johnstone – I touched Derek Johnstone! The experience added a new dimension to the game, and just wet our appetite for more.

On the road home we thought, having made it to the reserve game, why not take the logical step and travel to see the first team away from home. And that's exactly what we did, away games became an integral part of our routine, but only those within striking distance. Paisley, Airdrie, Motherwell and Kilmarnock were all visited. Exotic locations such as Edinburgh and Dundee were still deemed to be just a little too far.

The season progressed and Rangers, long since out of the league race were at least building a decent cup run. Falkirk, St. Mirren and Aberdeen all put to the sword. Only Hibs stood in the way of a place in the final and, after a dreary 0–0 draw, were overcome 2–1 in a replay.

Hampden that night resounded to the victory songs of the Rangers' support. As was common, the current 'pop hits' were modified to suit the occasion. That night John Lennon's 'Power to the People' became 'Power to the Rangers', though given the ex-Beatle's background and political beliefs I doubt he would have been best pleased. Supporters were creative in the 70s and always seemed to be on the ball converting songs to their cause. Not always in the most sporting or politically correct manner it has to be said.

The Piglet's 'Johnny Reggae' became "Johnny Greiggy, Greiggy, he'll break your fucking leggy".

Lee Marvin's "I was born under a wandering star" to "I was born under a Union Jack".

Later on the lyrics of 'Jesus Christ Superstar' would morph into "Dixie Deans, Superstar, walks like a woman and he wears a bra".

It's something missing from the modern game. The originality, diversity and spontaneity of supporter's songs falling victim to the all-seated stadia, political correctness and sanitised game, it's kind of sad really. It may also be down to the lack of decent new tunes about these days – or am I just being an old codger and showing my age?

The Scottish cup run posed a problem, Celtic had beaten Airdrie in the other semi-final and as a consequence we had another Old Firm final. Given the tragedy of the Ibrox disaster my mother was very reluctant to let me go to any more Celtic games – understandable I suppose! I tried to reason with her, but she just wasn't for budging, she did however leave the final decision to my dad. Not good, as he was by now back in Pakistan. In desperation I sent him a pleading letter, stating my case, begging to be allowed to go.

The days passed with no reply and I was becoming more and more frustrated, especially as by now I had a match ticket carefully hidden away in my bedroom. Anticipating bad news I pondered how I could escape, get to the game, and home again, without my mother noticing. Deep down I knew there was no chance of that happening. Would it be the radio again for me on Cup Final day? Then an envelope dropped through the letterbox, covered in Pakistani stamps – it was from my Dad. His long letter rambled on and on, scanning over it I just wanted an answer to my question, was it a yes or no? Then I reached the decision, against his better judgement he said yes. Yes I could go, but only if I was careful. Of course I'd be careful – Ya beauty!

Cup Final day finally arrived and I made my way to Glasgow Central Station. On arrival I was astonished, amazed, astounded at what I saw and heard. The station reverberated to Rangers song, the sounds echoing off the high glass roof, cascading over the assembled masses. Everyone in Glasgow seemed to be heading to Hampden and they were all wearing Rangers colours. Packed into the blue train like sardines, our carriage bounced all the way to Mount Florida station. Spilling onto the platform we marched as one, to the ground, our numbers growing with every step, joined by those from buses, from other trains, from everywhere and anywhere, and there was still two hours to kick off!

Then into the ground where a pocket of supporters gathered behind the goal under the vast cover of the Mount Florida end. Across the pitch a similar scenario was unfolding where the Celtic support gathered. Where had they all come from, I wondered? As time passed the pockets of support grew, and as both sides chanted and sang in defiance, the crowd swelled to over 120,000. Eventually the game started, and started so well. Rangers were terrific and played Celtic off the park. In the first half, chance after chance was created, and chance after chance was missed. In my first cup final I thought this was marvellous, it was only a matter of time before my team would score. Andy Penman cut into the penalty box, his low cross found Willie Johnston at the back post. An open goal ... this was it ... the crowd surged forward in expectation. Bud lifted his foot and unbelievably the ball rolled under it. A gilt-edged chance was gone. I soon learned one of football's fundamental rules: You have to take your chances. Celtic went up the field and Bobby Lennox rattled the ball into the Rangers net. Stunned silence from the blue half of Glasgow, what a racket from the other end. Just who invited that lot?

The second half drifted towards a Celtic victory, though there was still time for Willie Johnston to miss another snip. Then with three minutes to go, Derek Johnstone, hero of the League Cup final raced onto a long ball and nodded it past the despairing arms of the Celtic keeper. Rangers were level, and their support erupted. Remembering my dad's words I tried to be careful in the bedlam that followed. As calm was restored I encountered a new phenomenon. The sky had grown dark, it was murky and grey. A cloud hung over the Rangers end, but it was no longer a cloud of despair. That had been replaced by the infamous Hampden dust. The Rangers end was constructed of what looked like old railway sleepers, the gaps between them filled with gravel and dirt. As the happy 'Gers fans bounced up and down the dust from that filler rose high into the air. Breathing in all that grime couldn't have been healthy, but it was always welcome. The sight of the Hampden dust meant one thing: a Rangers goal, and that could only be good news. So we went home after a 1–1 draw, honours even, but it somehow felt like a victory. Another game was required, when the job would surely be completed.

The replay was four days later, and after a nervous day at school I set off for Hampden, supremely confident that I would be seeing big John Greig lifting the trophy. Alas it wasn't to be, twenty four minutes into the game Celtic scored, and a minute later their lead was doubled. Even I, as a novice, knew this wasn't good. As the green and white hordes celebrated, the crowd behind the Rangers goal swayed, a gap appeared in front of me and I leapt into it, angry and frustrated I directed a venomous verbal attack towards the Celtic end.

I spat out, "Fuck off you ... you ... you rotten things".

My mate David looked over at me, his eyes said it all: rotten things? It had been my chance to prove my credentials as a real Rangers fan and I'd blown it big style!

The 'Gers did pull a goal back, and despite a late chance to equalise, it was Celtic who won the game. Down but not out, it was time for me to continue my apprenticeship as a fan. Billy McNeil lifted the trophy in front of his jubilant supporters, but also in front of a packed Rangers end, blasting out support for their team. As Celtic paraded their trophy the ground reverberated in song, but not of the Celtic variety, they were Rangers songs. "We are the people" boomed from our end, loud and proud, and I joined in with gusto. My first real season may have ended in defeat and disappointment but I was hooked … and I just couldn't wait for the next one to begin.

Chapter 2:
Barcelona Here We Come

The close season saw me take an extended holiday, leaving second year at Clydebank High a few weeks early to join up with my dad who was still working in Pakistan. I had no problems missing the end of term, and three months in the Karachi sunshine was most welcome. The down side however was that I wouldn't return to Scotland till mid-August, missing the start of the football season.

On my return home I gave David a quick call to ensure he'd kept his promise and secured me a ticket for the League Cup tie against Celtic. He had, although after a torrid ninety minutes at Ibrox I was kind of wishing I was back on the Indian sub-continent as Celtic tore a sorry Rangers side apart, winning 3–0. The start of the league season saw no improvement and the opening game was lost away to Partick Thistle, followed by another Old Firm defeat. That Celtic defeat was a particularly sore one as Rangers had actually played well. At 2–2 they scored what looked to be a perfectly legitimate goal when Colin Stein lofted the ball over the advancing keeper and into the net. The goal then bizarrely chalked off for 'high feet', by a referee who had already reduced my team to ten men. Celtic's winning goal coming in the final minute, scored yet again from the head of five-foot-nothing Jimmy Johnstone.

David and I were by now full-time members of the away support, travelling to games on special trains known as football specials. The special was an integral part of the 'away' experience. Packed into some of British Rail's oldest and mankiest carriages, we were transported across the country. Generally there were a couple of policemen on board, but they kept a very low profile and allowed the support to get on with what they knew best. Some drinking, some card playing and a lot of singing – on the outward journey it was generally good natured, the return leg not always so.

One of our early excursions was an eagerly awaited trip to Edinburgh, to Tynecastle, to play Hearts, whose supporters had quite a quite fearsome reputation. Excitement grew as we joined the crush at the turnstiles, subject for the first time to a police search before squeezing into the ground. We stood behind the goal and watched in amazement as the hardcore sections of the Hearts and Rangers support fought a pitched battle for control of the terracing under the television cameras. Any lull in the warfare was broken by a hail of bottles and cans. Watching the missiles fly back and forward, it crossed my mind, that the police really needed to improve their search techniques as there appeared to be an ever plentiful supply of ammunition. Disappointed by the 2–1 defeat on the park, we took some solace in the fact that the Rangers support had clearly won the off-field battle by claiming that small area of terracing.

Exhilarated by the experience at Tynecastle, David and I joined what was known as 'The Choir' or 'The Derry' and stood with the hardcore boys at Ibrox, under the covering, opposite the Main Stand. We joined them also at away games, though not right in the centre of the congregation, that was deemed to be just a little too dangerous. As part of the Choir, I soon became familiar with their full repertoire, the Rangers songs, the party tunes, and a few more questionable chants. The latter two were officially not acceptable, but almost always tolerated. It wasn't just Rangers of course, all teams, had their own collection of official, and more objectionable songs.

One Monday morning at school, during a French lesson, I was feeling particularly bored. I detested this class and especially hated being in the language lab, having to repeat phrase after phrase, parrot fashion into a tape machine, only to listen back. I suddenly had a thought, why not ignore the rather tedious French and sing a few songs instead, and see how it sounded. It was a great idea, and for a good ten minutes or so I had my own personal sing-song blasting out "No Surrender", "Follow Follow", "The Billy Boys" and other assorted ditties – even attempting at one stage to translate them into French.

"Allo, Allo, nous sommes les garcon de Billy"

It was enormous fun until I realised that the teacher, sitting at the front desk had the facility to monitor what was happening. She was listening to me, and by her facial expressions wasn't best pleased. She clearly wasn't a Blue Nose!

Dragged off to the Headmaster's study, I was given a sermon on social responsibility and warned about my future conduct. He then went into his desktop drawer, and out came the tawse, a heavy leather belt used at the time to emphasise any lecture given to a wayward pupil. With my arms stretched out, I was whacked three times on the palm of each hand. It wasn't the first time I'd been belted and wouldn't be the last, I put on a brave face, but it was bloody sore. Walking away, blowing on my hands to gain some relief from the pain, I pondered on the social responsibility of a middle aged man thrashing a schoolboy with a leather belt, but it didn't seem the time to pursue the point.

I was now experiencing European football for the first time. Rangers were playing in the Cup Winners' Cup and were into the second round of the competition, having already disposed of Rennes, of France. Sporting Lisbon were the visitors, and were given an especially warm welcome as they entered the playing field at Ibrox, wearing their green and white hoops, a strip favoured by our 'friends' from the east end of the city. Rangers played quite magnificently that evening, and swept the Portuguese team away, racing into a 3-0 lead. Unfortunately the visitors struck back with two late goals to place the tie on a knife edge. The most noticeable effect of those goals was the deathly silence with which they were greeted. 60,000 people inside Ibrox and when they scored, you could literally have heard a pin drop. It was positively eerie!

Three days after the Sporting game and Ibrox was bouncing again, under very strange circumstances. Half time sounded in the game against Motherwell. It had been a dire, goalless first half and the home side were jeered from the field. As the supporters settled down to their pie and Bovril there was a sudden commotion in the main stand. I was directly across the field standing in a very disgruntled choir and watched as the commotion slowly spread to the Copland Road end, rippling round the ground like a human tidal wave. We watched, bewildered as to the reason, then we were leaping about in joy – Celtic were playing Partick Thistle in the League Cup Final and an announcement had been made that the half time score was: Celtic 0, Partick Thistle 4! Never have Thistle had so many jubilant supporters at Ibrox, and not one of them was a wearing red and yellow scarf. Rangers were cheered back onto the park and must have wondered what on earth was going on as the supporters roared their approval. The team responded, and scored four times to win the game, but the day belonged to the team from Maryhill, and not one of us grudged them that.

The games were now coming thick and fast and it was European night again, with Rangers in Lisbon for their return match with Sporting. I watched the football highlights on TV that evening: *Sportsnight with Coleman* was the BBC's flagship sports programme. As it opened, David Coleman, the veteran commentator, announced that he had a tremendous night of football for us. He always said that, even when the games were, well … crap! With the Rangers game kicking off late, news from was slow to filter through, and when it did, it wasn't good. Sporting had won 3–2 and the game was in extra time. Waiting up till well after midnight the news got progressively worse, the game had ended 4–3 to Sporting, 6-6 on aggregate, and they had won on penalties. My team was out of Europe.

Next morning I got up, and was both surprised and delighted to hear that far from being out of Europe, Rangers were actually in the draw for the quarter-finals. A sharp-eyed journalist had recalled the new UEFA rule that away goals scored in extra time counted double in the event of a draw. The referee had got it wrong and the game shouldn't have gone to penalties. Rangers had in fact won! As was traditional in those days, I looked out my Rangers scarf and wore it to school. No matter the weather, the scarf went on after a good result, and this one was certainly good, if totally unexpected.

The next big match was a much anticipated trip to Easter Road, to play Hibs. The Scottish League however, in their infinite wisdom had scheduled the game for Christmas Day. Indeed there was a full league programme that afternoon, spare a thought for Aberdeen who were asked to make a 300-mile round trip to Falkirk. The timing of the game could not have been any worse. My dad was home for the holiday period and my mother wanted us to have a special Christmas, a family day, with everyone present. I just wanted to go to the football and asked to be relieved of my domestic commitments. The answer to my request was a firm "NO", and no matter how hard I pleaded, I was denied permission.

David received the same answer but he just went anyway – I wasn't that brave. I sulked throughout that Christmas dinner and spoiled it for everyone, something I now regret, but I wasn't to know what the future would bring. Later that evening David phoned to give me the story of the day. A great match, Rangers victorious, 1–0, with a last minute Colin Stein goal. There had been running battles throughout the whole game, bottles and cans flying. I was so jealous.

I loved the excitement of the match day experience, and loved the football violence, but only from a distance. Neither David or I were really brave enough to get into the thick of the action. We were perfectly happy to stand on the fringes chanting: "Come and have a go with the Ibrox agro!" We did have the odd minor scrape though. Coming home from a cup tie at Brockville we found ourselves on a train with a couple of Celtic fans. With safety in numbers we sang our songs, and taunted them, it was great fun. What we failed to notice however, was the number of Teddy Bears dwindling as the stations came and went, and pretty soon David and I were the lone Rangers. It was time for the Celtic fans to extract their revenge; on leaving the train one of their number smacked me in the face.

"Fuck off you Orange bastard" he snarled, as another one gave me a slap. Football violence suddenly didn't seem so exciting!

The league season was proving to be a disappointment but Rangers were doing well in cup competitions. The Scottish Cup semi-final was reached, and after beating Italian side Torino, the Cup Winners' Cup semi-final also achieved. That game matched Rangers with old rivals Bayern Munich.

The two semi finals brought mixed success. Our Scottish Cup adventure came to an end. A very good Hibs side outplayed Rangers after a replay and made it through to the final where they would frustratingly freeze, and hand the trophy, on a plate, to Celtic. The Bayern game was different though and was a special night in Glasgow. The City was hosting two European semi-finals simultaneously. 80,000 would watch Rangers, whilst 75,000 would see Celtic take on Inter Milan. It's something that just wouldn't be tolerated these days. The authorities in the 70s however just accepted the circumstances and coped with little real bother.

After a day of much anticipation I found myself outside the gates of Ibrox, waiting for them to open, my 30p ticket clutched tightly in my hand, not wanting to miss a moment. What followed was a quite magnificent night in Rangers history. Sandy Jardine scored in the first minute, young Derek Parlane added a second, the men in blue were simply unstoppable. The Germans had no answer and were a beaten side. They knew it, Rangers knew it, and the supporters – well, we certainly knew it. A chant started to swell round Ibrox; it grew to a crescendo, and continued long into the night:

"Barcelona here we come"

David and I made our way home, excited, planning how we would make our way to that far away Spanish city. A European Final was not to be missed. Stopping off in Partick our thoughts turned to the other game; how were Celtic getting on? There had been rumours that their game had ended 0–0 and gone into extra time. That was confirmed when we nervously popped our heads into the public bar of the Hayburn Vaults, the Celtic game had not only gone to extra time, but was in fact going to penalties. We watched through a haze of cigarette smoke at a small TV behind the bar, we were chased away by the barman but returned so often that he gave up. He didn't want to miss the action either. Were we being good Scots and cheering on our countrymen? No way – c'mon the Inter!

Dixie Deans, the Celtic forward, stepped up to take his team's first penalty and blasted the ball high over the crossbar. How we cheered, as did most of the bar! We clearly weren't the only ones routing for the Italians! With Inter netting all five of their penalties it was all over, Celtic were out. This night just couldn't possibly get better. I made my way home thinking that Dixie Deans didn't really walk like a woman, but he may, for all I know, have worn a bra!

In three games Rangers had played before nearly 220,000 supporters. In their next three, the final league games at home to Hibs, Ayr and Dunfermline, there would only be a combined attendance of 16,000. I just couldn't understand it. Why didn't the fans turn out for these games? 'Follow Follow' was our anthem after all. Perhaps everyone was saving for the European final, and a trip to Barcelona. That's what I should have been doing but my mother, anticipating the inevitable question told me quite firmly that there was no way I was going to Spain for a football game – no way.

I pleaded. I begged. I sulked. I didn't get to go!

Rangers played a couple of pre-final friendlies, one of which was at Love Street. It wouldn't really have rated a mention were it not for a post match incident. I was approached by a couple of fans and ordered to hand over the Union Flag that was draped over my shoulders. I declined the request and was promptly headbutted. I ran away, blood streaming from my nose, still clutching my flag, but confused as to why I should have been attacked by one of my own. There are, as I was to find out over the years, lots of arseholes in the world, and some of them wear Rangers colours.

The day of the final came, and with it an insult from the football authorities, the game would not be broadcast live on TV. Scotland were playing Wales at Hampden, the SFA wanted a big crowd, and Rangers live on TV would inevitably cut the attendance. So whilst the rest of the continent settled down to watch a Scottish team in a European final, we got Coronation Street. The game was however to be shown on delayed transmission, so I made the decision to avoid radio coverage, and watch it later that night. Without knowing the score, it would be just as good as being live. So for all that evening I hid in my room, isolated from the world, anxiously waiting for the final to end and the programme to start.

At about 11pm I settled down in front of the TV to watch the 1972 European Cup Winners' Cup Final: Rangers vs Moscow Dynamo, optimistic but very, very nervous. The first half was like a dream come true, Colin Stein blasted a shot into the Russian's net, then just before half time, Willie Johnston headed home. My favourite players had scored, and Rangers were two goals up. Two goals up in a European Final, it was fantastic! The game was on Scottish television, STV, so they took the opportunity to go for an ad break. Bill Tennant, their news reporter and anchorman for the evening announced:

"Well it's been a great game and the second half is just as good, you have another three goals to look forward to."

I sat stunned. Another three goals … what did he mean? My mind raced, would we win 5–0, or would they win 3–2? The second half started and within four minutes Willie Johnston scored again, I leapt for joy and then realised that we'd won the cup, there were only two goals left in the game and the Russians couldn't come back. I sat down with an overwhelming feeling of anti-climax. The rest of the game was played out but with little excitement, Dynamo's gallant but unsuccessful fight back immaterial – thanks a lot STV!

School was attended the next day, wearing of course my trusty scarf. The playground chat though was not so much about the victory, but whether there would be a replay. The Russians were a little miffed about the pitch invasions that broke up the end of the game. UEFA in turn were not impressed with the pitched battle that had occurred between the Rangers supporters and the Spanish police.

Our support had indeed invaded the pitch after the final whistle, though this was a common occurrence in European finals during the 60s and 70s. They had, however, also been on the park in the minutes before the end of the game, nervous excitement and anticipation of the final whistle, rather than any hooligan intent. Faced by the victorious pitch invasion the Guardia decide that their honour was at stake, and they drew batons with the intention of clubbing the fans back off the park. That may have worked against local football supporters, subdued by forty years of General Franco's fascist regime. A Glasgow support tanked up no doubt on some fine wine were not going to accept that, and the rest, as they say, is history!

UEFA convened a hasty meeting and announced that the result would stand. That evening I went over to Ibrox to welcome my team home, thousands cheered from the terracing, some coming directly from the airport, still proudly wearing their sombreros. In torrential rain we watched the team, lead by John Greig, do a lap of honour round the Ibrox track on an open-backed lorry. It wasn't exactly the Lord Mayor's carriage but no one complained. The Rangers were home and they were Champions of Europe.

Season 72/73 was thrown into major doubt for me. My dad was ending his contract in Pakistan and would soon be moving to Turkey. With a large American presence in that country there were plenty of English-language schools available to educate me and my sisters, and a plan had been formulated to unite the family. Self-centred as ever I was only thinking of myself, and I didn't want that, I didn't want to live abroad and miss the football.

Our summer holidays were once again spent in Pakistan, but we did make a couple of trips to Turkey to check out the availability of schools in Istanbul. I tried my best to look disinterested, and became increasingly uncooperative. Eventually places were found for my sisters but, because I was going into my O Grade year it was decided that I would continue my education in Scotland. It was the only solution really, I'd been so stroppy and downright rude at the interviews I don't think any of the Turkish schools wanted me. I was delighted with the decision, though looking back I was clearly a selfish spoiled brat, and frankly needed a good slap!

Summer in Pakistan, and the Turkish school hunt meant that I missed all the pre-season friendlies, but I was home in time for the official opening game; an Ibrox League Cup tie against Clydebank. Willie Waddell, last season's team manager and now General Manager took the opportunity to give the home support a right good rollicking. The club had received a one-year European ban in the aftermath of the Cup Winners' Cup Final and Mr Waddell was under no illusions as to who was to blame – I suppose he had a point. We stood like naughty schoolboys listening to what we should and should not do, and to be honest, it wasn't the most inspiring start to a football year. As the game began the choir tried to get a singsong going but it just fell flat. It would be a while before normal service would be resumed in the Derry.

With Parkhead under reconstruction, Rangers met Celtic at Hampden in a lunchtime league game. The noon kick-off was an attempt to keep the supporters sober and, in theory, curb any crowd trouble. This game would prove to be the worst in my experience as a Blue Nose. Celtic toyed with Rangers, like a cat with a mouse. Going into the last minute it was 3–0 but could easily have been six or seven. John Greig, Captain Courageous through the years, pushed forward and scored a consolation goal. In a final humiliating moment he was ironically cheered by an ecstatic Celtic support, milking the moment for all it was worth. It was awful.

The master plan to avoid crowd trouble failed miserably. Instead of fighting at a quarter to five, the respective supporters squared up at a quarter to two, and fought a pitched battle outside Hampden's North Stand. The Rangers support giving as good as they got, putting up a much better fight than their team had on the pitch.

Wins over Stenhousemuir and Falkirk hinted that a recovery may be in progress, but a league defeat at Kilmarnock only served to increase the gloom. Things, quite frankly, could only get better. Things in fact got considerably worse.

I lost my friend and mentor David when he decided to leave home and seek his fortune in London. He had just turned 16 and it was a bold move, not one that I would have made, that's for sure. He did well though and would return for big games in the following years, but for now I was on my own. So on Wednesday 4th October 1972 I went to a game for the first time on my own. Not a big game for Rangers, but an important one for me, a League Cup quarter final against Stenhousemuir. Having won the first leg 5–0 this would be a stroll. Well it was – for Stenhousemuir, who deservedly won 2–1. The next day my hero Colin Stein was transferred to Coventry City, my other favourite Willie Johnstone would also move away, in his case to West Bromwich Albion ... my world was falling apart!

The bottom had been reached, though at the time I didn't realise it. Some new signings were made and one of them, Tam Forsyth, would play a big part in the season's finale. I still attended the games of course, that is, after all, what supporters do. Mid-November we were up in Dundee. An eventful afternoon passed, with sporadic fighting to and from the ground. In between, Dens Park hosted a super game of football, with Alfie Conn scoring a quite amazing goal. This sparked off some of the worst violence I had yet seen at a game. Still hyper from the terracing warfare, the support took their frustrations out on the football special, and it was well and truly trashed by the time it pulled into Glasgow. Seats ripped out, toilets smashed and light bulbs thrown from the now broken windows.

Returning to Glasgow was always one of the highlights of any trip. As the train pulled into Queen Street Station the carriage doors were flung open and supporters spilled from the still moving train. Marching down the platform, the station was always given a bellowing chorus of the Billy Boys before we all dispersed to our various home towns.

The New Year brought a little joy - for the first time in eight attempts, I was to see my team beat Celtic. Rangers dominated the early stages of the game and it was good to watch, but I'd learned by now that pressure means nothing, it's goals that count, and we needed one. Twenty-five minutes into the game the breakthrough arrived, via the penalty spot, and even the most conspiracy-ridden Celtic fan had to admit that this decision was correct: rugby tackles in the penalty box are most definitely not allowed! Derek Parlane, normally deadly from the spot, took the kick, but drove it too close to the keeper who blocked. The Celtic fans started to roar their approval and were in mid-celebration when Parlane pounced on the rebound, controlled the ball and drilled it into the net. Their celebration froze in mid air, and then crumpled in silence. Cue bedlam at the Rangers end.

Celtic scored with a second-half deflection, and yet again it looked as though we would be denied a victory. Then in the final minute Quentin Young burst down the wing and swung over an inviting cross. Alfie Conn out-jumped the defence and met the ball with his head. It rose over the outstretched arms of the keeper, hung in the air for a tantalising moment then dipped into the net. There was a split second of silence before the ground, well 70% of it, went absolutely mental.

Rangers were now on a terrific run of form, winning twenty games out of twenty one, the exception being a 1-1 Scottish Cup draw with Hibs. The replay at Easter Road was a tense affair and a terrific game of football, played in front of an amazing 49,000. The Ibrox men must have used up a season's worth of luck in winning that night. Hibs were outstanding, and only heroic goalkeeping from Peter McCloy kept them at bay. Rangers: two attacks, both breakaways, two goals. Sometimes a most satisfying, if nerve-wracking way to win a game!

The winning run continued all the way to the end of the season, giving Rangers an outside chance of the title. Celtic were away to third placed Hibs, a difficult game, but they only needed a draw – unfortunately they won. Rangers did their bit with a 2–0 win over East Fife but the cataclysmic start to the season had come back to haunt them. Once again though the supporters showed their loyalty and stood on the terraces, singing and chanting – only leaving when a line of policemen physically ejected them from the ground.

With the league title gone there was only one game left in the season, The Scottish Cup Final. Parental permission was no longer required for such games and I took my place in the Mount Florida end, joining in with a rousing chorus of the National Anthem to welcome Princess Alexandra to Hampden. With Royalty at the game we surely couldn't lose.

The cup final would prove to be one of the finest games of the season with play swinging from one end to the other. Dalglish scored for Celtic but Derek Parlane soon levelled, and the teams took a half time break at 1–1. The second half could not have had a more dramatic start. From the kick off a through ball was played into the Celtic half, despite giving Billy McNeill a five-yard start, Alfie Conn outstripped him and tucked the ball past the advancing keeper and into the net. Celtic hit back and were denied when John Greig dived full-length to push a goal bound shot off the line. It was a great save, or would have been if Greig had been the Rangers keeper. Unfortunately he wasn't, and Celtic scored from the inevitable penalty.

On the hour-mark came one of those iconic Hampden moments. Tommy McLean swung over an inch-perfect free kick; Derek Johnstone met the ball and bulleted in a header.

The ball crashed off one post, rolled along the goal line and bounced off the other. Running in at the far post was Tom Forsyth, a man who had yet to taste defeat as a Ranger. He swung at the ball, and from about six-inches scuffed it with his studs. The ball trundled into the net, though subsequently on TV it looked frighteningly close to missing the target. Big Tam ran away, arms in the air in full joyous celebration. We in the Rangers end were equally jubilant.

Further chances were created but no more goals were scored and it was John Greig who climbed the Hampden steps to get the Royal seal of approval and collect the Scottish Cup. Once again Hampden rocked to the sounds of cup final Rangers songs but this time they were of victory, and not defiance, and no one sang louder than me, celebrating my first trophy as a Rangers fan.

Chapter 3:
The Long Arm of the Law

With my dad still working in Turkey, it was back to Istanbul for the summer holidays. Istanbul was an exciting place; bordering Europe and Asia and full of contrasts and contradictions. Towering minarets with the call to prayer of a mostly Islamic population, coupled with bars and nightclubs on the neighbouring streets.

Having just turned sixteen, my dad decided it was time for some father and son bonding and he took me to a Turkish belly dancing show. Well that's how he sold it to my mother and sisters. The show certainly started out with some traditional dancing but as the evening wore on the very pretty Turkish girls removed more and more of their attire. With a few beers thrown in, it was quite a night, and still brings a warm glow some forty years later!

It was also in Turkey that I discovered the joys of the BBC World Service, their radio broadcasts keeping me up-to-date with British and world news and more importantly, the football results from back home. Not only that, they had commentary matches, so, imagine my delight when it was announced that they would be covering the Old Firm game at Ibrox. Perched on an Istanbul balcony, overlooking the

Bospherous, I listened as the game unfolded. It was a close run thing, and had me on the edge of my seat, 0–0 'til the final minutes when Celtic scored twice. The second of those goals sparking off a disturbance in the Rangers end which culminated in a pitch invasion. That perked me up just a little; at least the Bears weren't taking it lying down! I wasn't to know it, but although I was nearly 2,000 miles away, the events at Ibrox would soon have a direct influence on me.

A few days later I was back in Scotland, ready and eager to get back to the football. My homecoming game was against Arbroath, and played in front of 8,000 was dull in the extreme. David and I stood under the cover of the Copland Road and started a few songs, but other than the small group alongside us, no one else seemed remotely interested. It was all so disappointing, I'd been looking forward to this game for ages, and it was turning out to be nothing more than a damp squib. That would soon change.

Midway through the first half, I felt a hand on my shoulder. Thinking someone was wanting past I moved a little but was shocked to feel my arm clasped and jerked up my back. I turned in protest only to find myself gripped by a big Glasgow policeman, then, with my other arm pinned firmly to my side; I was dragged up the terracing steps. Looking back I saw David in a similar position … we'd been lifted!

We were manhandled round the back of the terracing and through a small wooden door that led under the main stand. As I was being pushed through that door, I had the bizarre thought that I was being cheated. Anyone else I'd seen being arrested had been taken round the track where they would be acclaimed by the support. I was being spirited away and denied my moment of glory. It just wasn't fair!

Any thoughts of glory soon dissipated as we were led into the police room and charged, 'Breach of the peace' – did we have anything to say? I just shook my head but David was much more composed and issued a firm "Not guilty". We sat silently as more supporters joined us in captivity and then, handcuffed, we were led out of the room, into the back of a big black van. A short drive took us to an old Victorian building that I would later discover to be Govan Police Station. Standing before an imposing desk sergeant, we were charged again. When asked if we had anything to say I followed David's lead and stated "Not guilty", though not nearly as forcefully as him.

We were then led to the cell block. Up a narrow metal stairway, feet clanking, echoing round the old building. Stopping outside a store room, we were each handed a very thin rubber mattress and a very scratchy sack-like blanket. One by one we were directed to a cell. My turn arrived and I was pushed inside. As I stumbled in, the big metal door slammed shut behind me. Spinning round, I heard the key turning ... and then silence. It was a horrible moment and I realised that I was alone, with no control over my immediate future. More prisoners were brought in and my despair grew with the sound of each crashing door. Lying on that smelly rubber mattress, I stared in the near darkness at the dirty tiled walls and sobbed a little. I wasn't a big bad football hooligan. I was a frightened little schoolboy.

After what felt like an eternity, my cell door re-opened. Dazzled by the light shining into my cell, I was told to get up and to neatly fold my gear, which I did. Following a policeman, I was led down to the main desk and handed a sheet of paper instructing me to attend Glasgow Sheriff Court. I was then shown the door and ordered to leave. So off I went, into the bleak and silent Govan air, with no way of getting home, bar walking.

Next day I found myself in Glasgow Sheriff Court, along with David, and a few relatives in tow for moral support. Our initial consultation with a court appointed lawyer produced a major panic. He told us that we would *probably* be released with a trial date, but bail may be requested, possibly £20 or £30 each. Not a huge problem in the modern days of cash machines, but in the early 70s there were none.

"What happens if we can't get the money", my mother asked.

"Oh," said the lawyer, very matter-of-factly, "then they will both go to Barlinnie 'til the money is raised."

My mother's face turned an ashen grey at the very mention of the place. I said nothing but was inwardly terrified of the prospect. The memory of that cell door slamming shut was all too fresh in my mind.

Our moment in court arrived and we were lead into the dock. Standing there, listening, as our 'breach of the peace' charge sheet was read out, the Clerk of the Court helpfully informing everyone that we had been "shouting and bawling, cursing and swearing, singing obscene and provocative songs". We pleaded NOT GUILTY to the charges, and that, pretty much was that. We were given a formal trial date, no bail required, and we were free to go. I was so relieved, and so very thankful that I hadn't been sent to Barlinnie!

The charges, however, had me worried. Thinking back to the night before, perhaps I was guilty. I had been "shouting and bawling", I'd certainly been "cursing and swearing" and I suppose, yes, I had been "singing obscene and provocative songs". But we did that every week at the football, why was it now an offence? I was confused.

My attendance at games was now in jeopardy. My mother wasn't keen on me returning to Ibrox, my dad, still working in Turkey, also expressed his doubts. I was distraught at the thought of having to give up the football and had to work hard on some kind of compromise, something that would allow me to continue my life as a supporter. I tried to convince my mother that the arrest had been one big mistake, I'd been in the wrong place at the wrong time, I'd been picked out as a Rangers fan by my colours. The police, I explained, were just out for a few easy arrests – It was all a big mistake – I was just a victim of circumstance. Most of that was a lot of tosh!

I continued the case for the defence and told my mother that the solution was actually quite simple: I would still go to the matches but wouldn't wear my team's colours. That way I wouldn't be identifiable as a Rangers fan. To seal the deal, I told her that I would no longer go onto the terracing but instead sit in the stand where I would be isolated from any potential bother. I played a blinder, not only was I allowed to continue going to the games but I was actually given an increase in my pocket money to help pay for the more expensive stand seat. My mother's only stipulation was that I should join a supporters' club, as that seemed a safer way to go to the game. I bought into that, no big deal really.

Two days later I was off to Parkhead for yet another Old Firm game. Wearing my Rangers scarf, which had been carefully hidden in a hedge down the road, I took my place on the terracing amongst all the other fans. Hey, I thought, what my mother doesn't know can't hurt her. To be honest, I didn't really enjoy the match as I spent most of it nervously watching out for policemen. I was convinced that I was going to be arrested again. A real shame as my team won 3–1, my first victory at Parkhead. Sadly there were no victory songs for me. I was the mute Ranger!

With the league season about to start, I followed my mother's instructions and joined the local supporters' club, the Hardgate Loyal. It actually made a lot of sense and was something I would probably have done anyway. The bus left a five minutes' walk from my home and was quicker and cheaper than getting the train, though not nearly as exciting.

In the weeks and months before the trial, we had various meetings with our legal aid lawyer. At the first meeting he made it clear that he wasn't really bothered as to whether we were innocent or not. Just as well, because to be honest David and I were pretty much guilty as charged! He followed up by outlining the expected prosecution case, telling us in a matter of fact way that we would be accused of shouting "fuck the Queen". On seeing our incredulous looks, he quickly altered that by saying "sorry, you are the Rangers boys – then you will be accused of shouting 'fuck the Pope'". David and I tried desperately not to laugh as our respective mothers looked on, wide-eyed, open-mouthed and aghast at what they were hearing!

Our lawyer seemed to know his stuff and primed us with all the correct things to say and do when we went to trial.

- Never accuse the Police of lying.
- Look innocent at all times.
- Get your story straight and stick to it.
- Rehearse all eventualities.

He also explained to our mothers that we had been picked up on the Wednesday as a reaction to the previous Saturday's Old Firm trouble, and that we were clearly innocent. It will be okay he told them. As we left his office he gave David and me a big wink – he knew the truth of it!

Wednesday 21st November 1973 was soon upon us: our day in court! Unfortunately we had a double booking that day, Rangers were also in action at Easter Road, and David and I were hoping to attend. It would be tight though, as the game had an afternoon kick off. November '73 saw the country in the midst of a miners' and power workers' strike. Electricity was being conserved. Hence the floodlight-free kick off.

We turned up at the Sherriff Court bright and early. I was dressed in my school uniform, white shirt, tie and blazer, hair combed and squeaky clean. David equally well turned out. We hung about for ages, waiting and waiting, our hopes of making Easter Road fading as the minutes and then hours passed. Eventually the moment of truth arrived and our case was called. We were in the dock with three other supporters, all a couple of years older, all dressed in denim and obviously no strangers to the court system. Gathered there we looked a totally contrasting group, which undoubtedly helped in the following hour or so.

The prosecutor outlined the charges, and a series of policemen came into the witness box to give evidence. One by one, they explained to the sheriff that the five accused; me, David and the other three, were disturbing the enjoyment of the other spectators with our foul-mouthed abuse and provocative songs. We were a group intent on causing trouble, and as a result, we had to be removed. Midway through their evidence, one of the policemen pointed directly at me and told the sheriff, "I apprehended him, after he had sung a song known as 'The Sash'."

I can't say I enjoyed that moment too much, with everyone in the courtroom looking directly at me. It was particularly uncomfortable as the evidence was progressively stacking up; I just hoped that our lawyer had a good defence in mind. As it turned out he did, and quickly set about placing doubts in the sheriff's mind. He pressed the police about us being a group. Were we really together? Had they seen it right? Couldn't they possibly have made a mistake?

We all had our turn in the witness box, and once again the contrast between the five of us was clear – three streetwise blokes from Springburn and two youngsters. My turn in the witness box arrived and I followed my lawyer's instructions to the letter.

"Were you singing those songs?"

"No, I wasn't. Some people were but not me."

"Do you know the other accused?"

"Other than David, no I don't."

"Were the police lying in their evidence?"

"No, I think they must be mistaken."

With the evidence complete the sheriff retired to consider his verdict. We had lunch and faced the fact that weren't going to make it to Easter Road, and to be honest, neither of us was really that bothered. We were putting on a brave face, worried far more about the impending verdict.

Back in court, we were asked to stand. The sheriff looked down on us and started to rant. He was fed up with football supporters being brought before him. He glared at us and proclaimed "Football supporters who misbehave should be punished to the full letter of the law". I was starting to get worried, very worried actually, visions of Barlinnie were forming in my mind again, but he then continued, "In this case I'm not convinced that the accused were all together in a group as the police maintain." He then pronounced his verdict on us: "Not proven".

'Not proven' – a quaint Scottish legal term which basically states: We know you did it, but we can't quite pin it on you. The sheriff in our case had pretty well got it spot on!

The remainder of the season was a huge disappointment, the only highlight being a 4–2 victory at Tynecastle when my new Ibrox hero Derek Parlane scored all four of the goals. That day was however special for another reason, a personal landmark; it was the day I bought my first drink in a pub.

The supporters' bus had stopped off in Harthill for an hour or so on the road home. In previous years I would have stood outside the pub, munching a bag of chips, waiting for the bus to leave, this season however I'd progressed to going inside. As usual I gave one of the older members some money and he bought me a pint. With time for another I decided to chance my arm and buy one for myself. Plucking up the courage, and with my knees knocking, I nervously caught the barman's attention. As a naive sixteen year old I thought it would be easier to get a half pint, so that's what I asked for. To my great relief the order was taken without question and a small glass of lager presented to me. It cost 8½p and tasted absolutely tremendous.

Chapter 4:
Tragedy and Joy

Domestically my family seemed to be in the process of reuniting. My dad's work assignments were gradually bringing him homeward. From Singapore to Thailand, Pakistan to Turkey. The journey was ever westwards. For season 74/75 he was based in Blackburn, Lancashire, only two hundred miles away, and close enough to visit at weekends.

Pre-season started with a Dryborough cup tie away to Stirling Albion, and my dad, for some reason thought it would be a good family day out if we all went along. I was horrified. Go to the football with my mother and sisters? He had to be joking! Fortunately, the female side of the family saw it the same way. They went shopping and it was just my dad and I who went to the game.

Next was a Dryborough semi-final in Edinburgh and my re-acquaintance with the football special. The outward journey was uneventful, and after a good win at Easter Road the return should have been the same, but for some reason the travelling support were in a particularly disruptive mood. Pulling the communication cord was a common trick on the specials and could be mildly amusing, watching the train guard trying to find out where it had happened and who had done it. That night, however, the cord was pulled no less than thirteen times, and a forty-five minute trip took well over three hours. It was tiresome to say the least.

Pre-season concluded with the Dryborough final at Hampden. Celtic won the trophy in an outstanding game of football but only after a nerve-wracking penalty shootout. You know, football fans can be a funny bunch. We clamour for entertainment, yet I went home disappointed. It had been an enthralling and exciting match, but I'd much rather have watched a tedious mid-field scrap with no goalmouth action, so long as my team had won. The truth of the matter is that it's only the neutrals, the TV armchair fans that want to see exciting, end-to-end action. Supporters of teams, like me, want victories, if it's done with style then so much the better, but at the end of the day its success that we crave.

I was now in sixth year at school. Most of my friends had already left and managed to find themselves jobs. Back in the 70s there were still plentiful apprenticeship opportunities in the various industries on Clydeside: The shipyards of Yarrows and John Brown, and the Singer sewing machine plant in Clydebank. I didn't really know what to do with myself – further education, a job? There was plenty time for all that. For now, I was really only interested in the football.

This was the year that Rangers were going to grasp the league title from Celtic and stop them winning ten championships in a row. Well, that's what we all hoped, but after an opening day draw with Ayr United, we feared it would be more of the same. That was to change with a trip to Parkhead. I went to the game by train, travelling firstly to Bridgeton Cross, then marching the few miles to Celtic Park as part of a Blue Army, ready to do battle for the cause. I was dressed as was the style for the younger supporter – Blue and white scarf round my neck, a scarf tied round my wrist with another tucked into my belt. Jeans turned up at the bottom to show off my Dr. Marten boots. In hindsight, I must have looked ridiculous but at the time it felt the bee's knees.

The game was eventful for a couple of reasons. Firstly and most importantly because we won! Secondly, because I finally got my walk along the track in front of the massed ranks of the Rangers support, the walk that the police had so cruelly denied me the previous year. I'd picked up an injury in the aftermath of the Rangers equaliser and had to be taken out of the crowd and round to the small medical room under the main Parkhead stand. Walking along the track I seized the moment, saluting the crowd with my arm raised, blood streaming from my head. Gesticulating to the Celtic fans as I went past them – it was fantastic. In the medical room I was patched up, the wound being very trivial, requiring a sticking plaster and no more. I was a bit of a fraud, but didn't care and took my bow and applause as I returned to the Rangers end. Just in time to see the winning goal – absolutely perfect!

Post-match we marched in full voice back into Glasgow city centre. Up to this point I'd always wondered where the Celtic support came from, and went to, on a match day. They just seemed to appear and disappear. That afternoon I was to find out. We reached the Trongate and were suddenly confronted by their massed ranks. They were thousands strong and it would be fair to say, not best pleased. So that's where they go, I thought, as a massed battle erupted on Argyll Street. Fist fights ensued, bottles, cans and various missiles were thrown, and at least one supporter was hurtled through a shop's plate glass window. I bravely shouted some encouragement from a suitably safe distance before scarpering as sirens and flashing lights signalled the arrival of the Glasgow Constabulary.

Rangers had now hit a winning streak and went top of the table at New Year with a most satisfying 3–0 home win over Celtic. With such an emphatic victory the Rangers end was jubilant, not so the other end and sporadic fights broke out.

Trouble on the terracing at these games always started in the same way. A small gap in the packed terracing would appear as two or more supporters squared up to each other, the crowd helpfully parting to give them room. I'd seen such skirmishes take place in our end, but they were usually over as quickly as they had started. At the Celtic end however, these very often developed into what looked like gang warfare. The gap on the terracing would grow into a huge no-man's land with missiles hurtled from one side to the other. We would roar our approval watching bottles spinning through the air, the contents spewing out as they flew towards their target. Eventually an uneasy peace would be restored and the gap would slowly close.

The friction between Rangers and Celtic supporters has been well documented, but Rangers and Aberdeen also have a fractured relationship. There are many theories as to why, where, and when it first started. Most point to the Alex Ferguson years, or the Souness years, or the Ian Durrant injury. For me, however, it started on January 25th 1975 when we were up at Pittodrie for a Scottish Cup tie. Queuing to get into the part of the ground known as 'The Paddock', I was aware of an ongoing commotion at the turnstiles. As I got closer I saw the reason. Spray-painted across the wall at the turnstiles was a slogan in big, bold red letters:

"THE BEACH END CELEBRATES THE IBROX DISASTER"

I found it hard to believe that someone could have taken the time and trouble to do such a thing. Why they should consider celebrating the death of innocent football supporters was so hard to comprehend. On a different day after all, it could have easily have been them. I so wanted to win that day, to stuff it right up them, but it wasn't to be. With a minute to go Willie Miller equalized for the Dons. A replay would be required.

Monday 10th February 1975 was to prove to be a momentous day in my life, and not just because Rangers lost that Scottish Cup replay. It was the day my dad died. The story however begins the day before. Sitting at home, my dad started to chat with me about the future – not something we had ever really done before. Together with my mother, we talked; about plans, hopes and desires, long into the night. As we got ready for bed he complained about having chest pains, just bad indigestion he said. I knew there was something wrong, my mother knew something was wrong and I'm convinced that my dad knew something was wrong, but it was like we all were helpless to intervene with what was laid down as fate. At 4 a.m. my dad had a massive heart attack and died almost instantly.

I woke at 7.30 a.m. and hearing voices in the house immediately sensed what had happened. I didn't need to be told, I just knew that my dad was gone. The day passed with everyone numb, visitors came and went, including the police who had to investigate a sudden death. Early afternoon my thoughts moved to the evening's football. I felt so guilty because I wanted to be there, it was wrong and I knew it, my place was with my family but I just couldn't help myself. My mother sensed my torment and said that I should just go. She told me, it's what my dad would have wanted and, frankly I was just getting under her feet. It was a poignant moment that mirrored our return to Scotland three and a half years previous, again without my dad being present, she had sent me over to Ibrox to watch Rangers play Aberdeen. So I went to the game and watched somewhat despondently as we were knocked out of the cup. Not surprisingly my heart wasn't really in it and in a strange way I was kind of pleased that we lost. It just wasn't a time for celebration.

In the days leading up to the funeral, I pondered my time with my dad. I wished I could have done more with him, wished we could have spent more time together. He was the man who introduced me to football, to Rangers, and in seventeen years I had probably only been to a dozen or so games with him. Most of all though I recalled that night in the Istanbul club, we'd been together, and for the first time ever, he'd bought me a beer. I sadly realised that I would never have the chance to buy him that drink back.

Life, of course, goes on, and for me that meant the football. Rangers were now on track for a league title. Easter Road was the place to be, five games to go and a single point was all that was required. A massive support assembled at the ground, the song of choice being a version of Pilot's "Its Magic".

"Oh, oh, oh it's magic, you know, you'll never get ten in a row."

It was a nervous occasion, particularly when Hibs scored to take an early lead. A Sandy Jardine penalty miss just added to the tension, then Colin Stein equalised with a bullet header, and thirty odd thousand fans erupted in joy. The game ended 1–1, a point had been gained, a point was enough and we were Champions. Celebrations started as soon as the final whistle sounded and continued all the way back along the M8 with champagne being quaffed on the bus. The dominant song had now changed to a version of Garry Glitter's "Oh Yes! You're Beautiful" – "Oh yes! We're Champions, Champions, didn't I tell you, didn't I tell you…" and it was sung over and over. It had taken eleven long years, but Rangers were on top again.

The season ended with a home defeat to Airdrie but the result was totally incidental. We had come to see the league trophy being presented, a trophy at last bedecked with red, white and blue ribbons. At the end of the game we were treated to the surreal sight of John Greig being paraded round the ground, league trophy in hand, standing on a chariot pulled by a big black horse. I allowed myself a smile and thought how my dad would have loved the moment.

Having left school, the summer of 1975 was spent job hunting. A lot of application forms were filled out and a lot of letters hand written before I got my first, and as it transpired, only interview, with James Scott, a Glasgow engineering firm. I was invited to their Head Office in Finnieston, and along with twenty or so other hopefuls undertook an aptitude test, followed by a formal interview. The test was pretty easy and I was confident I'd done well. The interview also went well and as it closed I remembered some of my father's advice and shook the interviewer's hand firmly, thanking him for giving me an opportunity. He seemed impressed and a few days later I got a job offer, to join James Scott Engineering as an apprentice electronic technician. It was time to join the big bad world.

For the first year of my apprenticeship, I was based at an engineering training complex in Coatbridge learning the basic skills of fitting, turning, welding etc. as well as a more intensive electrical training. At the centre I started to mix with the other apprentices and discovered that not all were Rangers fans, in fact in Coatbridge hardly any. There were a lot of Celtic fans, a few Motherwell supporters and even an intrepid follower of Albion Rovers.

Football season 75/76 got off to a flyer with a victory! Rangers' first opening day league win since 1968, a result made all the sweeter as it was over Celtic – bragging rights to me at the training centre! The good start continued, and a month or so later Rangers lifted the League Cup, with yet another win over the old enemy. The league was proving to be a close contest with Celtic in front for most of season, but Rangers tracking them, always a point or two behind, but ready to pounce on any slip up.

I was by now a member of the Clydebank Loyal and attending games, home and away. With a growing membership, a lot of the younger members fancied a night out after a game, Aberdeen being the ideal location. Those were the days when the Teddy Bears were welcome in the Granite City. A midnight stay in December was proposed but roundly dismissed by the old guard on the bus. Down but not out, a plan was formulated.

The club's March monthly meeting was due to start with the usual suspects in attendance, when a dozen or so of the younger membership entered the room, about to attend their first ever meeting. They played no part in proceedings until bus times were discussed. Aberdeen away: 9am.

A hand shot up, "propose we stay 'til midnight", quickly followed by, "seconded".

A furious argument ensued but the old guard had been well and truly outflanked and the vote was won. The bus would be staying. Mission accomplished!

In April we had our jaunt to Aberdeen and a good time was had by one and all. The younger members of the bus had a pub crawl, ending up in one of the city's dancehalls where we all tried very hard with the fair maidens of Aberdeen, but drew a blank. The old guys who had been so dead set against the trip found a bowling club and, by the looks of them at midnight, had drunk the place pretty well dry. The journey home was boisterous to start off with, but soon calmed down as we all gradually passed out. The final action of the night was spent at the back of the bus where we all sheepishly pulled out the condoms we had optimistically brought with us. One by one they were blown up balloon-like, and flicked up and down the bus, mine included. It would be a while before I would find any other use for a condom!

The season drew to a close and Celtic at last faltered, winning only four of their final ten fixtures. With three games remaining Rangers travelled to Tannadice, and with a goal inside thirty seconds, won the championship. To cap a wonderful season Rangers then beat Hearts in the Scottish Cup Final. It hadn't been a bad year really. I had passed the first year of my day release ONC, completed my training course in Coatbridge and my team had claimed the treble.

Chapter 5:
I'm Rangers 'til I die

It was 1976, and I was now working in the main James Scott factory in Carntyne, just along the road from Celtic Park. Factory life was a bit of an eye opener. The workforce was 90% female, mostly from the east end of Glasgow and quite unlike any woman I had ever encountered. I was used to the Women's Institute-type like my mother, who knitted and made cakes. The factory women swore like troopers, told dirty jokes and liked to tease innocent young guys who were starting their first job. At times I was terrified to go onto the shop floor, especially after a Friday lunchtime drinking session when they were particularly boisterous. At the end of the day though they were all good honest people who just liked a laugh and I grew to enjoy their company, even if I did remain just a little afraid of them!

For a while now, I'd been feeling more and more uneasy about football violence, it simply seemed so un-necessary. The season's first Old Firm game only served to focus those thoughts. As Rangers scored a fight broke out in the Celtic end, and as usual bottles and cans flew across their terracing. Rather than cheer, as I would once have done, I wondered about the welfare of some of my Celtic supporting workmates. Hey, they might be Tims but they were friends as well. Were they involved in the trouble? Would they be okay? Those thoughts about football violence were reinforced in the final minutes of the game when a bottle whizzed over my own head; an angry response from one of my fellow supporters at the sight of the Celtic equaliser. *What was the point of that?* I wondered, it's probably hit and seriously hurt one of our own. It was the seeds of doubt that would grow inside me as the season progressed.

October saw us make a little jaunt down to Birmingham to play a friendly against Aston Villa, though as it transpired it was friendly only in name. I travelled south with some friends on the overnight train from Glasgow Central. In Birmingham early, we wandered about the famous Bullring for a while, and then settled down for a few beers. The day took a somewhat bizarre turn when a coach load of Morris dancers entered the pub we'd chosen, dressed head to toe in white, with bells on their ankles, jingling as they walked. We viewed them somewhat suspiciously at first, not quite sure what to make of it all. My mate Peter, not the most liberal of chaps, gave us his forthright opinion; "fuckin' poofs!" Actually they were a decent bunch of guys from Yorkshire, who sank as many pints as we did and kindly shared their buffet with us.

Two o'clock found us outside Villa Park, a couple of thousand strong and all with the same intention, to enter the Holte End, the traditional standing area of the Villa support. For the 1970s football fan this was the supreme triumph, to claim a home end, and no one was going to stop us. As I entered the ground a policeman told me not to settle down as we would soon be re-located. I had a little smile and shook my head at that comment; he obviously didn't know that we were merely the advance party! By kick off there were probably between five and ten thousand Rangers fans in that end of the ground. Any Villa supporters who'd managed to gain entry were given the ultimate insult of being led away, to join their countrymen in the 'away end' – victory was ours!

Not for the first time, and certainly not the last, the events of a game became a little hazy. I remember the first half being pretty uneventful bar a lot of singing and taunting; a very simple, but effective, chant of "We're in the Holte End", reminding the Villa fans of who was in charge.

The real action of the day started at half time with a couple of solo pitch invasions, Villa fans running onto the pitch waving Irish tricolours. A few of our boys went on to teach them the error of their way, and the police got their warm-up for the main event which was soon to follow. We watched from the back of the vast terracing, enjoying the spectacle with a few bonus beverages. A couple of lads had broken into the (not surprisingly) closed beer stall and liberated some crates of best Midlands' bitter.

The second half started with a couple of quick Villa goals and at last the home support had something to crow about. Another incursion from a green, white and gold flag-waving Villa fan was met by a major response from the Rangers end and the pitch was invaded. The Villa support accepted the challenge and poured onto the park, but, on seeing the vast numbers haemorrhaging from the Holte took the sensible decision and retreated to the safety of their terracing. That left the police to deal with the interlopers from Glasgow, and some skirmishes ensued on the park as arrests were made. The police gradually forced the pitch invaders back onto the terracing, and were rewarded with a hail of missiles – those liberated bottles of beer now finding a secondary use.

The game had long since been stopped and abandoned, but the action continued with more and more violent scenes and injuries on both sides. I watched as missiles rained down on the advancing police. The trouble was that a big proportion of them were falling on Rangers fans. We were hurting our own and that just didn't make sense (not that, in hindsight, chucking bottles at the police made a lot of sense either). The police eventually restored an order of sorts, and we were pushed rather unceremoniously to the exits. Ejected from the ground we made our way back, under escort, to the city centre. Unable to leave Birmingham 'til our late train we decided to keep a low profile, not easy as almost all the pubs had been closed under police orders. We did manage to find an Indian restaurant happy to accommodate us, a curry and some overpriced bottles of beer keeping us going 'til departure time. It was a subdued train that arrived back in Glasgow, the traditional chorus of the Billy Boys curtailed by the sight of TV cameras and reporters searching for a story. It had been a journey of reflection for me. I was beginning to doubt what being a football fan, what being a Rangers fan, entailed.

I was now in my second year at work. James Scott was a small engineering firm owned by a chap who ruled with an iron fist. Wages were low, with few benefits other than the statutory legal minimum. When the boss cut overtime rates the workforce decided to fight back, and became unionised, joining the AUEW. My terms and conditions were guaranteed under my apprenticeship agreement but I joined as well, and became actively involved.

This was also the start of my brief flirtation with revolutionary socialism. On a Friday evening I would go down the pub with friends, around about closing time, a group would come in selling the Socialist Worker newspaper. Being an active trade unionist I thought it my duty to buy it and to be fair it was a decent read. With news from home and abroad it tweaked memories of my days in Pakistan and the Far East where I had seen some genuine poverty and deprivation. I became quite friendly with one of the girls who sold the paper; she was very pretty and always took time to chat, letting me buy her a drink or two. Without realising it, I became sucked into the International Socialist organisation, soon to become known as the Socialist Workers Party. I was the victim of a honey trap! Within weeks I'd given up my Friday drink and started to tramp the streets of Clydebank, helping that girl sell the newspaper, eventually becoming a card-carrying member. In joining, I managed to increase the local membership from four up to five!

I had gained myself a new set of friends, or comrades, as we liked to refer to each other. What became immediately clear was that I was the only member of the group who was a Blue Nose. Indeed when we had a conference of all the Glasgow branches I discovered that I was the only Rangers fan in the entire organisation! We had many an evening in the pub; drinking, analysing the world's problems, plotting the road to socialism ... and discussing why I should give up Rangers. Eventually their persistence paid off and I was convinced that it just wasn't politically correct to be a 'ger. I became a 'football fan', picking and choosing a game each week, going for entertainment and not out of blind loyalty. It hadn't been an easy decision to make but I'd been troubled by the violence I'd seen at Rangers games and I just didn't want to be a part of that any more.

My first game as a 'non-fan' was on Christmas Day when Clydebank entertained St Mirren. It was a super game with both teams battling out an entertaining 2–2 draw, but not at all festive. Clydebank had organised a group of Santas to hand out sweets to the local youngsters at half time. When the collection of Santas reached the covered terracing they were pelted with cans thrown from the Clydebank hooligan fringe, next to them were the travelling Buddies who gleefully joined in. Within minutes they were firing cans and bottles at each other, a fight broke out, and a small pitch invasion followed. So much for Christmas spirit! At that point I should have realised that my concerns about football violence were not unique to Rangers Football Club. The problem was in fact endemic in the game as a whole. It would take me a while to come to my senses.

A week or so later I was back at Kilbowie, home of Clydebank FC, marvelling at the skills of a young winger by the name of Davie Cooper. He scored a hat trick that day in an 8–1 win over Arbroath. Perhaps my decision to pick and choose games was a good one. I did make a return to Ibrox for the New Year game, going without my colours. I was, after all, a neutral now. Rangers lost 1–0 to a Colin Jackson own goal, and neutral or not, I wasn't happy looking over at the celebrating Celtic support. Old habits die hard and although I didn't know it, there was a spark still inside my belly, just trying to escape.

My football travels took me to Dumbarton for a Scottish Cup tie, the home side entertaining a Hearts team who were somewhat down on their luck and about to be relegated from the Premier League. I was impressed with the Hearts support, a seriously hard bunch who took no prisoners. Within minutes of entering the ground they had kicked the Dumbarton fans out of 'their end'. Once again the penny should have dropped about football violence. Watching the Hearts support, I cast my mind back to my childhood. With my dad away from home my grandfather would come over to watch over my sisters and me. Originally from Broxburn in West Lothian, he was a Hearts man through and through and would spend hours telling me about the great Hearts teams of the 50s and early 60s. Indeed for a while I was the only child at my Elgin Street primary school with a maroon and white scarf, I was in danger of becoming a Junior Jambo!

My attempt to be a neutral football fan only lasted a few months and came to an abrupt end in March. I found myself at Parkhead with some of my SWP comrades, watching Celtic who were on the cusp of another championship. They beat Dundee United 1-0, the biggest roar of the day however came not from the Celtic goal, but when a score was announced at full time: Kilmarnock 1, Rangers 0. I watched, as the ground wildly celebrated, and felt quite ill. It was as though I had suddenly been awoken from a bad dream. What was I doing here ... what had I been thinking? My heart belonged at Ibrox, and that's where I wanted to be. I couldn't get away fast enough. My romance with the Rangers was back on again!

My return as a supporter certainly went with a bang. It was an evening game against Motherwell, pretty routine actually, until midway through the second half when there was a huge, ear-splitting explosion from the back of terracing. Cue mass panic; the IRA were on yet another mainland bombing campaign and everyone had jumped to the conclusion that the terrorists had finally got round to targeting Ibrox. The pitch was quickly invaded as everyone tried to escape the 'bomb blast' and any follow-up explosions. Most supporters decanted to the Centenary Stand, I stayed on the Copland Road – I was a fan again and I was moving for no one, not even the IRA!

The police moved in and it soon became apparent that there had been a fault in one of the gas canisters. A pipe had worked loose, burst into flames and set the pie stall alight, which resulted in the canister exploding. Fortunately no one was hurt and the game continued with the support, now feeling safe, vociferously expressing their dislike of the IRA. There was a fringe benefit of staying on the terracing. In their understandable haste to evacuate the pie stall, the staff had forgotten to remove the cash box, and in the explosion loose change had been blown all over the terracing. I managed to gather enough shrapnel to pay for my train fare home!

This was the year that I started to develop an interest in music. I was in Sauchiehall Street's White Elephant Club with a girl from work. The DJ for the evening stopped playing his disco music and announced that he had a copy of the newly released single from the Sex Pistols, "Anarchy in the UK". It was the period of their infamous appearance on the Bill Grundy TV show and they were pretty much Public Enemy #1. The DJ stuck the record onto the turntable, and in came the thrashing guitars, then the Johnny Rotten vocals:

"Right ... now ... I am an antichrist."

The DJ then ripped it off the turntable and smashed it into pieces. "Its rubbish isn't it?" he yelled, and we all roared our approval. Actually, I thought it was pretty damned good. The girlfriend didn't last long, but my interest in music, alternative music, did. My Eureka moment came when listening to the debut album from The Clash. It just blew me away and immediately took pride of place in my record collection, pushing my previous favourites to one side. Barry White, The Stylistics and The Carpenters (yes really!) would, from now on gather dust.

The final game of the season was the Scottish Cup Final at Hampden. I stood on the terracing and watched Celtic win the trophy, their goal in a 1–0 win coming from a disputed penalty. It wasn't pleasant, and it hurt, but it was a good hurt, because it meant that I cared. It meant that I was once again a true Rangers fan. I may have come to my senses football wise, but back in the real world I was still a confused and mixed up young man. Still involved with the SWP, I spent one Friday night selling the Socialist Worker in the pubs of Clydebank, wearing my "Stuff the Jubilee" badge. Less than twenty-four hours later I was standing on a Glasgow street corner, watching the annual 12th of July parade, Loyal Orange Order members commemorating the Glorious Revolution and the British monarchy. As band after band passed, I tapped my foot in appreciation of their tunes – I just couldn't see the irony.

The new season started with me entering the third year of my apprenticeship at James Scott. I was enjoying my time there, though I was receiving very little training, really just being used as a bit of a dogsbody. It was a worry, and I knew that at some point I would have to address the problem, but not being the most assertive of people, I just let the situation drift. Anything for an easy life.

Rangers made two encouraging signings: that super young winger, Davie Cooper, from Clydebank and striker Gordon Smith from Kilmarnock. The squad was looking good and we approached the season with some degree of optimism, and hopefully an opening day victory – we should have known better. Rangers just didn't do good starts, two games into the league campaign and they had zero points. A couple of weeks later I was at Ibrox, watching despondently as Celtic raced into a two goal half time lead ... then Rangers woke up and rapped three into the Celtic net to win 3–2. We were back in the title hunt.

The SWP were heavily involved in a 'Right to Work' campaign, protesting against youth unemployment, and had organised a march from Manchester to Blackpool to lobby the TUC conference. In support, a contingent from Glasgow were joining the march and I had been put under some pressure to join them, but had managed to wriggle out of it with a few excuses. In actual fact, I was heading up to Perth that weekend for a League Cup tie.

On the Friday night however that plan was to change. It was whispered that the Sex Pistols would be playing a gig in Wigan to entertain the marchers. On hearing the news I quickly decided that it was my duty to support my comrades, if the Sex Pistols were performing, well, that was just a bonus. So, on Saturday, as the Clydebank Loyal set off for Perth, I headed in the opposite direction to Wigan. Arriving in the town it became clear that I wasn't the only one who had heard the rumour that the SPOTS (Sex Pistols on tour secretly) would be playing, there were hundreds of punks mingling about the town centre. What followed was a good, though ultimately disappointing evening as the Sex Pistols, inevitably, I suppose, did not play. The Drones and the Nosebleeds entertained an audience that consisted of some curious locals and a lot of Northern Soul boys, resentful that a bunch of punks and political activists had invaded their famous venue, the Wigan Casino. The evening ending as so many did with a big scrap, that evening it was Soul Boys vs Punks. I kipped the night in a freezing cold 'Right to Work' tent before sneaking away after breakfast. Marching to Blackpool just didn't appeal to me. Anyway, I had a job to get back to. Once again I just couldn't see the irony in my actions.

That trip to Wigan had kindled the punk spirit in me and I wanted more, but that just wasn't possible in Glasgow. The city's council leaders would not allow punk bands to play – Punks were undesirable, dangerous and violent. Strange as the same council had allowed Glasgow's two biggest tribes to do battle for the previous hundred years, all in the name of sport. Eventually the embargo was lifted, and a series of bands would come to play, usually at the Apollo. October was an especially good month with Elvis Costello, The Stranglers and The Clash all playing. It was however an expensive time, tickets for concerts and the associated drinking costs were eating into my still meagre wage packet, and something had to give. So I decided to skip the League Cup tie with Aberdeen convincing myself that it wouldn't be much of a game. The following morning I read newspaper reports of a 6–1 victory, each one raving about one of Rangers' best performances in years: outstanding, majestic, awesome, dazzling – bloody typical I thought.

For the next year or so I was a Rangers supporting punk rocker, though to be honest I never really mastered the punk look. The ripped T-shirt was easy, on it the statutory safety pins and zips. I had a chain round my neck padlocked a la Sid Vicious, so far so good. Unfortunately being money conscious, stingy some might say, I refused to give up my flared jeans and continued to wear them, until they had worn out – a total no go for the "real punk". My biggest problem though was on my head; punks had spiky hair and my hair just refused to cooperate. It was curly, not in a wavy way but frizzy afro. Try as I might, I could do nothing with it. I was depressingly more Jackson 5 than Generation X!

For all my years as a Rangers fan I had learned to look out for the Celtic score, they were always the team chasing, or to be chased. This season was different, Celtic were frankly rotten, camped in the bottom half of the table. Beating them however, no matter their league position, was always satisfying. A particularly memorable game came in the New Year fixture at Ibrox.

Rangers, a goal up, were under a lot of pressure from a Celtic side who were playing disturbingly well. During an attack one of their forwards was bundled over in the process of shooting. I groaned in expectation of the inevitable penalty award, as it looked a stonewall decision. The referee, bless him, disagreed and awarded a goal kick. A decision not well received by the Celtic players who crowded round the official in protest. As the irate hoops pursued the man in black, the men in blue raced up the park. After three or four passes the ball was at John Greig's foot, right in front of an open goal, and he wasted no time in gleefully slotting it into the empty net. A few years previous the green and white supporters had cheered a John Greig goal … well they weren't cheering now! A section of their support spilled from the terracing and onto the pitch, whilst the inevitable fight broke out – this was marvellous!

Jock Stein, the Celtic manager, had to intervene to try and restore order, at the same time his players argued and complained to the referee. Clearly not happy the Celtic players tried to leave the field, like wee boys at school; "we're not playing anymore!" – could this get any better? Having persuaded his supporters to return to the terracing, Jock Stein then had to coax his players back onto the field to continue the game. In a final show of petulance they kicked off by blootering the ball up the park, the dummy well and truly spat out. It was simply fantastic and if there is a better way to score in an Old Firm game, then I've yet to see it!

The Rangers support, to be fair, were no angels, and had their moments of petulance as well, never slow to express their displeasure. In February their actions were to provide a boost in the league title race. Two goals down at Fir Park, the crowd reacted badly to an ill-advised gesture from one of the Motherwell players who was celebrating their second goal. The fans surged forward in anger, the crush pushing spectators onto the park, followed by others intent on causing bother. The game was disrupted and the holdup gave the men in blue time to regroup, Motherwell in turn lost any momentum that they had gathered. When the game was restarted Rangers took control and overturned a 2–0 deficit into a 5–3 victory. A vital two points had been gathered, with a big helping hand from the support, though no one would openly admit that.

The League race continued with Aberdeen mounting a challenge to the final game of the season. On that day Rangers only needed a point against Motherwell to claim the title, a 2–0 victory over saw both points won and the Rangers were Champions again. There was no time to celebrate however as I had a date in London, Rock against Racism were holding a march and carnival in Victoria Park, and with The Clash performing it just wasn't to be missed. So after the game I drove, along with a few friends, down to London, stopping off midway for a few beers and a sleep in the car. Driving south I pondered my mother's parting remarks. She was away on a week's holiday and had told me: No parties or using her car for long journeys as it was due a service. I wasn't too worried. Let's face it, she'd never find out.

We made it to the carnival and being a political animal I went on the march, the rest of my party headed to the pub. The concert was superb with The Clash in blistering form, joined by Jimmy Pursey from Sham 69 in a rousing "White Riot" climax. Well worth the trip. Reunited with my friends it became clear that we had a problem. I was sober, and they were all pissed, so it would be only me driving, London to Glasgow. I could manage, but only if we put some petrol in the car. Another problem, my pissed pals had drunk all their money. No money = no petrol = no trip home. The problem was solved after a lot of thought by calling the AA and getting them to sub us some petrol money. They weren't keen but could see that there was no other option; all they needed was my mother's AA membership number so they could send her the bill! Driving home in the early hours of the morning I turned on the radio to keep me awake. Tuned to a local BBC station I heard Nat King Cole singing "There may be trouble ahead…".

In May, Rangers lifted the Scottish cup to complete another treble. We thought the season was all over … we were wrong. Not long after the final, manager Jock Wallace resigned from his post. Questions were asked as to why, over and over, but big Jock would not reveal his reasons. The new manager was soon unveiled. It was team captain John Greig. Could he make the transition from player and friend, to manager and boss in one swift move? Only time would tell.

My SWP phase was also over, I'd grown bored with the routine of selling newspapers, become disillusioned with the politics, and weary of all the left wing in-fighting. It all seemed so stupid and pointless, and totally detached from the real world that I lived in. Possibly I'd just grown up a little!

Chapter 6:
Heading into the Doldrums

I was now in my fourth year at James Scott, still going to the football and attending concerts, The Jam, The Clash, The Damned, The Buzzcocks, and Stiff Little Fingers amongst many others playing at the Apollo. I also discovered Glasgow band, The Zips. They were superb and over the next few years I would follow them about the city, their gigs occasionally conflicting with my Rangers duties. The Zips were a great band, who played some good punk with clever and thought provoking lyrics. After a while I became friendly with the guys in the band, helping them load and unload their van, sometimes even operating their light system. It might have only been five or six coloured lights and a strobe lamp, but it made me feel so important, I could kid on I was part of the band. Some great nights were enjoyed in places like the Burns Howff and the Amphora. For a while they even played closer to home, in Clydebank's Atlantis Bar. Unfortunately the band didn't attract hordes of teenage groupies; still, they were happy days!

Ibrox, as a stadium, was now starting to change. Willie Waddell had vowed in the aftermath of the Ibrox Disaster that such a tragic event would never happen again. He had a vision of an all seated stadium, where spectators would be comfortable and safe when watching their team, and in season 78/79 that vision was put into action. During the close season the Copland Road had been bulldozed and foundations put down for a brand new stand. The end of the ground where I'd been arrested had disappeared, the exploding pie stall, gone. No longer would we keep warm by gathering up all the discarded newspapers, and burning them on a cold winter afternoon. The guy who wandered round selling the Macaroon bars and spearmint chewing gum would have to find a new pitch. The woman who sold the cheese rolls from an old egg box would have to decant to another part of the ground. Just how old were some of those cheese rolls? If the cheese wasn't mature the rolls certainly were. The new Ibrox was starting to grow and as the season progressed the new structure would tower over the rest of the ground.

I was, by now, well used to bad starts and realised that it didn't always lead to a disastrous season. This time however, our start wasn't so much bad as calamitous with only one win in the first eight league games, no goals in the first three. Undaunted I decided that it was time to step up my support for the 'Gers; I was going to follow them into Europe. The first round of the European Cup had paired Rangers with Juventus, the Italian Champions. To be honest, if I wanted to travel to Europe then I had better choose this game, as we were unlikely to progress any further, their squad containing no fewer than nine of the current Italian World Cup squad. The best, and by far the cheapest way to travel was by supporters' bus, so I scanned the Rangers News and Evening Times, for busses who would be making the trip, and from the five or six available I chose the Partick Loyal, simply because it was closest to home.

We left Glasgow on a Monday evening, with the target of Turin early on Wednesday. As I was to discover over the years, these trips rarely go as planned and our departure was delayed as the bus convener explained to one traveller that yes, he did need a passport to travel abroad! Passing through London early on Tuesday morning, our journey was further delayed. Taking a slight de-tour, and by special request, the bus went twice round the Queen Victoria memorial in front of Buckingham Palace. We all stood for a chorus of the National Anthem as we passed the Palace for the second time. It seems quite bizarre now, but at the time it was a perfectly reasonable thing to do.

The long journey through France was broken up by a stop in a small town just outside Grenoble. Settling in the main square, one local café owner had a dream evening; his rivals looked on enviously as we descended, en-mass into his establishment and set about spending as many French francs on as much French beer as was humanly possible. Before leaving we had a march round the town square, in full voice, led by the café owner waving a red, white and blue tricolour. We had made at least one Frenchman very happy.

We arrived in Turin very early on Wednesday morning and wandered about, taking in the sights and partaking in a few Italian beers – just, you understand, to compare them to the quality of the previous evening's French fare. During the afternoon we bumped into some Scottish journalists led by Ian Archer, a thoroughly disagreeable man, in my humble opinion. Celtic had been playing Burnley in the Anglo Scottish Cup the night before and we wanted to know what the score had been. Archer made it perfectly clear that he knew the result, but wasn't going to tell.

Sneering at us, he instructed his colleagues: "tell them nothing".

We shouldn't really have been surprised as Archer was a man, quoted in the Glasgow Herald as saying: "This country would be a better place if Rangers did not exist."

For the record, Celtic lost 1–0 to Burnley and their fans initiated a mass riot. So it wasn't only Rangers fans that were involved in crowd trouble, but Archer just couldn't, or more likely just wouldn't, see that. Anyway, his intransigence only postponed our mirth for a few days.

As kick off approached, we gathered outside the Stadio Comunale di Torino, and I suddenly realised what being an 'away fan' was all about. With Rangers I went to away games but as part of a support that were almost always in the majority, outnumbered at Parkhead perhaps, we were still a good 20,000 strong. That night in Turin we were 300 in a crowd of over 60,000.

We were kept together in a small pocket, guarded by a ring of Policemen, bordered on all sides by crazed Italians. Fireworks exploded in the no-man's land that surrounded us, and not your Astra type squibs, these were like sticks of dynamite. Fortified by a few bottles of Italian plonk we put up a good show of defiance, singing loud and proud whilst dodging the bombs! Whether the Rangers team could hear us I don't know but they also put up a great fight. Losing the game by a single goal, they fought, scrapped and battled for the entire ninety minutes. The referee's final whistle sounded an end to the player's endeavours, but for the supporters on the terracing there was extra time to be endured, we had to get back to our buses. Not an easy task with the Juventus Ultras spoiling for a fight.

I became separated from the main group of supporters and had to make a solo dash for the bus park. At one point stopping to fend off an attack from a group of Juve hoodlums. Swinging a flagpole at them I managed to escape, in hindsight though, waving a Torino FC flag may not have been my smartest ever idea. Adrenalin pumping, I triumphantly made it back to the Partick Loyal and was surprised to see everyone cowering behind seats or lying on the floor. What was going on I wondered ... and had an immediate answer when a police rubber bullet crashed off our bus. We were under attack not only from the Ultras but also the Carabinieri. Our bus escaped from the mayhem unscathed, but others were not so lucky and had to cross the Alps with missing windows. September it might have been, but at that altitude it was very cold. I certainly didn't envy them during that part of the journey.

The second leg was two weeks later: Rangers 2, Juventus 0. Six of that Juventus team would go on to win the World Cup with Italy. At Ibrox they were soundly beaten and it was the Scottish Champions who proceeded into the next round.

European Cup second-round opponents were PSV Eindhoven and plans were immediately made to travel to the second leg, a booking made this time on the Old Kilpatrick Loyal RSC. A disappointing 0–0 draw at Ibrox put a slight dampener on the trip to Holland, but we set off ever hopeful that Rangers could get a good result. The Philips Stadion was a totally different venue to that we had encountered in Italy; much more compact, holding a relatively small 28,000. With a couple of thousand fans making this trip there was a tremendous atmosphere in the ground. Pre-match I turned to one of my friends and said, "We just have to keep it tight for the first ten or fifteen minutes". The game kicked off, and after about five or six passes the ball was in the Rangers net. I glanced up in dismay, at the big electronic scoreboard, and saw that thirty six seconds had elapsed! Not quite the start I'd envisaged. An epic European tie then followed.

Rangers drew level … PSV took the lead again … once again Rangers equalised.

With the game on a knife-edge Rangers then scored a quite sublime goal. Gordon Smith sprinted from the edge of his own penalty box. He swung a crossfield pass to Tommy McLean, who waited for a few seconds before slipping an inch-perfect pass into the path of Bobby Russell. The young Ranger ran in on goal and coolly slotted a shot under the advancing keeper. We watched from behind the goal as the ball trundled towards the net, every one of us willing it to go in. After what felt like an eternity, the ball slipped inside the post. My team were 3–2 ahead, and how we celebrated. Three minutes later, the game was over, and PSV Eindhoven had tasted European defeat on their home soil for the very first time.

The Dutch supporters were to prove very different from their Italian counterparts, and the walk back to the coach park was surprisingly friendly, with some scarf swapping and hand shaking. There was even time for a few beers in a groundside bar, something that would have been completely unthinkable, and extremely foolhardy in Italy.

I now thoroughly disapproved of football violence, throwing missiles was just stupid, particularly when they were raining down on fellow Rangers fans. It didn't, however, stop me bringing in the ammunition; it was a time when drinking at the game was commonplace. Whilst alcohol was officially banned from football grounds it was relatively easy to gain entry with it. Some cans stuck inside your trouser belt, a couple more tucked inside your socks, would allow a reasonable cargo for the game. Along with my friend Peter, I would smuggle a couple of beers into the ground: cans of Tennants Lager and McEwans Export. Many supporters added a bottle of Lanliq or Eldorado fortified wine to their stash. Peter and I had a much more educated palate and preferred a bottle of Emva Cream. A cheeky wee sherry would add a lovely glow to a winter's afternoon.

Drinking at the game meant a trip or two to the toilet, inconvenient in a big crowd and always carried the risk of missing a goal. The solution to that problem was to open up the top of a can of beer, just enough to allow the desperate supporter to relieve himself. Once full, the can would be discarded onto the terracing, its new contents soaking into the dirt or seeping away through the cracks in the concrete steps. Unthinkable now, but in the 70s it was standard practice. I was always wary of the semi-opening method, fearful of the consequences of a goal being scored when in "full flow", so I became adept at removing the top completely off of a can. With a 50p piece and a quick flick of the wrist it could be achieved in a few seconds and so much easier to use. I was clearly an early advocate of Health and Safety!

The league race was now in full swing and, recovering from their poor start, Rangers were actively involved. The table did, however, have an unusual look to it, in mid-February, St Mirren were top! This was a St Mirren side that would sack their manager at the end of the season. Their manager being a certain Alex Ferguson, a man who would go on to have some success in the game!

The European Cup run continued and in March we were in Cologne for the quarter final, now feeling confident of going all the way. Cologne was an interesting city, its centrepiece being a quite majestic cathedral. It was a building that had somehow remained untouched during the Second World War, amazing really as the RAF had pretty much flattened the rest of the city. A message to certain Scottish journalists – it remained untouched after our visit as well! Rangers went down 1–0, but we returned home ever hopeful. After all, we had achieved the same result in Turin and overcome a technically better Juventus side. The dream of European glory was still on.

The return leg was scheduled for a Wednesday evening in Glasgow but an unexpected blizzard put paid to that and the game was called off, the Ibrox turf covered in a few feet of snow. Volunteers helped clear the pitch and twenty-four hours later the game was played, but the momentum had been lost, and with a 1–1 draw the European dream stuttered and died.

European failure was soon forgotten as Rangers claimed the first trophy of the season, beating Aberdeen in the final of the League Cup. It had been a close-run thing though, the winner coming from Colin Jackson in the final minute. It was nice to see him getting the crucial goal after witnessing so many of his own-goals. Little did I know what was to come!

As the football season drew to a close, the league table took on a more familiar shape with the Old Firm in the top two positions. Celtic's final game was at Parkhead against Rangers, and a win would give them the title, any other result would inevitably propel the league flag to Ibrox. In a hugely disappointing night of drama Rangers took the lead but were pegged back. Playing against ten men for over half an hour they failed to capitalise, but with five minutes left, with the score tied at 2–2, they still had the title in their grasp. Then it was lost, Rangers scored, but into the wrong net. Yup, it was a Colin Jackson own-goal yet again! An injury time fourth for Celtic was academic, other than to rub salt into our already painful wounds, and we trudged despondently back to our buses. It had been a bad, bad night.

The season ended with a Scottish Cup final, though for a while it seemed that it would go on forever. Saturday afternoon, and I watched Rangers and Hibs play out a pretty dreadful goalless draw. I'd smuggled a bottle of champagne into the ground to celebrate the expected cup win, well, it was actually a bottle of Asti Spumante, but same difference; the cork popped out, it fizzed and was alcoholic. With a draw I couldn't pop my cork, so for the first time ever I had to smuggle some alcohol *out* of a ground! Four days later Rangers and Hibs contested the replay and produced a game even more dismal than the first. My bottle of Asti was smuggled into the ground and unbelievably back out again. Enough was enough, the bottle was cracked open and the contents drunk on the bus home, but tasted as flat as the game had been.

The replayed replay was pushed back to the end of May and became the fixture that no one wanted, not even covered by television, no highlights, nothing. A shame really as it was a cracker, Rangers winning by the odd goal in five, though it did take a Hibs own-goal to send the trophy Ibrox-bound.

Season 79/80 started with me on holiday and although I didn't know it at the time, I was about to miss its only highlight. One of my friends, Alan, had snagged himself a job in Hamburg, and I went over to stay with him for a few weeks in the summer. As I was sipping Holsten Pils, and sampling the dubious pleasures of the Reeperbahn, Rangers were taking on Celtic in the final of the Dryborough Cup. The Ibrox men won 3–1 and Davie Cooper scored arguably the finest goal ever seen at Hampden. Picking the ball up wide, he flicked it over one defender after another, playing 'keepie uppie'. He worked his way into the penalty box, glided past a final opponent before slipping a shot into the net. I would later see some grainy film of the goal and had to marvel at the sheer brilliance of it. Now, if only he had done it at Parkhead back in May of last season…!

An opening day win at Easter Road was to prove a false dawn for Rangers' League Championship campaign. In the next game, in front of the newly opened Copland Road Stand, they threw away a two goal lead to allow Celtic a draw. Once again Rangers couldn't finish off ten men. They were then to stumble their way through a quite dismal season; indeed it would be December before two league wins in a row could be strung together.

Life wasn't running too smoothly for me either. My training at James Scott had become pretty well non-existent. I'd temporarily moved into their Production Engineering Department, for some work experience, and never left. After a while it became clear that I was simply being used as cheap labour, to keep production moving, my electrical training, my apprenticeship had effectively ended.

The football season ground on with Rangers in dire form. To their credit the support kept faith with the team, clinging to the forlorn hope that things may somehow get better. Sadly nothing changed, though on the final day of the season Rangers had the chance to redeem themselves and snatch a bit of silverwear. They had made their way to the Scottish Cup final to play, inevitably, Celtic. It was a day that Scottish football would never forget. Played out to the world, live on TV, the Old Firm fans excelled themselves, and fought a pitched battle on the Hampden turf. Crowd trouble on the football terracing is often referred to as rioting when in truth it's little more than a bit of a skirmish. Today was different; this was a riot in the literal sense of the word.

It hadn't been the best of games, and after a goalless ninety minutes went into extra time. With time running out, a replay was looking more and more likely. Then, with ten minutes remaining Celtic scored with a deflected shot. It was a horrible moment, and a terrible way to lose a goal, and we all knew, deep down, that it was all over. Rangers, sadly, just didn't look like getting back into the game. We were unfortunately proved correct, and the final whistle sounded with Celtic victorious.

I applauded the Rangers players as they received their runner-up medals, and despondently turned to leave the ground. Walking up the terracing steps I watched over my shoulder as Celtic paraded the cup to their fans, some of whom invaded the park. One of their number provocatively made his way into our half. Having found a ball from somewhere he proceeded to run to the goal at the Mount Florida end, and, gesticulating to the Rangers fans, he slammed a shot into the net. "Light the blue touch paper and stand well back", well that's what that individual did. The outraged Rangers fans spilled onto the park, in ones and twos, in dozens and then hundreds. They charged at their rivals, driving them back onto their terracing. With the police caught unawares the Celtic support counter charged, and a mass battle erupted on the park.

The riot was finally quelled by a third pitch invasion, this time by mounted Glasgow police, their horses showing no respect for the colour of scarf or strip. A few heads were cracked with truncheons, and eventually the pitch was cleared. As calm was restored, a TV camera, broadcasting to the nation, panned round the ground: the abiding memory being a pitch strewn with bottles and cans of all description. It was a scene that was to herald the conception of the Scottish Criminal Justice Act. Alcohol would no longer be allowed into grounds, or permitted on transport to or from the match. Football as we knew it was starting to change.

Chapter 7:
European Adventures

My time at James Scott was drawing to a close, I realised that I had no real prospects there. Indeed the way the electronics industry was developing, the company itself had a limited future. Having achieved some academic success over the years, I decided to continue along that path. I applied for, and was accepted onto, a full time degree course in Electronic Engineering at Paisley Technical College, sad to be leaving some good friends at the factory, but excited at the new challenge ahead of me. It was ultimately a good decision because within a year the factory would close, the workforce made redundant.

The previous season's calamitous league placing meant no European football for Rangers. In fact they were relegated to the humiliation of the Anglo Scottish Cup, a competition shunned by all of England's top sides. In 1972 Rangers won the European Cup Winners' Cup. In 1979 they were battling for a place in the European Cup semi-final. Now, in 1980, eighteen months later, they were playing the mighty Chesterfield from England's third division, in a 'Mickey Mouse competition'. How we had laughed at Celtic's misfortune in losing an Anglo-Scottish tie in Burnley. Now we were to suffer a similar fate ... what goes around comes around!

Second rate competition or not, I still wanted to go, so I set off for the exotic delights of deepest Derbyshire, travelling on the Tradeston bus. For most it was a trip to be forgotten, for me it was literally a forgotten trip. The bus stopped off for the afternoon in Blackpool, and I remember going into a few pubs, my next memory is drinking neat vodka from a Smirnoff bottle. After that it's a complete blank, though I have vague recollections of Colin McAdam missing a penalty. We lost 3–0, the rain was tumbling down, and I was drenched to the skin, not the best of trips.

Performances didn't improve, and the season stumbled on, with Rangers slipping further and further behind in the title race. They were at least putting together a Scottish Cup run, but even that required a last minute equaliser to salvage a replay against lower league St Johnstone. Rangers made the final, but in-keeping with the season as a whole the game was a dismal affair. Rangers drew 0–0 with Dundee United, even managing to miss a last-minute penalty. However, the replay was entirely different; a Davie Cooper inspired Rangers suddenly found some form and won an exciting and entertaining game 4–1.

I looked back on the season, and considered it to have been relatively successful. We had after all won a trophy, but I was kidding myself on. Celtic had won the league, whilst my team were fighting St Mirren for fourth place. It just wasn't good enough.

During the long college holiday I earned myself some money doing odd jobs round the neighbourhood, painting and gardening; enough to finance a jaunt to Scandinavia, to watch Rangers' pre-season tour. The tour started in Sweden, and was totally unlike any European trip I had ever been on. With games in small towns and villages there was an opportunity to mix with the players, and, with a small band of travelling supporters, it was a very relaxed, and surprisingly sober experience. Not that I'd suddenly become health conscious, far from it, it was simply because Swedish beer was outrageously expensive. In an attempt to curb a severe alcohol problem, the government had quadrupled the cost of drink. It certainly curtailed our boozing … well; it did once the bottles of beer and vodka brought over from Denmark ran out.

The first game in Trelleborg gave me the novel experience of being a footballer. Wearing a tracksuit, I was approached by a small boy who clearly thought I was part of the Rangers squad. I was twenty-four years old, fit and athletic (well, kind of), so an easy mistake to make! The boy pushed a scrap of paper and a pen into my hand and asked me to sign it. I tried to explain that I wasn't really a player, just a supporter, but he looked so crestfallen at my refusal that I decided to humour him. I scribbled my name onto the bit of paper, with a postscript of Rangers FC. I may have been a fraud, but at least the boy went away happy – and I felt pretty good as well. From then on I quite happily signed programmes and autograph books, even posing for the odd photograph. I was though, I'm quite sure, the only 'player' on the tour who settled down post match in a tent, cooking rashers of bacon on a small gas stove.

A win over Ooland was followed by trip to Karlsham where I evolved from being a footballer into a rock and roll star! The crowd at the match were entertained by a local band, their amplifiers wired up to the stadium sound system. One of my fellow supporters had jokingly said to the band that he'd join them for a song. I said I'd join in, but never thought for one moment that it was a serious proposal. Just before kickoff, the band made an announcement that they were to be joined on stage by a couple of Scotsmen. I was mortified but, having backed myself into a corner, there was no going back. I nervously crossed the field with my knees knocking, quietly cursing my sidekick for getting me into this predicament.

We asked the band in they knew "Follow Follow", they didn't, but soon got the idea when we hummed a few verses. Then off we went, belting out the club anthem to a somewhat bemused Swedish audience. The nerves soon dissipated, and once I got used to my voice booming out, I started to enjoy it. "Follow Follow" over, we went right into "The Billy Boys" and various other medleys (sanitised obviously for the family audience). As a double act we weren't exactly Simon and Garfunkel, but without wishing to brag I think our performance received louder applause than the introduction of the Rangers team a few minutes later. As a huge bonus, we were then taken to the hospitality tent, and treated to a few cold Swedish beers.

After three games in Sweden we crossed over to the Danish capital Copenhagen, for the final game of the tour, playing Hvidovre IK. Post-match we went to the Yankee Bar, whose owner had sponsored the game, reflecting on the tour which had been a great success. Manager John Greig came over to our table, pulled up a chair and chatted for a while, all of us having a chuckle as we watched a youthful and somewhat inebriated Glasgow Evening Times reporter trying, and failing miserably to feed money into the jukebox. The reporter, a certain Chick Young, finally gave up declaring the machine broken and useless. A few minutes later the sounds of "Blue Suede Shoes" blasted out, prompting John Greig into a mighty fine Elvis Presley impersonation!

As Greig left our company, he went into his wallet brought out a couple of hundred Kroner, and told us to have a few beers on the Rangers, thanking us for our support. It was a quite superb and totally unexpected gesture, and much appreciated, as funds were starting to run dangerously low.

Over the years as a fan it has become a standing joke that whenever you go to a friendly; at home or abroad, first team or reserves, there will always be some idiot in attendance wearing a Celtic top – they just can't help themselves.

Confession time: I once became an equivalent halfwit. On my way home from Denmark, I stopped off in Hamburg to visit my friend Alan, who was still based in the city. Hamburger SV were entertaining Celtic during my stop over, and we decided to head over to the Volkspark Stadion for the game. Hamburg play in blue, Rangers play in blue, I had my scarf with me so wearing it seemed perfectly logical.

The game went well, standing on the West Curve, scarf on display, I was enthusiastically embraced by the Hamburg fans. The home side winning by three goals to one just made it all the better. Celtic had a reasonable number of fans at the game, but curiously they displayed little support for their team, preferring to sing song after song about the royal wedding of Charles and Diana. Based on their song lyrics, it would be fair to say that they wouldn't be sending a present to the happy couple!

After the game, we got a U-Bahn back into the city centre, sharing a compartment with a group of Celtic supporters. I had my colours well and truly hidden at this point, but was formulating a plan for a wind up. The train pulled up at our station, and we got off. I waited for the train doors to close, and the departure tone to sound, this high pitched noise indicated that the doors were now firmly locked. I'd seen, many times before, people trying to open the doors after that tone but unable to do so … so I knew I was safe.

This was my moment … feeling secure, I stood on the platform, and unveiled my scarf, banging the train window to get some attention. Giving the Celtic fans the finger; I stood bravely showing them the Rangers badges on my scarf, laughing as they all scrambled to get at me. Then, in an awful moment, the tone sounded again, and the doors sprung open. I was now face to face with a group of extremely irate Tims. Their intentions were perfectly clear, and I wasn't hanging about to allow them to indulge their frustrations on me. I turned and ran, closely pursued by the green and white mob, escaping only by virtue of Alan's local knowledge. We ducked into a side street bar, and lay low till the coast was clear. A couple of schnapps were downed to calm the nerves, as Alan gave me a lecture on what an arsehole I was, and to be fair he was 100% correct.

Just before Christmas, the new all-seater Ibrox was formally opened with a friendly match against Liverpool. I wanted to go to the game, but it posed a dilemma as Altered Images, local band made good, fronted by the wonderful Claire Grogan were playing at Tiffanies on the same night. I had a bit of a hankering for Miss Grogan and really didn't want to miss the gig. I was so keen, that I'd queued up on the first day of ticket sales, managing to secure brief #0001. The solution to my problem was to go to Ibrox and watch the first half of the game, and then leave, to ensure a front row vantage point for the concert. That's what I did, and as a result I saw Rangers draw 0–0 with Liverpool, missing the two goals that the Reds scored in the second half. As for the concert, Altered Images were superb and the wonderful Miss Grogan was, well … wonderful.

On the downside musically, after a few years of good gigging, the Zips decided to call it a day. Punk was now giving way to the New Romantics, and with it a new style and fashion. Leading the way for this new movement were bands like Duran Duran and Spandau Ballet, I just couldn't stand those Spandau boys, more about that later.

The league season was to end somewhat bizarrely. We were at Pittodrie playing an Aberdeen side that could still technically win the championship, but only if Celtic lost at home to St Mirren and Aberdeen could win, and at the same time overturn an effective goal difference of six. A Colin Jackson own goal gave Aberdeen a good start, and by half time they were four goals ahead. A terracing rumour then filtered through that St Mirren were leading Celtic 1–0 and excitement mounted. If Aberdeen could score just one more goal they would deny Celtic the championship. Incredibly some in the Rangers support started to cheer on Aberdeen. I didn't want Celtic to be crowned champions any more than they did, but I sure as hell wasn't going to will my team onto an even more embarrassing defeat. Some tense moments were endured as arguments raged over the merits of supporting Aberdeen, 'til Celtic scored a couple of goals and made it all academic.

League season 82/83 started with the usual mess up, a 2–2 draw this time at newly promoted Motherwell. Worryingly at this game there was crushing in the crowd, the sheer weight of numbers causing the Rangers support in one corner of the ground to spill onto the park. Not a new occurrence, and not crowd trouble, simply too many people crammed into too small a space. For football clubs, numbers meant money, and more numbers meant more money. It's how the game worked and occurred at grounds all round the country whenever the Old Firm were playing. Take their cash and squeeze them in seemed to be the common mantra.

Rangers made their first trip to Pittodrie at the end of September. I travelled up to Aberdeen on the Clydebank Loyal, on my own, the rest of my friends having left earlier by train; they had an overnight stay planned. I was so jealous, I really wanted to be part of that but the train fare and accommodation costs were just too prohibitive for my miniscule student grant. It was regrettably the football, and straight home for me. Well that was the theory.

I met up with my pals in Aberdeen and had a few drinks, then off to the game, which had a most unusual outcome, a victory. The first Rangers win at Pittodrie since December 1974! In the euphoria of victory I was persuaded to stay the night. Dossing down on a hotel room floor, I would only need the cost of the train fare home and some beer money. Just about manageable, and if my grant ran out before the end of term, my ever helpful mother would undoubtedly bail me out. We had a good few beers in the city, and then I had to bid my friends a good night. They were going to the dancing, and, being unprepared for an evening stay, I stood no chance of getting in, wearing as I was, trainers, jeans and a Rangers top. So I went for one last drink on my own before heading back to the hotel. Wandering about Aberdeen on a Saturday night wearing Rangers colours, quite unthinkable now! Having that final beer, I met up with a local girl, and we chatted for a while. It was the perfect way to end a very good day. This isn't a kiss and tell story, so I'll stop here. Other than to say: Sarah, you made a skint student very happy that night!

My third year at Paisley Tech had gone well and I was on track to enter the honours degree stream, the only drawback was a failure in a minor subject, Financial Management of Industry. Without that pass I couldn't continue on the course. I still had the lifeline of a re-sit, which shouldn't have been too much trouble, but before that exam date. I had another European tour to look forward to. Season 83/84 was about to start with a trip to Sweden.

Travelling overnight from Glasgow, I got a train to Folkestone and boarded the Hydrofoil bound for Oostende. Settling down, I became aware of some commotion amongst the passengers, with teenage girls particularly excited. Looking up, I saw to my horror that the guys from Spandau Ballet were on board and holding court. I watched with distain and then spotted Gary Kemp, who I really wasn't keen on. He was rumoured to be stepping out with the lovely Claire Grogan and there he was, in a clinch with some admiring blonde. It just wasn't right! *Ignore him*, I thought, but my annoyance grew and grew 'til I had to take action. I'd had enough and I marched up to the front of the boat, determined to give the toe rag a piece of my mind. But it was all rather feeble. Being aggressive just wasn't my style.

"Kemp," I spluttered, "you're a wanker."

Unfortunately it was one of those 'he who laughs last, laughs longest' moments. He took a drink from his chilled Stella Artois and held onto the girl, looking at me with disinterest. His look said it all; he had the continental beer, the money, the fame and the girl – I had a warm can of Tennants!

The tour started with a fine 11–0 win over Arlovs. A Swedish train then took me up the coast to the town of Solvesborg. After pitching my tent, I took a stroll down to the football ground, joining the fifteen or so others who were on the tour. Kicking a ball about we were approached by a Solvesborg IF official, initially it looked as though we were going to be ejected from the pitch, but quite the contrary, he actually wanted to know if we fancied a game. We did, and an hour or so later we lined up, a motley crew in an assortment of blue tops verses a semi official looking Solvesborg XI. It was a hard, hard game, played in the searing afternoon sun. Not being the fittest bunch of players we struggled towards the end of the game, but did receive some unexpected encouragement. The Rangers team had turned up, and were standing on the terracing, watching us play. In a bizarre role reversal they were cheering us on! We put up a good fight, but unfortunately lost 3–2.

Later that evening, the normal order was restored, and we settled down to watch Rangers run up another impressive score, winning 12–0, Sandy Clark scoring five goals. Not bad, but not enough to grant him immunity from criticism. After missing a late chance, one of the supporters expressed his displeasure at the quality of the finish, telling Sandy that he … wasn't terrible good. Sandy wandered over and called out "well at least we're winning", then jogged off chuckling – there was no answer to that!

Rangers returned to Scotland after two further games in Sweden. I stayed in Europe and toured a little. There were further games to enjoy as the team were due to play the Metropole tournament in Antwerp ten days or so later.

I've always believed in trying local dishes and drinks when abroad. Never really understood the mentality of those who go to Spain, for example, and have a full English breakfast every morning and sup best bitter at night. Trying different meals and drinks could be a bit of an adventure and often brought pleasant and unexpected surprises – although not always, as I was to find in Antwerp. I'd met some friends and we settled down for an evening meal. Everyone ordered hamburgers. Not me, I scanned the menu and spotted 'steak américain', some form of steak I reasoned, bound to be okay, and worth a try.

The meals arrived, mine to some hilarity. On my plate was a dollop of raw mince topped by an uncooked egg yolk and surrounded by a green leaf salad. As the laughter grew I called the waiter over and explained that I couldn't possibly eat this … was there any chance it could be cooked? This created some commotion and the chef arrived at our table in obvious distress. I'd ordered his signature dish, the house speciality, and seemingly just insulted it. He grabbed my plate and in a blind fury stormed over to his open plan kitchen. With flames rising and smoke billowing he glared at me, and dramatically cremated the dish. Returning, he slammed my meal back onto the table and stood over me, demanding that I eat it. I crunched my way through the burnt offering, washing it down with as much beer as was humanly possible. With honour satisfied, I complimented him on his cuisine and beat a hasty retreat. Hamburgers and hot dogs for the rest of the Belgian stay. I then returned to Scotland, and the small matter of that re-sit exam.

I'd taken my financial management notes with me on my month long soiree round Europe, but they had remained buried in my rucksack, inevitably untouched. So I sat down to the re-sit unprepared, but still confident. When I opened the exam paper my heart sank. It was set on obscure parts of the course, stuff that I'd never seen before.

I failed the re-sit, and as a result would have to repeat the entire third year of my course. I was annoyed and angry, the exam seemed unduly hard, and it didn't seem fair. In truth though, it was my own fault, I'd stupidly put supporting Rangers before my own future. Getting blootered in Antwerp, thirty six hours before a career defining examination, probably wasn't the wisest of preparations!

The domestic season started well with a Glasgow Cup win over Celtic, not the world's most prestigious tournament but a springboard to a league challenge, surely this year. An opening day draw and eight defeats in the first twelve games gave us the answer ... no!

John Greig was now under immense pressure as manager, and in October he bowed to the inevitable and resigned. A great and inspirational captain, he just couldn't quite transfer those qualities to the manager's chair. The quest for the new manager started and Alex Ferguson was targeted. I was appalled; I didn't want him anywhere near the Rangers job. I didn't like what he had done to Aberdeen, turning them into an aggressive, snarling bunch of whingers. What I was clearly overlooking was the fact that he'd also transformed them into winners. In eight years he'd guided Aberdeen to three league titles, five domestic cups and a European trophy! He was in fact the perfect man for the job.

In November I set off for Portugal to support the still managerless Rangers against Porto, travelling this time on the Kinning Park bus. We left on Sunday morning, ten o'clock-ish, after a few beers in the specially opened Red Lion pub, a long, long journey in front of us. On the bus I double checked that I had everything with me: a change of clothes, washing gear, walkman, tapes, passport, money and match ticket. Also, my supply of food: some tins of beans, ravioli, corned beef, biscuits and some beer of course. Spotting my larder a few of the guys on the bus ridiculed me.

"Check out this arsehole," they mocked, "he's brought beans with him!"

The bus journey through England was always the worst part of any European trip, the motorway scenery not very inspiring. But a few beers helped and soon enough we were in Dover in time for the overnight ferry. With a tight schedule to maintain the bus travelled directly through France without stopping. Midway through the afternoon I tucked into a tin of cold ravioli and had a few biscuits, watched enviously by the same guys who had been laughing at me some thirty hours earlier. I'd been on enough European trips to know that you had to be prepared for all eventualities – the ravioli was delicious!

We had an overnight stop in the Spanish city of San Sebastian, giving us time to recharge the batteries with some beer and warm food before setting off for Portugal on the Tuesday morning. San Sebastian to Porto was only 370 miles but it would take over twenty-four hours to cover that distance. The plush French motorways had been left behind, giving way to a more basic Spanish highway. On reaching Portugal we were clearly entering a completely different part of Europe, with the standard of road degenerating rapidly. Travelling over mountain tracks it was quite frightening looking down at the huge drops, picking out the wreckage of burnt out vehicles that hadn't quite made the tight turns in time. Imagine Michael Caine in the Italian Job and you will get the picture!

At the more hazardous bends there were little shrines with candles burning, a Virgin Mary or some other figurine guarding the danger spot. A lot of the guys on the bus ridiculed these offerings as Roman Catholic mumbo jumbo. Personally I just hoped that, RC or not, they were looking out for us. These roads were downright dangerous and I was willing to take help from any source. We made it safely to our destination and spent a pleasant afternoon in the city of Oporto, sampling a few cultural glasses of port and as kickoff approached, we set off for the Estadio Das Antas. Unfortunately things didn't bode too well at the ground with large groups of Porto fans on the lookout for trouble, any hopes that the teeming rain would cool their passions were sadly misplaced, and the arriving coaches were systematically bombarded with missiles.

Inside the ground the penned-in Rangers support were showered by coins and various other objects launched by the extremely hostile home support. We had been searched on entry, and the Porto fans clearly hadn't, a fact confirmed when an iron bar crashed onto the terracing. This was getting serious. I wanted to support my team but frankly wasn't willing to die for them. I moved as far as I could from the firing line but there was nowhere to safely go, the missiles were raining in from all directions. In the meantime that iron bar had been commandeered by an enterprising fan and used to smash pieces off concrete from the crumbling terracing, providing a steady supply of ammunition. With the game becoming incidental missiles were exchanged. I had long since renounced football violence but on this occasion I joined in. I had no qualms about injuring any innocent Porto fans as they all appeared intent on causing us some severe GBH. I do regret those actions now, I'd hate to think that I hurt someone, but you had to be there to understand how it felt.

Eventually the police restored some semblance of order and we could concentrate on the football. Leaderless off the park, Rangers looked lacklustre on it, and lost 1-0, going out of the competition on the away goals rule. This heralded the most disappointing part of the trip. The Rangers team left the field, without even an acknowledgement of their travelling support. Okay, it wasn't exactly the evening for a lap of honour, but a simple wave of recognition would have been nice. Locked in the ground for a good hour after the game we were eventually let out. The delay was in theory to allow the Porto fans to disperse; they of course did no such thing and merely tooled up for an ambush. As we made our way back to the bus park we were pelted with various items from a car scrap yard, an old exhaust pipe just missing me! The joys of supporting your team in Europe!

The vacant mangers' chair at Ibrox was eventually filled by the returning Jock Wallace. I was pleased with the decision, and personally delighted that Alex Ferguson hadn't got the job. He would of course go on to boss, and do rather well, at Manchester United – it just shows how much I know about football! For a while it looked as though the appointment of Jock Wallace would be a success, Rangers started winning games and managed to regain the League Cup, beating Celtic in the final, Ally McCoist netting a hat trick. The striker was loudly cheered that day, a few weeks earlier however he'd received a quite different reaction. The Ibrox men had tumbled out of the Scottish Cup to Dundee and Ally wasn't having one of his better games. In fact he picked this game to have a real stinker, missing chance after chance. Patience having run out, the disgruntled fans in the Copland Road Stand chanted a clear and unambiguous message to him:

"Ally, Ally – get tae fuck."

I didn't join in, never having seen the point in publicly berating a player. It's hardly going to make him perform any better after all. The vocal criticism didn't bother the bold Ally in the slightest, and he plugged away, popping up late on to miss yet another sitter!

Sadly, the Jock Wallace-inspired recovery faltered, with six draws in the final eight games. The season fizzled out in disappointment yet again. For me the year's highlight came not on the football field but at the Glasgow Penthouse where Altered Images played what turned out to be their final gig. I was there, of course, once again with ticket #0001, my flame for Claire Grogan still burning strong. The band was superb and to cap it all I managed to blag my way into the post-concert party, sipping a beer I sidled over to the lady herself to have a quick chat. I had a lovely few minutes 'til my lack of tour ID was spotted by an eagle-eyed bouncer and I was persuaded to leave.

"Take care Duncan", Miss Grogan said, and gave me a kiss – I thought I'd died and gone to heaven! And, I know. I know she supports that other team in Glasgow – but hey, none of us are perfect.

Back at college I successfully completed my re-run of third year, passing my financial management with flying colours. Academically it had been a bit of a wasted year but at least I was back on track for my degree.

Chapter 8:
If They Go To Dublin!

Another football year started with another pre-season tour. This time the destination was Switzerland – first stop being the small mountain village of Einsiedeln. The game was a decent one, with Rangers winning 9–1. After the match had ended I strolled across the pitch, looking for a few photos and autographs. On a whim I approached one of the Einsiedeln players and offered to swap shirts with him, and to my surprise he agreed. He got my new Rangers top and in return I received his rather sweaty red and white shirt, a shirt very much in the Arsenal style. I wore that Einsiedeln shirt the next day, after washing it of course, and immediately took some good-natured abuse from my fellow supporters on the tour who took great delight in re-naming me Charlie, after Charlie Nicholas; the playboy Celtic player who'd recently been transferred to Arsenal. I have to say this irritated me intensely as I was definitely no Nicholas fan. I tried my best to ignore the jibes as I knew the more I protested, the more they would persist, unfortunately it didn't work, and persist they did!

The next game was in Solothurn. Drinking in the beer tent after the game, I was being wound up yet again with all that Charlie stuff. I'd had enough and foolishly retorted by singing the Celtic song "It's a grand old team". Don't ask why – it just seemed a good idea at the time. The first line had barely left my lips, when I was abruptly stopped and grappled in a bear hug, the air squeezed out of me.

A gruff voice boomed out, "I don't ever want to hear that song again".

I was gripped firmly for a few seconds, and then released. Looking up, I saw my assailant. It was manager, and ex-jungle fighter, Jock Wallace.

"I was only joking", I wheezed, "I'm a Rangers fan".

Big Jock glared at me. "Don't ever joke like that again son. Never forget who you are". Beating his chest, he continued, "Rangers, son, Rangers". The lesson was learned, and to be fair Jock forgave me and we shared a beer or two. I decided after that, to retire the Einsiedeln shirt 'til I got home, it had caused quite enough bother!

The final part of the tour took us to the city of Sion, and then over to Kaiserslautern in Germany. Better and more testing games for the team, but not as enjoyable for the supporters. Small town games were more intimate, and often brought about the unexpected. An example being a friendship I struck up with John McLelland, the big Ulsterman and club captain. He was a lovely guy, always willing to spent time with the travelling fans. His final act of the tour was to slip me a few beers as he boarded the team bus after the 2–1 win in Kaiserslautern, a much appreciated gesture!

Follow Follow, we will follow Rangers,
Everywhere, anywhere, we will follow on,
Follow Follow, we will follow Rangers,
If they go Dublin we will follow on.

The UEFA cup draw gave me a chance to put that line from the club anthem to the test, matching Rangers with Bohemians of Dublin. I wasn't going to fail that test.

Travel-wise, the most obvious route was through Northern Ireland, and then south into the Republic. I decided to do it differently, going with the Edinburgh Union Jack; they had an alternative plan, to go via Liverpool and sail directly into Dublin by ferry. This would avoid any of the potential flashpoints that might be encountered when crossing Ulster's border bandit country and looked to be the safer option – it didn't quite work out that way!

We left Edinburgh early on Tuesday morning, and arrived in Liverpool at lunchtime, spending the afternoon and evening in the city. The bus was booked into the Derry Club and most of the travellers settled down for a few pints, a good few pints! Not fancying an eight-hour drinking session, I went for a stroll round the city, taking a look at Anfield and Goodison Park. I did have a couple of beers, but only a couple. Deep down I had a feeling that this was a European adventure where a clear head might very well be advisable. Eventually, it was time to head over to the port, and board our Dublin-bound ferry.

We were immediately welcomed by some Irish youths making gun and rifle type gestures. Pointing imaginary pistols at us they gleefully announced that the Provos would be waiting in Dublin. Ignoring them we settled in the bar, knowing that pretty soon the ferry would be full of Rangers fans, and the youths would be well outnumbered and unlikely to be quite so cocky. The ferry left on schedule, and we were on our way across the Irish Sea. The first indication that all was not well came an hour or so into the crossing, when the bar was suddenly shut. This was always a bad sign, as the bar is a big money spinner for the ferry operator and is only closed as an absolute last resort. It seemed that there had been some bother on one of the decks. I guessed it involved those

Irish youths and some of our less tolerant supporters. Whatever had occurred though had clearly been serious enough to necessitate the return of the ferry to Liverpool.

Back in Liverpool, the police came aboard to investigate and some arrests were made. With tempers raised, trouble erupted and the police retreated, calling for back-up. What followed was like a scene from a swashbuckling pirate movie. The police re-enforcements tried to board the ferry, but were repelled by angry supporters who bombarded them with deck chairs, life belts, anything in fact that wasn't nailed down. The battered and bruised police retreated, but soon returned, this time in battle gear, their shields raised to deflect the barrage from the decks above. Gaining the upper hand, they swamped the ferry and rounded up all the passengers. Everyone was herded into one small area; supporters then separated from other passengers.

We were corralled into a corner, formed into a single file, and then marched away like prisoners of war. Sensing what was about to happen, I took my scarf off and discretely stuffed it into my travel bag, then slipped on the casual jacket I'd thankfully brought with me. We were clearly going to be ejected from the boat, and I wasn't having that, I was determined to follow-follow my team to Dublin. My chances of escape though were diminishing with every step. Under the watchful eye of Merseyside police we were led closer and closer to the exit sign. In front of me supporters were being directed to the right, towards the gangway. The situation looked hopeless, then, at the very last minute, one of the policemen turned his head away. I grasped my opportunity, took a deep breath, and kept walking straight on ... waiting for a hand on my shoulder, or a shout to return to the line, but nothing happened. So I walked ... and walked ... desperately fighting the urge to run ... heart racing, 'til I was out of view. I then searched out the darkest and quietest corner that I could possibly find. Cowering behind a discarded Irish Times I managed to blend into the background, so well disguised that I managed to elude a further police sweep of the boat.

With calm restored and after an age, the ferry made its second departure. I kept a low profile for an hour or so, before eventually feeling confident enough to venture away from my sanctuary. Wondering if I was alone, I searched out any friendly faces. Spotting a few, we exchanged knowing looks, without actually saying anything. The sound of a Scottish accent would have been a huge giveaway. This was now more like a scene from *The Great Escape*! Morning dawned, and we docked in Dublin. Once safely on dry land the escapees gathered outside the dock. From the bus load of fifty that had left Edinburgh, eight had made it to the Irish capital.

We spent a very quiet and uneventful day in Dublin, it was clear though that we were the only supporters in the city. The buses coming from Ulster and Scotland were obviously being held back 'til closer to kick off. We visited a few pubs, and as it was Dublin I felt obliged to sample a Guinness. I bought a half pint of the stuff but struggled to finish it, perhaps it's an acquired taste! At this point all the Dubliners we had met were very friendly. That sadly was to change. As kick off approached, the tension started to mount. More Rangers fans were appearing in the city, and as they did, the atmosphere grew more and more hostile, with gangs of local youths looking to pick off any unsuspecting supporter.

Inside Dalymount Park the atmosphere was no less tense. With the Garda lined up around the Rangers section of the ground, it was becoming quite clear how this day was going to end. Supporters from the Bohemians end seemed to gain access to the pitch with impunity, to wave Irish tricolours, and to burn Union flags. Anyone foolish enough to try the same from our end was swiftly set upon by the police. The sporting tussle on the park was mirrored by persistent battles between the Rangers fans behind the goal and a tooled up

Garda, quite clearly spoiling for a fight. It has to be said though, that the Ulster boys in our support, no strangers to civil disturbance in their homeland, were easily giving as good as they got.

Rangers lost 3–2, with Nicky Walker not having one of his better games. Hardly surprising, as he spent most of the first half some thirty yards off his goal line, trying to avoid a constant barrage of bricks, bottles, coins and golf balls. The police, for some reason, totally oblivious to this bombardment. Game over, we made our way back to the port, trying desperately to avoid the swinging Garda truncheons as we left the ground. Our troubles, however, were far from over!

At the port the police were waiting, and quickly culled the Rangers support from the other passengers. They were pretty efficient and managed to snag all eight, pushing us into a corner – we clearly weren't getting onto the ferry. At this point I started to get a little concerned – no, a little frightened. The police were in full riot gear and looked to be in the mood for a spot of retribution. My mind went into overdrive – were we about to be beaten up, or worse? A black van with darkened windows drew up, and we were pushed towards it. My mind went into hyper drive – were they about to take us to some downtrodden Dublin ghetto? Maybe the Provos were waiting for us after all!

We were bundled into the back of the van, and driven away. In the gloom, we all sat in silence, contemplating our fate. After twenty minutes or so the van stopped, and its doors flung open. We climbed out, fearing the worst. Those fears quickly turned to relief, though. We weren't in a downtrodden Dublin ghetto. We were in fact parked in a leafy suburban street, outside a small hotel. The police advised us, no, ordered us, to book in, to take to our beds and not to leave 'til the morning, when we were to board the first train for

Belfast. As an alternative to being shot by the Provos, it seemed like a good option, and that's exactly what we did!

I was glad I'd made the trip, pleased that I'd followed my team to Dublin, and wouldn't have missed it for the world. Would I do it again? Probably not. No, definitely not!

The return game was won at Ibrox, with two late goals. The highlight of the evening was the overreaction of the Glasgow police, ringing the Broomloan Road Stand with officers, determined that there would be no repeat of the Dublin violence. They manfully protected the three Bohemians supporters who attended the game.

The European draw then paired Rangers with Inter Milan. A trip to the San Siro was not to be missed, so it was time to dig out the passport. Despite some reservations, I travelled by supporters' bus, knowing full well that this form of transport was always unpredictable, but it was also cheap, which was important, as I was still on a student grant. The outward trip passed off uneventfully, and we arrived in Italy as scheduled, which allowed plenty time for a bowl of spaghetti. Mindful of my previous time in Italy, I didn't partake in too much vino.

The match was, I'm afraid to say, entirely predictable, with Inter running out winners by three goals to nil. It could have been so much better though, if Ally McCoist hadn't missed an absolute sitter. Super Ally was a wonderful player, and a prolific goal scorer. We loved him dearly, but bless him; he just couldn't head a ball to save himself. A thirty-yard Ian Redford shot crashed off the crossbar and up into the air, with the Inter keeper lying prostrate on the ground, Ally ran in for the rebound. All he had to do was wait, and head into the empty net. Ally however elected to jump for the ball, and hopelessly mistimed it. He was on his way back down when it bounced off his head, and rolled harmlessly away. An away goal would have made so much difference to the second leg.

The journey back to Scotland looked to be passing off quietly. Then we hit France, and stopped at one of their autoroute service stations. Despite a strong warning from the bus convener, a lot of thieving went on, cheap souvenirs acquired for wives and girlfriends, I suspect. The bus pulled away and all appeared to be okay. However, a few miles up the road we were pulled over at a tollbooth, and asked to disembark. The police were in attendance, accompanied by the service station owner, who was apparently a little concerned about the unexpected and dramatic reduction in her stock. The police boarded our bus and conducted a full search. They returned about ten minutes later, with a bag full of swag – Eiffel Tower shaped bottles of perfume being the most popular item. The service station owner surveyed the goods, but still wasn't happy. She claimed that there was a silver plate missing, and she wanted it back.

A further search produced nothing, which left the local Inspector Clouseau scratching his head. He then deduced that there was only one place that the missing item could be, it had to have been pushed into the bus toilet! Discussions followed and it became patently obvious that none of the gendarmerie were going to investigate that possibility. It was made clear that one of the supporters would have the unpleasant task. Shock-horror, no one volunteered, and after a standoff it was announced that unless the item was found, the whole busload of us would be locked up for the night. Eventually a patsy was found to do the deed – me! I'd simply had enough, and just wanted to get back on the road again. With a big bin bag encased round my arm, I delved into the bowels of the bus and fished out yet more, not so sweet smelling Eiffel Tower perfume bottles, a couple of Arc de Triomphes, and eventually the offending silver plate. I somehow managed the task without barfing, but it wasn't easy.

We were thankfully then allowed to continue our homeward journey. Our passports, which had been confiscated earlier on, were returned, with a message stamped onto them. I can't read French so don't know what it said, but, I suspect something along the lines of: 'Not welcome in France!' Now, you'd have thought that I might have got a few thanks for doing that dirty deed, but no! Everyone on the bus gave me a wide berth for the remainder of the journey – I was, after all, the guy with the stinky arm! I vowed that my next European trip would be by train, or I'd fly, definitely no more supporters' buses for me!

All was not well at Ibrox. My favourite player, John McLelland, was in dispute over his contract, and Rangers were, for some reason, determined to make an example of him. He was stripped of the captaincy and then transfer-listed. The big man kept his head down though and continued to give one hundred percent for the team, as I would have expected, having got to know him quite well in Switzerland. However, it was clear that his days at Ibrox were numbered.

Rangers were to win the League Cup in one of John's final games. During the presentation, all the players raised the cup in celebration. Well, all bar one – John didn't. He looked at the trophy, then over to the supporters, and simply passed the cup away. He was clearly a troubled man, and, significantly, he didn't celebrate on the pitch. Not long afterwards, he was transferred to Watford. It didn't seem right somehow, a Rangers captain moving to a team like them. No disrespect intended to the London club. John later wrote a letter to me, explaining his reasons for not celebrating the cup final win, and expressed his regret at leaving the club. It was a nice gesture from a nice guy, and in my opinion a player that we just couldn't afford to lose.

Academically, this was my final year at college, and it was time to see about getting a job. I applied for a number of posts, but really only targeted one company, Ferranti in Edinburgh. The reason: well, I would be able to keep attending Rangers games – what else! With all my eggs in one basket, I struck lucky, and in January was offered a place with that very company. The only condition being that I passed my final exams.

It had long been my ambition to attend every first team game in a season, home and away, friendly or competitive, anywhere in the world. This looked to be the season that I was going to achieve that goal. I'd attended all the pre-season friendlies, all the European ties, all the testimonials and benefit games, all the hard work had been done. I'd managed fifty-one games in a row, with only seven or eight games left in the season. It was surely in the bag. Then Rangers announced a snap three-match tour of the Middle East. Playing games in Iraq and Kuwait, right at the height of the Iran–Iraq war, I couldn't believe it. I obviously couldn't go and it was dream over for another year!

We travelled to Easter Road on the final day of the season. Having watched the first half of a very poor game, I decided that enough was enough, and left to join a few friends in a local bar; they hadn't even made it to the ground. I got into the pub in time to see some television pictures coming in from the Bradford City game, not sporting pictures unfortunately, but news coverage of a terrible fire. The main stand at Valley Parade was ablaze, and before our very eyes, football fans were dying. It was a terrible sight. Once again Bill Shankley's comment about football being more important than life or death was shown to be nonsense.

Football clubs in general had done little to improve facilities over the years, with the majority of grounds having changed little over the decades. What happened at Bradford was an accident just waiting to happen, and could have occurred at any number of places around the country. Ibrox was one of the few grounds to have been upgraded, and that was as a direct consequence of the events of 1971. It's a shame that it takes tragedy for improvements to be made and safety to be looked at.

A few days later Rangers travelled to London to play Chelsea in a benefit match for the victims of the disaster. I didn't go. It was in the middle of my final exams, and I knew that they were much more important than a game of football. So, I wouldn't have made it to all the games in that season after all!

The football season was to end with another tragedy, once again played out on live television. This time however, it could not be deemed an accident. Liverpool played Juventus at the Heysel Stadium in Brussels. Heysel was another one of those grounds that had seen little, if any improvements over the years, and was frankly not fit for purpose. It was certainly not up to hosting a game such as the European Cup Final. The state of the ground, however, does not excuse what happened that night.

As pre-match tension rose, a section of the Liverpool support charged at a group of Juventus fans. The fleeing fans were crushed against a perimeter wall which collapsed and in the ensuing crush thirty-nine people died, the youngest being an eleven year old boy. As people lay dead and dying, UEFA made the shameful decision to proceed with the match. The reason given was security, but it smacked of 'the show must go on'. Football really needed to take a good hard look at itself: supporters, the clubs and the authorities – everyone connected with the game.

Away from the football, I managed to pass all my final exams and graduated with a B.Sc in Electronic Engineering, I was no longer a student at Paisley Tech. It was time once again, to join the real world. I would soon be moving to Edinburgh, to work for Ferranti.

Chapter 9:
The Times They Are A Changing

One of the first repercussions of Heysel was the withdrawal, and ultimate banning of all English teams from European competition. It shouldn't have affected Scottish clubs, but did have a knock-on effect. Rangers had arranged a pre-season tour of Germany but cancelled it at the last minute, fearful I suppose of some sort of post Heysel backlash. This was bad news as I'd already made plans to go. With my German train pass already purchased, I decided to continue with the tour on my own. I'd no other plans for the summer anyway.

Keeping more or less to the dates of the aborted tour, I turned up in Saarbrücken, and took a trip over to the stadium. I was met by a groundsman, who, on seeing my Rangers top tried to explain that the game had been cancelled. He seemed very apologetic, so I played along, pretending I didn't know. Out of sympathy he showed me round the stadium, and treated me to a meal and a few beers in the local pub. A result! One of the other scheduled games had been against TSV München 1860, a game I had been looking forward to. Unfortunately, no meal or beer when I went for a wander round their ground!

During my spell in Munich I visited Dachau concentration camp which is about ten miles north of the city. It would be wrong to say it was an enjoyable trip, but I felt a necessary one. It's to Germany's credit that they don't try to hide the most horrific period in their history, and they showed the camp as it had been, nothing hidden or covered up. Walking through the gas chambers and crematoriums where so many people lost their lives was a sombre and thought provoking experience. As I left that terrible place I signed the memorial book, and felt deeply depressed and ashamed to be a British football fan. A few entries above me, someone had scrawled:

'CHELSEA FC – NATIONAL FRONT – NF'

What kind of person does something like that, in a place like that, where so many innocent people were murdered?

Holiday over; it was time to head over to Edinburgh, to find somewhere to stay. I spent a week or so visiting some hovels and dingy bed-sits, getting more and more hacked off, before stumbling on a nice flat just off Easter Road. Renting a room would cost me £100 a month and was an absolute bargain considering what I had been looking at previously. I would be sharing with my landlord, Jim, who was a Celtic fan, but other than that, he was a decent guy!

Living away from home for the first time was a bit of a culture shock. I'd to start helping out with housework, making my own meals and washing up. I began to appreciate what my mother had been doing for me for so many years, though that still didn't stop me going home every weekend, with a bag full of dirty washing, returning to Edinburgh with clean and freshly ironed clothes. I wasn't that domesticated!

In September the Scottish national team manager Jock Stein died and a minute's silence was arranged for football grounds round the country. A lot of eyes were on Kilbowie Park in Clydebank on the day of the tribute, Rangers being the visitors. Jock Stein had of course been the Celtic manager, leading them to numerous trophies, nine championships in a row and a European Cup – how would the Teddy Bears respond? As the referee's whistle sounded the assembled journalists waited, pens poised, and a minute later had to report an impeccably observed silence – as it should be.

Settling in at Ferranti I was required to go along to Heriot Watt University to attend an 'induction course' along with all the other new graduates. During the course, we were asked to write down the name of the person we most admired, and to give a reason for our decision. At the end of the day the course organiser asked us to read out our personal selection. The answers came thick and fast.

"Margaret Thatcher: she's a decisive leader"

"Sir Clive Sinclair: he's a trendsetting innovator"

"Richard Branson: he's a great entrepreneur"

"Basil de Ferranti: he started this fine company"

Then it was my turn. Realising I had possibly misjudged the mood of the occasion; I took a deep breath and said:

"Davie Cooper: he plays for Rangers!"

Later that night, and to back up my decision, the very same Davie Cooper scored a terrific free kick against Hibs in the League Cup semi-final at Ibrox. Unfortunately the Edinburgh side had won the first leg 2–0, and Rangers went out of the competition.

My first year in Edinburgh was not proving to be a good one on the football front. Having already been dumped out of one competition by Hibs, the capital's other side Hearts then eliminated my team from the Scottish cup. Hearts were in fact having a terrific season and were looking like possible champions, something Rangers had sadly not been for many years. My team were in fact looking like a rudderless ship, heading for oblivion. With only one win in eight games the supporters were becoming restless. A friendly match with Tottenham, and a 2–0 defeat, proved to be the straw that broke the back of many, and a demonstration was mounted outside the main stand, a new manager demanded.

The board of Directors were clearly of a similar mind and within days Jock Wallace was sacked. It was sad to see Jock leave in such a manner, but the club desperately needed a change in direction, that was obvious. Mirroring his previous departure, Jock made no comments or criticisms. At the end of the day he was a Rangers man through and through and would always have a special place in the hearts of the supporters. With almost indecent haste Graeme Souness was announced as his replacement. It was a coup that any South American dictator would have been proud of! The football world was caught unawares and stunned by this bold and imaginative move. Whether it would succeed was, of course, another matter.

The league season ended with a home game against Motherwell, Rangers hoping to claim fifth spot, and a European place. Fifth place, for heaven's sake! They achieved their target, but only goal difference stopped the Ibrox club from ending the season in the bottom half of the table.

The summer of '86 was an exciting time to be a Blue Nose as signings were made. Not the usual run of the mill players though. Terry Butcher, the England captain, was snatched from under the nose of Manchester United, England's stand-in goalkeeper Chris Woods joined, as would Graeme Roberts, the Tottenham captain.

The new season started with a tour of Germany, a real one this time! What became immediately clear was that there was a more professional attitude at the club, more disciplined. Graeme Souness and his new assistant Walter Smith were not going to stand for any nonsense, either on or off the park. This new attitude was amply demonstrated to me in Würzburg. Wearing my Rangers tracksuit, I had blagged my way into the post-match reception. With a smattering of German at my command, I was enjoying myself, chatting to a few of the Würzburg officials and sipping some free beer. All was well 'til the Rangers party arrived, and I was spotted by Walter Smith. On previous tours I would have been left to my own devices, but not now! Walter kept his eye on me, then came over and told me quietly, but firmly that I'd had a good time, but that it was now time to leave. Feeling brave, I told him that it was okay, I'd just stay for a bit longer. Walter looked at me, gave a long hard stare and said one word.

"No".

It was clear he meant business, and I knew it was time to go. Uncle Walter was clearly not a man to be messed with!

Back in Scotland, the league started in rather dramatic fashion at Easter Road with the traditional opening day defeat. Graeme Souness was sent off for a quite dreadful tackle on George McCluskey, though assault may have been a better description. This incident sparked an on field brawl, which resulted in something like twenty retrospective yellow cards being handed out. Inevitably the press had a field day, declaring it a 'shame game'. The spectators apparently shocked at the scenes. Truth is that the spectators loved it and were in a frenzy of excitement. It's great when the players get stuck into each other! The three points would have been nice though! The following weekend Rangers managed to squander a two goal lead at Ibrox and lose to Dundee United. We were playing catch up once again and worryingly, it looked like brand new manager, same old story.

The best way for a new manager to ingratiate himself with the Rangers support is to get a win over Celtic. Graeme Souness managed that task not once, but twice in the first three months of his tenure. A fine league win at Ibrox was followed by an even better League Cup final victory at Hampden. With league points now consistently being gathered, we started to believe that Souness might just be the real deal.

It was UEFA Cup time again. With enough holidays left and money to spare I decided to travel over to Germany for the second leg of the tie with Borussia Mönchengladbach. This time making the trip by train, I'd more than had my fill of supporters' buses by now.

The Borussia match was pretty much standard fare for an away game in Europe. The supporters roared their team on, the team in return huffed, and puffed, and fell short, going out of the competition on the 'away goals' rule. The journey home was going as planned, and I was congratulating myself on arranging a hassle free trip, when the guy sitting beside me on the train suddenly awoke from his slumbers, bolted upright, looked over and – let me explain:

I had caught the train at Euston Station in London, travelling north with a couple of other fans. Sitting next to us was a strange chap, who looked a bit dishevelled and down on his luck. We shared a few beers, and he told some tall stories, one of which involved him deserting from the French Foreign Legion! He seemed harmless enough though, and eventually fell asleep. We'd crossed the border into Scotland when the guy suddenly woke up, looked very startled, threw a bit of a wobbler, and then headbutted me! A bit of a scuffle followed out as the guy lashed out at everyone and anyone. Calm was restored, but not for long, He wanted another couple of rounds with me and my pals. The train guard intervened and he was set upon as well. The 'fun' was eventually halted at Motherwell, when the police intervened and took the guy away. The reason for his outburst remained a mystery, though perhaps he really was ex-Foreign Legion, reliving one of his old battles. Who knows! So much for that nice relaxing train trip – maybe I should have gone on a supporters' bus!

Enjoying my life in Edinburgh, and with money to spare, I started to have an active social life, out on the town virtually every night, eating in restaurants, going to concerts, to pubs, and drinking – a lot of drinking. Looking back now, it's clear that I was drinking far too much, and far too often. But at the time I just couldn't see it. Matters came to a head one day in March. I was in work, sipping a cup of coffee, trying to fight off a raging hangover, when I overheard some workmates talking about a terrible accident. I asked what had happened and they were amazed that I didn't know. It had, after all, been front page news for days.

On Friday 6th March 1987, the cross-channel ferry "Herald of Free Enterprise" capsized just outside Zeebrugge, with 193 fatalities. Four days after the event I had no idea. I wracked my brain, trying to think what I had been doing that weekend, but I just didn't know, I couldn't even remember if I had been to the Rangers game, or even if there had been one … I sat there, and realised that I had a problem. Something had to be done! I pondered my situation and resolved to lay off the drink for a period of at least one month. I knew it wouldn't be easy, but I had to sort myself out.

My period of abstinence was made somewhat easier by a forthcoming change in my circumstances. Jim, my flatmate and landlord, had decided to sell his Easter Road flat and move on to a different location. It was a decision that would soon render me homeless, unless I took some action. Jim wanted to sell his flat, and I wanted somewhere to stay. The solution was staring us in the face and we pretty quickly came to the agreement that I would buy the place from him, subject to a decent offer, and my getting a mortgage. It was obvious though, I couldn't meet lawyers and bankers whilst hungover and smelling of drink. So I gave up beer and took up another beverage, Irn Bru. For six weeks I restricted myself to Scotland's other national drink. By the end of that period I had pretty well sorted myself out, and saved a fortune in the process. I did start drinking again, but more responsibly. I wasn't going teetotal!

The deal to buy the flat went through quickly and smoothly, and a month or so later I had a £24,500 mortgage, and a place of my own. Being a home owner I quickly discovered some basic facts; toilet rolls don't replace themselves, and dishes left overnight in the sink are still there in the morning. Not for the first time, and certainly not the last, I marvelled at how my mother, widowed, with three kids, had managed to keep a tidy home for all those years.

On the football front, Rangers were now stringing an impressive number of results together. With an unbeaten run of nineteen games, Celtic's lead at the top of the league was gradually overcome and in March the 'Gers went top.

At home, my life was further changing. I started going out with a girl from work, Jacqui. To be honest I hadn't really noticed her during the working day, more fool me, but we bumped into each other on a night out, and kind of clicked! As the days followed we would see more and more of each other – romance was in the air.

There were only two games left, and the league title was now in sight. Two points at Pittodrie, possibly less, depending on the Celtic result, would clinch the league flag. The season was to draw to a close just as it had started, with a fired up Graeme Souness receiving a red card, for a somewhat exuberant tackle. A Terry Butcher goal had us celebrating, but a quick Aberdeen equaliser put a dampener on that. Late into the game, news of Celtic's demise filtered through. Falkirk were winning at Parkhead, and a draw would be enough. A draw was gained, and at last, Rangers were champions.

Eight years of frustration and disappointment had been cast aside, and in delirium the Rangers support spilled from the stands and onto the park to party. From all sides of the ground they poured. It seems that it wasn't just Aberdeen fans in the home end! I wasn't going to hold back and joined the throng on field, singing and dancing. It was all very good natured, unless you were the Aberdeen groundsman, who must have been tearing his hair out as he watched the unfolding scene. The crossbar at the Beach End collapsed under the weight of supporters swinging and sitting on it. The goal net was torn apart. The pitch dug up, souvenir divots of turf ripped from it. Eventually the field was cleared, and I returned to the stand with a large bit of Pittodrie turf in my pocket, and a piece of the goal net safely tucked away in my wallet. Later to be sown onto my scarf for posterity. Next day, I planted the piece of Pittodrie turf in my Easter Road window box. Unfortunately the grass didn't take, and soon died off. The memories of that day will never die though!

Over the football free summer months Jacqui and I grew closer and closer. I didn't realise how serious it was becoming 'til the pre-season tour of Switzerland arrived and I actually considered staying at home. I was going to give the football a miss, for a girl – this was serious indeed! I did, of course, go on tour. Well, it had already been booked, and anyway, Jacqui had her own Spanish holiday planned.

The Swiss trip started with a game in Solothurn, then a train journey to the town of Delémont. After pitching my tent, I took a stroll down to the football ground which was part of a large sports complex. Walking past the tennis courts I noticed Davie Cooper knocking a ball about, waiting for his playing partner. Davie had in the past played a few sets with supporters, so I thought I'd chance my arm and offered to give him a quick game, just 'til his partner arrived. Not a good move in hindsight as Super Cooper was no mean tennis player, he sent me scrambling about the court for a few minutes before I retired, exhausted, seeking refuge in the bar.

We then hit the big city, and on a wet and miserable evening watched Rangers lose 5–0 to FC Zurich. My biggest defeat so far watching the Teddy Bears. Back on winning ways, a 3–2 victory in Wettingen was followed by the final match, a game that took us to the mountain village of Charbonnières, to play Lausanne Sports. The attendance that evening boosted by various members of the Scottish press, all travelling over to get their first sight of our latest English signing, Trevor Francis. Interestingly, all bar one of those reporters spent the entire game hidden away in a far corner of the beer tent. Ever wonder why match reports in different newspapers seem so similar?

As I packed my gear to return home, it was as though the football gods were trying to tell to me something. Firstly, my trusty tent, which had served me so well, died, the outer sheet ripped in a high wind rendering it useless. Then the main frame on my rucksack snapped. My two constant companions on European trips for nearly a decade had reached the end of the road.

Booked on the 8am flight to London, I had to spend the night in Zürich. Tentless and penniless, I intended to sleep on the floor of the Hauptbahnhof and then catch an early train to the airport. It was a good plan, with one fundamental flaw – the railway police did not approve of people sleeping inside their station, and I was swiftly escorted outside. It may have been the Swiss summer, but it was bitterly cold so I was delighted to discover a nearby warm air vent. Settling down in my centrally heated spot I was disturbed for a second time, this time by a group of Zürich tramps who were none too pleased at me squatting in what was their prime location. The situation was looking confrontational, 'til I produced a spare bottle of schnapps from my wilting rucksack. That was an acceptable trade it seemed, and we all shared the five star location. To be honest it's not a lifestyle I'd like to embrace full time, and I felt a lot better for a shower and a cup of coffee over at the airport.

Although I'd enjoyed the Swiss tour, I was glad to be heading home to see Jacqui, as I'd missed her a lot. It soon became clear what the football gods were trying to tell me. Jacqui and I got engaged a few weeks later. That trip to Switzerland would be my last pre-season tour.

Rangers may have been league champions, but it didn't stop them having their traditional bad start to the season. 87/88 kicked off with only one win in the first five games, no way to set about retaining a league title.

October saw another of those 'shame games', the type the press so love to hate. It also came close to being my last ever game at Ibrox. In the highly charged atmosphere of an Old Firm game there is some responsibility on the players to behave themselves. Celtic's Frank McAvennie clearly hadn't read the script, and got into an unnecessary spat with Chris Woods. After a scuffle, both players were sent off. It was ten-a-side now, but hardly a fair contest as Rangers were without their goalie. Celtic raced to a two goal lead and the situation looked bleak. No one amongst the Rangers support wanted to say it, but we were all thinking the same terrible thought – this could end up as a six or seven goal drubbing.

In the second half, an already desperate situation deteriorated when Terry Butcher was very harshly sent off – Rangers were now down to nine men. I'd had enough, and decided that something had to be done. I'd spent the morning of the game in a Clydebank pub, and had clearly flung back far too many beers for my own good. With my judgement clouded, I leapt from my seat, pushed my way to the aisle, and stormed down to the front of the stand. I was quite clear in what had to be done. I was going onto the park to let the referee know what a shocking game he was having, with my persuasion, he would retract Butcher's red card. In my befuddled state it was a perfectly rational course of action. Fortunately one of my fellow supporters had read my intentions, and intercepted me en-route. He dragged me back up the stairs, to the edge of the pie stalls, and held me there 'til I came to my senses. My thanks will always go to that man.

Without his intervention I would have been arrested, locked up, banned from Ibrox, and probably lost my job. Not only that, I would have missed a grandstand finish!

The nine man Rangers, fuelled by a sense of injustice, attacked incessantly. With a few minutes left, Ally McCoist pulled a goal back. Celtic retreated, looking nervous, and Rangers lay siege to their goal. Deep into injury time, Richard Gough slammed home an equalizer and Ibrox went bonkers. There was still time for stand-in goalie Graham Roberts to conduct three quarters of the ground in some victory anthems. Okay, to be precise it wasn't a victory, but it certainly felt like one!

On Saturday 31st October 1987 I missed the home game against Motherwell. My excuse for non attendance was however a reasonable one, Jacqui and I were married at Leith Registry Office. It was a hugely happy and enjoyable day, and I never once thought about the football – well that's not strictly true. I did nip away from the afternoon reception to sneak into a next door bar, to catch the final scores on TV. Rangers won – a good day indeed!

In November, Rangers suffered a big blow when captain Terry Butcher broke his leg during a midweek game with Aberdeen, a double blow in fact as the Dons went on to win that game. The loss of Terry Butcher didn't affect the team as badly as was first feared though. In fact they won their next five games in a row, but were still trailing in the league race. In an attempt to claw back some ground, Souness made an imaginative signing: Mark Walters from Aston Villa. Walters was a fine player, but wouldn't have made front page headlines, bar the fact that he was black. Scotland hadn't had any black players in my memory, so he was breaking new ground.

England had a long running problem with racism in football, but it hadn't really been an issue in Scotland – we were above that sort of thing. Or was it because we didn't have any black players in the country? Rangers made the trip to Parkhead for the New Year game, with Mark Walters making his debut, and in a shameful day for football north of the border, he was subject to some prolonged and dreadful racial abuse, all of it emanating from the vast Celtic support. Jeers, boos and monkey noises were heard whenever he touched the ball. Bananas were thrown at him, not just 'the odd piece of fruit', but a constant and concerted barrage. Curious, as the Celtic support, self-styled 'greatest fans in the world', normally align themselves with any minority cause that they can find. It was apparent on that day; their dislike of racism was overwhelmed by their hatred of anything in blue.

Unfortunately Mark Walters couldn't revive Rangers league title aspirations and a disappointing season ended with Celtic, in their centenary year winning the double. Many pointed to their success being lucky, they seemed to win countless games with last minute goals, but, through gritted teeth I had to admit it was more to do with determination and team spirit than good fortune. They simply wanted to win more than anyone else. It was frustrating, but true.

Chapter 10:
A Dark Day in April

During the summer of 1988 Glasgow hosted the annual Garden Festival, a celebration of all things horticultural. Not really my cup of tea, but my mother wanted to go, so Jacqui and I took her over. One of the first things we saw was a huge floral Celtic crest, across from it a stall selling Celtic souvenirs. Impressive, I grudgingly admitted, and looked forward to seeing the equivalent Rangers version, which would surely be on display elsewhere. I hunted high and low but just couldn't find it, or any stall selling our goodies. It soon became apparent that Rangers were not represented in any way, shape or form at this international event.

The Garden Festival was situated in Govan, virtually in the shadow of Ibrox, and attracted 4.3m visitors in 152 days. What an opportunity for the club to boost their profile. They could have offered stadium tours; a chance to visit the superstore, an opportunity to learn about one of Glasgow's best known institutions. What those millions of visitors were offered was exactly nothing; it was as though Rangers didn't exist. I wrote to the club shortly afterwards expressing my opinion that this had been a great opportunity missed, and asked why they hadn't made some kind of contribution. I got a one sentence answer to my question.

'We did consider this matter previously but decided not to go ahead after discussion.'

Words failed me at that correspondence. It was symptomatic however of the direction that the Rangers PR department were heading. Celtic were sadly leading the way, both on and off the park.

My admiration for Graeme Souness grew in the lead up to season 88/89. The Daily Record ran their traditional poll of managers, asking them who they thought, outwith their own club, would be crowned champions. Of the twelve premier league managers, six went for Rangers and five for Celtic. What of the missing vote? Graeme Souness of Rangers FC didn't select a team. He stated, "I never contemplate coming second to anyone." I liked his style!

Before the season started I indulged in a bit of culture, going to, of all things, the ballet! As part of the Edinburgh Festival, Michael Clark, a Scottish contemporary dance artist put on a show which was vaguely based around King William of Orange, charting his accession to the English throne in 1689. The ballet dancers were backed musically by Manchester industrial punk veterans, The Fall. It was a bizarre concept but one that worked very well. The highlight of the evening, for me anyway, was an on stage Old Firm game. Two teams of dancers dressed in the respective club colours, chasing after an enormous ball. How sad was I, when I started to cheer on the team in blue, and then celebrate their single goal victory – you had to be there!

A few weeks later, I was celebrating goals against Celtic for real, five goals to be precise in a quite outstanding 5–1 victory. It was a fantastic day, yet in the days that followed there were twinges of regret. It seemed a little churlish to complain, but it could have been more! Rangers had scored those five goals in the first hour of the game, and there were still thirty minutes left. Plenty of time surely, to score again and again. Graeme Souness however, preferred to 'take the piss'. Sure we cheered the showboating, and of course it was good at the time, but a final scoreline of 7–1 or even 8–1 would have been so much more satisfying – complaining after *only* beating Celtic 5–1, who'd have thought it!

Rangers had, for once, started the season well, with only one point dropped in their first eight games. That good run was to end at Pittodrie, in a bad tempered and tempestuous game. However, the day will always be remembered not for the result or the football, but rather for one specific incident when Aberdeen's Neil Simpson took centre stage, and quite literally stamped his personality on the game. Midway through the first half the studs on his right boot smashed into the knee of young Ranger Ian Durrant. It was a thoroughly disgraceful challenge, with absolutely no prospect of the defender winning the ball. Quite what was going through Simpson's head at that moment simply beggars belief. Ian Durrant played no further part in the game; in fact it would be two and a half years before the talented youngster would kick a ball again.

As stated previously, for me, the long running Rangers–Aberdeen feud started in 1975 with those Ibrox disaster comments, but for a new generation of fans it began at this game. Regrettably, it also gave the Aberdeen hardcore some new anti-Rangers songs to add to their repertoire, with Ian Durrant bizarrely becoming the villain of the piece!

Fate dictated that the two clubs would meet again very soon. In fact it was just two weeks later at Hampden, in the League Cup final, and revenge was in the air. In a highly charged atmosphere, the big Rangers support was just willing someone to 'do' Neil Simpson. It didn't happen, and rightly so, as two wrongs don't make a right. I'll be honest though; I, for one, would have been delighted if Simpson had been stretchered off. The fans had to settle for winning the trophy. A victory made all the sweeter by virtue of the fact that the winner came in the very last minute. Ally McCoist's goal could not have been more exuberantly celebrated, both on, and off the park.

Success on the park would hopefully be mirrored by success in the board room. In November, Rangers acquired a new owner, when David Murray, an Edinburgh businessman bought the club for £6m. To be honest, none of us had ever heard of Mr. Murray, so he was a totally unknown quantity, but having a hands-on multimillionaire in charge could only be a good thing.

With one trophy secured, Rangers set their sights on the other two domestic prizes. The league championship campaign was going well with the Ibrox men top of the table and by New Year they were odds-on favourites to regain the Premier League title. Rangers were also making good progress in the Scottish cup. April brought cup semi-final day, both north and south of the border. Rangers were at Parkhead, drawing 0–0 in a quite dreadful game with St Johnstone. Two hundred and fifty miles away, Liverpool were playing Nottingham Forrest at Hillsborough. It was April 15th 1989, a date forever etched into British football history.

The build-up at both grounds was the same. Supporters queued up to gain entry. As the kick off approached, the crowds gathering outside the grounds grew bigger. At this point, the circumstances north and south of the border diverged. In Glasgow, the fans filtered into the Parkhead, directed by stewards and police who were well used to this type of fixture. Down in Sheffield the Liverpool fans were shepherded into the Leppings Lane end of Hillsborough, an area of the ground divided into pens. With little co-ordination or guidance, the majority moved into the central pen, which rapidly became dangerously overcrowded, and crushing occurred. Totally unaware of the growing problem, the

Liverpool fans continued to squeeze in. Conditions on that terracing became intolerable. Terrified supporters were having the life squeezed from them, men, women and children were dying. In desperation, in an attempt to reach safety, the Liverpool fans started to climb the terracing fences, the fences that caged them.

From the other side of the touchline fences, the police watched. They saw supporters clambering over the fences, and years of programming kicked in. They assumed it was hooliganism, and responded in the only way they knew – they stopped them. To quote Peter Jones, the veteran BBC reporter who was commentating live on the radio:

"The teams have just left the field ... the trouble away to our left, where there is a packed enclosure of Liverpool supporters. Two and a half minutes after the match started, they really came over the top of the fence. Police are trying desperately hard to hold them back ... at the moment it is simple mayhem! I should stress incidentally, it's not so much a question of crowd trouble. It's just they were packed in far too tight, they went over the top. People got frightened ... they then tried to climb out."

The fences round the Hillsborough terracing had been placed there to prevent spectators gaining access to pitch, and they did their job with deadly efficiency. Supporters were being crushed, supporters were dying, and the police response was to hold them back.

Eventually the enormity of the situation became clear and supporters were allowed access to the field, access to safety. It was at this point that the much maligned Liverpool supporters took charge. They built makeshift stretchers from the advertising hoardings and carried the injured to safety, trying desperately to find medical help. The police, in the meantime, stood on the half way line, hundreds strong, seemingly unsure of what to do, to stop the supporters or to help them.

From subsequent video clips it looked as though they did neither, they just stood by and watched.

In the days that followed, the football authorities, the police, the media and the government all closed ranks, and shamefully scrambled to blame the Liverpool fans for the tragedy. The F.A. forgot all the pre-match concerns issued by Liverpool FC. The main worry being that their numerically larger support was to be located in the smaller end of the ground. The Sun newspaper mounted an unforgivable campaign of hate. Police incident reports were altered to reflect the 'official' version of the disaster. CCTV video footage of the incident mysteriously went missing.

The Liverpool supporters were not to blame on that tragic day; they were victims for heavens sake. They were simply used as an easy scapegoat for the inadequacies that had crept into football. The sad fact was, once again, this was a disaster just waiting to happen, and like the Bradford fire of 1985, could have occurred at any number of grounds round the country. Over the years football had backed itself into a corner. Hooliganism had been a growing cancer in the game. To combat the problem, the authorities had decided to treat every single supporter as a potential troublemaker, and introduced more and more draconian measures. The reinforced fences which penned supporters together like animals was just one of their actions. It was a downward spiral that resulted in ninety-six deaths that day in April.

Football had to change, and it did. Prompted by the Justice Taylor Report, football grounds at the top level became all seated. Those lethal fences were torn down, and conditions for the supporters improved. An all-seater stadium was much easier to police, and as a consequence, hooliganism, at least inside the ground, was greatly reduced. Football had finally been dragged into the twentieth century! Sadly, once again, it took tragedy to prompt those changes. Hillsborough was an event that touched all supporters, regardless of their allegiances, because we all knew: there but by the grace of God, it could have been us, it could have been me.

The effects of Hillsborough were immediately obvious on football. The following week I was at Love Street. The Rangers end of the ground was packed solid, whilst the St Mirren side was half empty. With crushing becoming a real problem, the police took action and decanted a large proportion of the away support to the other terracing, to the St Mirren end. Properly policed, a potential problem had been alleviated. A simple solution, and easily achieved, yet, had this had occurred a few weeks earlier the police would have done nothing. The supporters would have been left to fend for themselves, jammed in like sardines.

Having regained the league title, Rangers were hoping to end the season with a domestic treble, and Celtic were equally determined to stop them – and stop them they did, winning the Scottish Cup Final by a single controversial goal. During a tense first half, the ball was knocked out of play, possession to the blue team, or should have been. Roy Aitken of Celtic leapt in and quickly took the throw. The referee for some reason allowed play to continue and Celtic broke upfield to score the only goal of the game. To compound our misery, Rangers had, in the final minutes, an equalising goal disallowed. You know, it's strange; the average Celtic supporter normally has an encyclopaedic knowledge of all football injustices, yet they always manage to overlook this game. Perhaps it's only certain games that they can recall!

As I looked back over the football year, I felt disappointed. Perhaps it was a hangover from the cup final defeat, I don't know, but the season seemed to have been a bit flat. How times change! A few years ago I was watching a team struggling to achieve fifth place in the league. Now I was unhappy that they had only won two out of the three domestic trophies!

Chapter 11:
Just Another Summer Signing

Iwas cycling to work one morning in July. As I passed a newsagent I glanced at a billboard that proclaimed 'Johnston signs for Rangers'. I cycled on, wondering who this Johnston was. Passing another newsagent, I saw another billboard; this one made it perfectly clear, 'Rangers sensation, MoJo signs'. I had to stop to investigate, and there it was, in black and white: Maurice Johnston signs for Rangers. I read the paper, over and over, scarcely believing my eyes – Maurice Johnston.

Maurice Johnston!

Now, signing a Scottish international forward would be news, but not national news. The problem was, and it shouldn't really have been a problem, but Maurice Johnston was a Roman Catholic, and not just that, he was ex-Celtic. Rangers hadn't had an RC on their books for many years, and certainly not one with a high profile. In fact, it was pretty well understood that they just didn't sign Catholics. That's how it had been for most of the century, and seemed destined to stay that way. Until now!

To be fair, Graeme Souness had made it clear from day one that he wanted the best players possible at the club, regardless of their background, but we'd heard all that before and took it with a pinch of salt. Souness, however, had clearly meant business. To be honest, I wasn't bothered at all by the religious aspect of the signing, having long grown out of that sort of thing. I was however a little concerned about Johnston's history; memories of him celebrating goals against Rangers were still fresh in my mind. Still, if Souness thought he was the man for the job, who was I to argue? Plenty did though, and crowds gathered outside Ibrox; some to protest, some just to watch for developments. Not too many, it seemed, to support the signing.

Camera crews and reporters camped outside the ground looking for a reaction, and inevitably they got it, with some supporters tearing up their season tickets. Some burnt blue and white scarves to express their displeasure. If no scarves were readily available, then reporters rushed to the club shop and helpfully supplied them – along with the matches ... just to fan the flames of discontent I suspect.

If sections of our support were upset by the signing, it was nothing compared to the fury unleashed in the green half of the city. They were incandescent with rage. There I was, thinking that they wanted Rangers to be more inclusive in their signing policy!

Pre-season saw Rangers at Broomfield, to play a testimonial match for a couple of Airdrie players. Those players must have been rubbing their hands with glee as the presence of 'you know who' ensured a bumper attendance. There was a strange atmosphere at the game. Uncertainty was in the air. How would the support take to the new signing? There were a few murmurs as Johnston's name was announced over the tannoy, but more cheers and certainly no jeers. The game started, and MoJo's first touch arrived, and passed, with little attention. Later on a few chants of "Mo,

Mo, Super Mo" were heard. All in all, the day had gone pretty well. The scores of reporters present had to go home disappointed, with just a match report in their note pads. The protests, the demonstrations, the boycotts, the catcalls, they just didn't happen.

The season then started for real with points dropped – don't all seasons start that way? St Mirren did the damage with a victory at Ibrox. Next up was an away game at Easter Road, but, just round the corner from my flat, so a home game for me! Unable to get a Rangers end ticket, I bought one for the Hibs' end. It wasn't ideal, but at least I'd be there.

On the day of the game I took my place amongst the Hibs faithful (obviously without my colours – this wasn't a suicide mission after all!) my intention was to keep a low profile and quietly watch the game. Maintaining that low profile actually wasn't too difficult, as Rangers were totally outplayed by a good Hibs team, and I had precious little to get excited about. The day didn't run completely smoothly though.

My troubles started when the home team scored their first goal, and a nearby Hibee noticed that I wasn't joining in with the celebrations. He deduced that I must be one of 'them', and insisted on letting everyone else know. Fortunately, the majority of the surrounding Hibs fans were far more intent on watching their team demolish the current league champions, and paid him little heed. This seemed to aggravate him even more. When the second Hibs goal went in he totally lost his rag, yelling that, there was "a hun" in here. Ignoring his team's moment of glory, he stormed away in a strop, to the back of the stand, returning with a policeman. In an absolute fury he demanded that I be arrested for being a hun. Keeping calm, I explained to the policeman that I was no hun, and I wasn't. No self respecting Rangers fan would ever accept that derogatory description. Being prepared for such an eventuality, I produced my Ferranti work badge and an

Edinburgh library card, which showed I was an Edinburgh resident.

"I'm a football fan," I explained, "simply here to watch a game."

The policeman accepted this, and warned the still irate Hibee that if there was any more bother it would be him, not me, that would be getting arrested. A minor victory for common sense, though I did linger in the ground afterwards, just to make sure that my adversary was long gone. I didn't fancy being reacquainted with him outside!

A season that started slowly, began to swing Rangers' way on the 4th of November. The game that day was heading for an uneventful 0–0 draw. With minutes to go, a cross ball was deflected to the feet of a Rangers forward. The forward turned, and drove a shot into the corner of the net – the game was against Celtic, and the forward was Maurice Johnston. An ecstatic Maurice ran to the Copland Road Stand, arms aloft, and then to the East Enclosure, whose occupants were in absolute delirium. It would be fair to say that MoJo had won over his critics. Three of the four Ibrox stands bounced in joy. In the fourth, the Broomloan Road, the disconsolate Celtic fans left, with a rousing chorus of "Mo, Mo, Super Mo" ringing in their ears.

In April, Rangers' 1–0 victory at Tannadice ensured that the league flag would still be flying over Ibrox. Once again though, the end of the football season did not mean the end of the football news. Last year's MoJo story stunned Glasgow, but that was nothing compared to the news that was to rock Edinburgh. Wallace Mercer, Hearts' owner and chairman, announced that he intended to take over Hibs; in theory, to merge them with Hearts, and form some sort of Edinburgh 'super team'. To most Hibs fans though, it looked like a hostile takeover, and the death of their club, a viewpoint that I had to agree with.

To be honest, Hibs have never been one of my favourite teams, but I sympathised with them greatly. They had, over the years, played a big part in Scottish football, and simply didn't deserve to be treated in this shabby way. The Hibs fans quickly mobilised a campaign of resistance to the takeover, which culminated in a rally at Easter Road, and as a football fan, I felt it was my duty to attend. So, I joined the masses on the Easter Road terracing to lend my support. I may not have been a great friend of Hibs, but their cause was undoubtedly just.

I went to the rally wearing my Rangers top, but covered by a neutral sweatshirt. The organisers had said that all supporters were welcome to attend, and to wear their club colours, but I was just a little nervous about that. Rangers and Hibs fans have never been great bedfellows, so I decided to play it safe. I stood in the ground and applauded the speeches, listened to the Proclaimers singing "Sunshine on Leith", then, after gauging the mood of the crowd I took my sweatshirt off to reveal my Rangers top. I stood there, extremely self conscious and very, very nervous: one Blue Nose in a sea of Hibees. I had of course nothing to worry about, the Hibs fans recognised a fellow football fan, and made me feel very welcome. It's a move though that I wouldn't be repeating on my next visit to the ground, that's for sure! I just wish that Hibs fan from earlier in the season had been there to see me. Would he still want me chucked out and arrested?

Wallace Mercer's bid to takeover Hibs eventually faltered and died – not on economic grounds, as his financial clout was sufficient to have swung the deal. It was, at the end of the day, people power that thwarted the Hearts owner. He had misunderstood and underestimated the attachment that supporters have for their football team. Mercer thought that the Hibs fans would swap allegiances as easily as changing from one flavour of potato crisp to another. He could not have been more wrong, football fans are non-transferrable.

The Hibs faithful had shown what a mobilised support could achieve.

Hands off Hibs – well done the Hibees!

The first home game of season 1990/91 was a friendly against Dynamo Kiev. I wasn't there. Having learned over that the years that pre-season games at Ibrox were almost always boring non-events, I decided to give it a miss. I went instead to Galashiels, to watch the reserves play in The Borders Challenge tournament. With two entertaining games against Gala Fairydean and Hawick Royal Albert it was a good decision, and not only that, the junior 'Gers won the tournament to lift the first silverwear of the new season. The following Wednesday, Rangers played Manchester United at Ibrox, and, disregarding my gut feeling about friendlies I went along – it was a boring non-event!

By the end of November things were ticking over nicely on all fronts, the three Rangers sides I supported were all doing well. On a Wednesday evening I was in Linlithgow to see the youth team beat Airdrie, on track for the Reserve League West; three days later, the reserves were beating Celtic at Ibrox, on track for the Reserve League; then Sunday, the big one: Celtic 1, Rangers 2, the first team were on track for the Premier League. Things just couldn't be better.

In January 1971, sixty-six football supporters died at Ibrox when leaving the ground after a Rangers–Celtic game. Twenty years later, the same two teams met at the same ground. In commemoration, Rangers unveiled a memorial plaque, and both teams gathered for a minute's silence. As the referee's whistle blew, a hush fell over the ground, but only for a few seconds; whistles, jeers and chants then emanated from the Celtic support in the Broomloan Road Stand. Derogatory and hurtful songs were sung. As anger mounted inside the ground, Celtic captain Paul McStay, and goalkeeper Pat Bonner ran to the Celtic end to plead for silence, which thankfully they eventually achieved. The damage however had been done, and the game was played out in a quite poisonous atmosphere. It was sad that a moment's reflection had been destroyed in such a manner. You'd have thought, and hoped, that the death of so many football fans would have transcended tribal rivalry. It was only for a single minute after all. It's curious, only two years before, Celtic had welcomed a Liverpool side, post-Hillsborough to Parkhead. Before that game, a silence had been impeccably observed to commemorate the football supporters who died on that terrible day. What was so different at Ibrox I wonder?

Rangers won that New Year game, and then went on a terrific run of form dropping only one point from a possible twenty-eight. A third league title in a row looked to be a certainty. Football, however, then took a back seat in my life.

We'd had some good news earlier in the year when Jacqui discovered she was pregnant. We'd been trying to start a family for some time and were obviously delighted, but having already suffered a couple of miscarriages, we tried not to get too excited. Not at this early stage anyway. As the months passed, we relaxed; everything seemed to be progressing normally. Then complications set in, and Jacqui was taken into hospital. At twenty-four weeks, it was a critical time. We were told if we could get to twenty-six weeks then everything would *probably* be okay. To be on the safe side Jacqui remained in hospital, and we just kept waiting, hoping and praying, thankful for each passing day that brought the twenty-sixth week closer.

I was called to the hospital one fateful morning in February. Jacqui had gone into premature labour and was in a great deal of pain. I rushed to the Eastern General, but on arrival was greeted by an empty bed. I was taken to one side, and a doctor explained that there was nothing that they could have done; our baby had been stillborn. I was then taken to a private room and reunited with an obviously tearful Jacqui. The doctor explained that the baby had been just too young, not developed enough to survive the trauma of the early birth. It was all so matter of fact and business-like. The doctor then, somewhat heartlessly, told us that "we were young and could try again"! I'm quite sure that he meant well, but at that emotional moment it really wasn't the kind of advice that we needed.

As is now common practice in hospitals, the baby, a boy, was wrapped in a little shawl and brought to us. To gain some kind of closure I suppose, rather than just whisk the child away as used to happen, which must have been very traumatic for the parents. Jacqui held onto the baby for a minute or so. I was offered the chance to do the same, but shook my head. I was numb, and just didn't know what to do. It's something I deeply regret now, he was my son and I didn't even hold him. I can't help but feel that I let him down at that moment.

A week later, on a cold and frosty morning, we were at Mortonhall Cemetery. They have a rose garden area there, specially dedicated to still born babies. Our baby son, named James, was buried there; I placed a Rangers scarf and teddy bear on top of his little white coffin before it was lowered into the ground. I don't know if it was an appropriate action, but I just didn't want him to go away without receiving something from me, something to show him that I cared. Each year we return to remember him.

The football season had of course continued, and a season that had been looking so good suddenly started to fall apart. Going into March, a dropped point at St Johnstone gave nearest title challengers Aberdeen a glimmer of hope. Rangers then went to Pittodrie. With an eight point advantage, a draw would most likely be enough to claim a third Championship in a row, and it looked as though the Ibrox men would get that point. Then, with the clock hitting ninety minutes, Aberdeen scored. The league race was back on!

Next stop was Parkhead, for what turned out to be a nightmare Scottish Cup tie against Celtic. The home side were two goals up and cruising, when Rangers' discipline snapped. Perhaps the pressure was beginning to tell. The referee flashed a red card, then another, then another. The men in blue had been reduced to eight men! Tension mounted on the terracing at the Rangers end, with some serious crowd trouble looking very possible.

In the final minute, the referee called Maurice Johnston over following an off the ball altercation. It looked for all the world like another red card, and how the green and white hordes would have loved that. The Rangers support, frustrated and angry, surged towards the track. The police responded and moved forward, ready to meet the challenge. For a few horrible seconds it looked as though we were heading for a major confrontation, until, thankfully, both sides backed off. On the park the referee took the sensible decision of blowing for full time, thus avoiding any further flash points. The game, after all, had long finished as a contest.

Everything was going wrong! The first team were struggling; the reserves and the youth team were losing. The three league titles that were "in the bag" back in November seemed to be slipping away. Hibs visited Ibrox, and left with a 0–0 draw. Rangers just couldn't force the ball past the Hibernian keeper Andy Goram, who played quite magnificently. Across the country, Aberdeen won again, and the gap was suddenly down to two points.

The league leaders were clearly struggling, two wins from seven games was a depressing statistic, particularly at this stage of the season. In an attempt to turn the situation around, Graeme Souness issued a rallying call. In a statement, playing hard on the theme of 'no one likes us we don't care', he demanded that the fans get 100% behind the team.

"Together," he said, "we can triumph."

The fans did get behind the team, and the next game, at home to St Johnstone, was comfortably won. Souness was right; together we could go on and win the title. Unfortunately we weren't together for long! On April 16th, a few days before a vital league game, it was announced that Graeme Souness was to leave Ibrox! Liverpool had come calling, looking for a new manager, and Souness just couldn't resist that call. A statement was issued, saying that he would be the next manager at Annfield.

Souness kindly said that he would remain at Ibrox, to try and help the club in the last few weeks of the season, but the bond between manager and supporter had been lost. David Murray, the Rangers owner, stepped in and made the brave, but correct decision, to tell Souness that if he wanted to go then he might as well go right now. So, Souness left, as abruptly as he had arrived, and in a quick transition Walter Smith was promoted to the manager's chair. We were about to enter the era of 'Walter Smith's Blue and White Army'.

As the season drew to a close, the first of the three league titles came up for grabs. The reserves had one last game to play at Ibrox, with a five goal victory required. On a frustrating afternoon, the second X1 got to within one goal of their target. Leading by four, they just couldn't get the fifth: the one that would have claimed the prize. As a result the league title went to Parkhead. The real frustration of the day was the perceived lack of effort shown by some of the fringe first team players, Dutch internationalist Pieter Huistra, in particular, just didn't appear too bothered about the result. I felt so sorry for the young lads in the team, players who had battled hard over a full season, only to be let down at the final hurdle by some of their more illustrious colleagues. One league title had gone. We surely we wouldn't lose the other two as well!

The penultimate game of the season took Rangers to Fir Park, still two points ahead in the league race. A good win would put real pressure on Aberdeen, leaving Rangers only needing a point to claim the championship. After a horrendous ninety minutes we left Fir Park, trying to come to terms with a score line that read: Motherwell 3, Rangers 0. Aberdeen were now on top of the table, only on goal difference, but they were top. There was one game to go, at Ibrox, against that very same Aberdeen. It was shoot out time for the championship.

Before that big game, the Reserve League West had to be sorted. The youth team were playing Falkirk at the Grangemouth Stadium, a big athletics type bowl. Rangers went into the game level on points, but two goals ahead of Clydebank. A decent win would set the Bankies a target later that night when they were to play Airdrie. The afternoon didn't start well with Falkirk racing into a two goal lead, but Rangers hit back to go 3–2 up. This put the Ibrox youngsters two points clear, but with a goal difference advantage of only three, not nearly enough.

It's often been said that supporters can be the 'twelfth man', spurring their team on to victory; well this was never more evident than on that Grangemouth afternoon. Rangers were desperate to score more goals but were hindered by constant breaks in play, the ball spending long spells on the running track, or in the vast expanse behind the goals. Time was quickly running out, when big Garry Lynch intervened. Garry was a larger than life, true blue supporter, who followed Rangers at all levels, everywhere and anywhere. Never shy to express his opinions, he bellowed over to the management team, telling them that they ought to "get the finger out and push for more goals ... how about getting the substitutes out to act as ball boys?" Garry's timely advice was acted upon, the bus driver even dashing out to lend a hand. With the ball being returned quickly into play, the pace of the game picked up and Rangers managed to score another four goals. Clydebank now needed to win by seven goals, and not just three.

Later that night, Clydebank, rather unfairly playing their entire first team squad, beat Airdrie by six goals to nil. A good win, but not good enough to deny Rangers the championship. Sure it was only the Reserve League West, and did it really matter? Well, it mattered to the young lads playing for the club, and it mattered to the supporters who followed the team. So, yes, of course it mattered – and I know it didn't happen, but Rangers should really have struck an extra medal for big Garry. He was without doubt man of the match that day! The young team had done the business. Three days later the mantle was passed to their 'big brothers'. Could the first team deliver the championship that we really craved?

I went to Ibrox for the league decider, more in hope than expectation. I'll admit I wasn't too confident. The momentum was with Aberdeen; they were the form team, they were in pole position and didn't even have to win the game. I may have had doubts, but the Aberdeen support didn't. They swarmed into the Broomloan Road Stand very early, blasting out their anthems as their team warmed up. Ironically this backing may have been counterproductive by lulling their team into a false sense of security. Aberdeen returned to the dressing room with Ibrox still half empty. When they made their reappearance, the ground was bursting at the seams, the noise deafening, the songs, loud and proud, and all in favour of the home side.

Watching from the Govan Stand, I knew, in one defining moment, that we were going to win. One of the Aberdeen defenders was warming up. He ran towards my section of the stand and was met by thousands of fired-up fans, out of their seats, hurtling some dreadful abuse. The player stopped and stood transfixed, he looked absolutely petrified. One of his more experienced teammates came over and pulled him away, but the damage had been done. I was now confident and believed. More importantly that Aberdeen player, wasn't and didn't!

The game went like a dream. In the early minutes Mark Hateley clattered the Aberdeen goalkeeper. A clear and premeditated foul, intended without doubt, to unsettle their young keeper. Not very sporting I suppose, but hey, all's fair in love, war and title deciders! And it worked. Not long after that, the big striker flew goalwards and bulleted a header into the net – Ibrox all but exploded in joy. A second half goal, again from Mark Hateley, put the icing on the championship cake, and we could relax, enjoy, and celebrate!

Going into the '90s UEFA introduced the 'three foreigner rule' to their competitions. Basically it meant that for European games a team could only play three 'non-nationals' in their side. It was a problem that Scottish teams would have to quickly address. In our case very quickly, as last year's European Cup side had seven non-Scots regularly playing.

Walter Smith started the squad readjustment in the lead up to season 91/92 by signing two Scots, full back David Robertson and goalkeeper Andy Goram. One of the victims of the new signing policy was goalkeeper Chris Woods. He was a fine keeper, but English, and consequently one of the more obvious players to drop out of the side. Strange, after years of being criticised for their signing policy, Rangers had opened up and were ready and willing to sign anyone, regardless of colour, creed or nationality. Now the club were being forced by officialdom to be restrictive once again!

The first team started the season playing in a tournament down in Kilmarnock, which didn't sound too exciting, so I decided to head north to watch the reserves. It was August, so doubled up as a sort of holiday for Jacqui and me.

The reserves beat Deveronvale, with Chris Woods playing in goals. After the game Jacqui and I went out for a meal, and then returned to our hotel for a nightcap, entering the bar we discovered a party in progress. The Deveronvale team manager co-owned the hotel with ex-Aberdeen striker Joe Harper, and they'd invited the Rangers coaching staff along for a few drinks. Jacqui and I joined the party, as you do, and had a few beers. I chatted a while with Chris Woods, and spoke to him about the goalkeeping situation. I was curious about his feelings, though also a little wary about asking. I wasn't quite sure how he would respond. Chris as it turned out, was a really nice guy, and was happy to chat. He was very pragmatic about what was happening, and explained that he didn't want to leave Rangers, but understood that it was a football decision, and if he left, it would be with regret. At around one o'clock in the morning we decided to retire for the night, wanting to be as fresh as possible for tomorrows drive to Aberdeen. It wasn't the end of the party though.

I woke up through the night; the quantity of beer I'd drunk necessitating a trip to the bathroom, which was situated down the hallway. I returned to my room to find the door latched shut with the key, unfortunately, on the other side. I banged on the door, trying to wake Jacqui, but she was sound asleep and didn't respond. Not good! I was stuck in the hotel corridor, stark naked!

I thought that there might possibly be a spare key downstairs so I returned to the bathroom, to try and find something to put on, hoping there might be a dressing gown, or something. All I could find though was a towel, a rather small hand towel. Not ideal, but hopefully sufficient to preserve my modesty. I ventured downstairs but had no luck finding a key; I did however hear some noises coming from the bar. Peeking round the door I saw the party was still in full swing. With no other options available I ventured in, and discretely asked the barman if he could help me in my predicament. The partygoers spotted me; I don't suppose I was hard to miss, since the towel wasn't big enough to cover my backside!

"Fooking 'ell," exclaimed Chrisy Woods, "I've seen it all now!"

As the barman searched for a key, I rejoined the party and had a few more beers before returning to bed – all free gratis as my towel didn't have any pockets! Next morning we set off, somewhat bleary-eyed, for Aberdeen and that afternoon's game against Cove Rangers. The Rangers from Glasgow lost 3–1, with Chris Woods not exactly at his best. Strange, because when I'd last seen him, at 3am, he was on top form!

The league season started with a win. The only concern was the form of Andy Goram in goals, who was having a shaky start to his Ibrox career. The goal he lost against Hearts was a particularly bad one. He stood and watched as a speculative shot drifted over his head and dropped into the net. Perhaps we should have stuck with the 'foreigner' Chris Woods!

In September I managed to wangle a four day pass from Jacqui and went over to Prague for a European Cup tie. The trip was a good one, spoiled as ever by the football. Ask any supporter about a European trip and nine times out of ten, he will say it was great, apart from the game! Rangers were poor and lost 1–0, the goal coming from a cross that sailed over Andy Goram and dropped into the net – another costly mistake from the new keeper.

Hibs and Dunfermline contested this seasons League Cup final. The Edinburgh side had disposed of Rangers in the semi-final, with yet another dodgy goal conceded by Mr Goram. I watched the Final live on TV, desperately hoping for a Dunfermline victory. Not because I was a great Pars fan, but I knew that if Hibs won I'd have to endure all their fans returning from the game. Living on Easter Road, that wasn't a prospect I particularly relished. Hibs did win. And sure enough, a couple of hours later, the Hibees started gathering, cheering the open-topped bus as it made its way to the Stadium. Despite closing all my windows, I could still hear the roars as the victorious Hibs team did their lap of honour.

After the trials and tribulations of the Wallace Mercer takeover attempt, I couldn't really begrudge the Hibs fans their moment of glory. In any case, I'd seen my team win plenty trophies, and knew that I'd see plenty more. Let them enjoy their moment I thought. I did, however, envy them one aspect to their win. The Hibs team had travelled all the way from the Edinburgh city boundary on an open topped bus, working its way along Princes Street, in front of their adoring fans. It was the perfect way to end the day, a pleasure always denied to Rangers and Celtic. Glasgow was just too divided a city to allow that to safely happen.

In October we found out that Jacqui was pregnant again. We were obviously delighted, but a little scared as well, the trauma from last year still fresh in our memories. All we could do was carry on as normal, take care, and hope that this time, everything would be okay.

Hearts were top of the league table, and to be fair, there on merit. Rangers, however, were in hot pursuit, looking for their fifth title in six years. One man who wouldn't be helping in that quest was Maurice Johnston; in November he left Rangers to join Everton. By far the majority of the support had welcomed Johnston to the club, and appreciated his 'never say die' commitment to the cause. Fifty odd goals and two Championship medals told its own story. There were a few, however, that could not, and would not, accept his presence in a blue jersey. They made their feelings known at Ibrox on the day. From the East Enclosure a sarcastic song was heard.

"Mo, Mo, Cheerio!" – There's just no pleasing some people!

By February normal service had been resumed in the league race. Rangers visited Tynecastle and beat Hearts by one goal to nil. That was the season's turning point and Rangers pulled away, another championship was on its way. Once again however, football had to go on the back burner. The pregnancy, which had gone so well, hit complications at almost the same stage as the last time. Surely history wasn't going to repeat itself! Jacqui had to go into hospital for observation, and rest, and once again we had to wait and pray that all would be okay. We agonised for a couple of weeks, taking one day at a time, then, thankfully, the doctors gave us the all clear. The problem had been resolved and Jacqui was allowed to return home. Too late for me to witness the league championship being clinched, not that I was concerned – some things are more important than a game of football.

The pregnancy thankfully went well after the scare, and by June it was just a case of letting nature take its course. In the early hours of Tuesday 30th June, Jacqui went into labour, I rushed her over to the Eastern General, and we settled in, unsure of what the next few hours would bring. Everything looked to be going well, the midwife in charge was very upbeat, but as time passed her demeanour changed and she started to look a little concerned – there was clearly something wrong.

"Nothing to worry about", she assured me. Then she called for assistance.

As more and more doctors gathered, I grew more and more anxious. The baby's position was constantly scanned, readings were taken, equipment was monitored – and then, with a shrill burst, an alarm sounded. In an instant Jacqui's bed was dragged away towards the nearby Operating Theatre, wires and tubes left dangling, gas and air bottles clanking onto the floor, leaving me and a couple of student nurses rooted to the spot, staring at the now empty space. Now, I'm no doctor, but even I knew this wasn't good!

A nurse clasped my arm and whisked me off to a waiting room. She assured me that "everything was fine". She didn't believe it, and neither did I. Alone, with only my thoughts and fears for company, I did the expectant father routine, pacing the room, up and down, over and over – at the end of each circuit I stopped to watch some tropical fish swimming carefree in their tank. After what seemed like hours, the nurse returned. It was a horrible moment, waiting to gauge whether the news was good, or bad, then she smiled, and I started to relax.

Her next words were, "Congratulations, Mr Whitelaw, you have a baby son."

I was taken into the delivery room, in time to see Jacqui being united with the child we thought we'd never have. It was a moment to savour, and quite unlike anything I had ever experienced. We did suffer a few nervous days as the baby was put into the special care unit, but all was well, and mother and child were allowed home. Two of us had driven to the hospital; three of us were driving home!

I'd been pretty mad with our old manager a year before, leaving us in the lurch like that, to go off to Liverpool, but I'm a forgiving kind of guy. We named the baby Graeme William, Graeme after Mr Souness, and William after Jacqui's Granddad.

It's Off To The Match I Go

Chapter 12:
Champions League Chicanery

A 2–1 home defeat by Marseille in a pre-season friendly (more about them later) was disappointing, as was the start of the 92/93 league campaign, with only two wins from the first five games. There was little to indicate that Rangers were about to embark on arguably their most successful season in living memory. The catalyst for the turnaround came with home and away victories in UEFA's new competition, the Champions League. Those victories over Danish side Lyngby set up a mouth watering clash with English champions, Leeds United – games that would inevitably be tagged 'the battle of Britain'.

Rangers hosted the first leg at Ibrox, and had the worst possible start, losing the opening goal in the very first minute. They fought back, however, and had Ibrox bouncing with two goals of their own. The atmosphere at the game was terrific, but could have been so much better if the Leeds fans had been allowed to attend. Terrified over the prospect of crowd trouble, the two clubs had come to an arrangement that neither would accept tickets for their away fixture. It was a shame, because football needs an opposition support to help generate that special atmosphere. If the Glasgow police could manage to control over seven thousand Celtic supporters at Ibrox, then they could surely handle eight or nine hundred Yorkshire men. It was, sadly, the two clubs showing deep distrust of their own support and taking the easy option.

Written off by the English Press as 'no-hopers', Rangers went to Elland Road for the second leg, and won 2–1, a truly outstanding victory. This game really marked the arrival of Andy Goram as a Rangers goalkeeper, the mistakes of the previous season now long forgotten. At Leeds, Andy made a string of magnificent saves, thwarting local hero Eric Cantona, time after time. Also memorable was Rangers' second goal, a quite superb flying header from Ally McCoist, the man I've already berated as one who 'just couldn't head a ball to save himself'. I was delighted, on this occasion, to have been proved so dramatically wrong!

Returning triumphant from Elland Road, Rangers made the much shorter journey to Parkhead. This was normally an eagerly awaited fixture and one of the highlights of the football year, but today it felt different. There was a perceptive feeling on the slopes of the Rangers end that this game was somehow no longer special, or at least not as important as it used to be. Rangers had qualified for the first ever Champions League, and were part of Europe's elite. Celtic were frankly so far behind, that they were, it seemed, only here to make up the numbers. That feeling was re-enforced when we cheered the announcement of the Celtic team, each player receiving his own ironic roar of approval. As expected the men in blue won the game, with Ian Durrant, free from injury at last, scoring the only goal.

Following that trip to Parkhead I had to cut down on away games. Graeme was now three months old and looking after him was pretty much a full-time occupation for Jacqui. I realised that it wasn't fair of me to disappear every Saturday and Wednesday, leaving her to hold the baby. She needed a break, so I stayed home every other weekend to help out.

Good grief, I was turning into a new man! As a part-time supporter, I now had to rely on the radio for my football fix. That involved tuning into Radio Scotland or Clyde, and waiting to find out which match they were covering. Perhaps my memory is playing tricks on me, but the announcement always seemed to be: "Today we will be going to Parkhead, to cover the Celtic game". That meant I had to listen to their game, and wait for the score flash from Tynecastle, or Pittodrie, or wherever Rangers were playing, holding my breath for the few seconds that felt like hours, before the news came through that my team had hopefully scored. To be honest the news was almost always good, as the Ibrox men were on an unbelievable run sweeping away all domestic opposition. In the coming months only two points would be dropped from a possible forty-four.

The good form needed to be more than just domestic; Rangers were in the group stages of the inaugural Champions League, competing with Europe's best. It was a real step up in class, light-years away from the Scottish League and games against the likes of Partick Thistle. A fact amply demonstrated when French champions Marseille came to Ibrox and gave us a quite comprehensive football lesson. They were better in every department, and totally dominated. Watching them race into a two goal lead, I sat back, admired their play, and thought this must be what it's like being an Albion Rovers fan, watching your team get humbled. Their small band of supporters at one stage whipped off their pale blue tops and turned their backs to the field of play, seemingly in disdain for their opponents. They bounced up and down, and chanted a song, which I suspect was the French equivalent of "Oh, this is so fucking easy". However, he who laughs last, laughs longest. If the French had the skill and technique, then the Scots had the grit and determination. In the final ten minutes, with the rain tumbling down, the two goals were pulled back and a draw somehow salvaged.

It was the start of a European adventure that would see my team a whisker away from the Champions League final. In the following games, CSKA Moscow were beaten away from home. A win and a draw gained over Club Brugge. Rangers then travelled to Marseille and came home with a well deserved 1–1. On match day six, the final round of games were played. Rangers and Marseille topped the group, level on points. We were at home to CSKA Moscow, Marseille having a tricky away game with Club Brugge. With the better head-to-head record the French side only need a single goal victory to progress, and that's what they got. At the same time, on a night of raw emotion, Rangers could only draw 0–0 with CSKA Moscow. They flung everything bar the kitchen sink at the Russians, but just couldn't score the goal that might, just might, have taken them to the final. On the final whistle the players slumped onto the Ibrox pitch, drained and exhausted, knowing that the dream had just died. The supporters stood, the ground still full to capacity, and applauded. In that instant, the stadium, the team, and the fans all seemed to be as one – I'd seen my team win trophies, doubles and trebles, but in that emotional moment, in defeat, I'd never been so proud.

That pride would subsequently turn to frustration when it emerged that whilst Marseille were a fine football team; their club was awash with corruption. Domestic matches had been rigged to help them in their European campaign. Following an enquiry the French football federation stripped Marseille of their league title, 'Le Championnat', and relegated them. There were rumours and allegations, that their final Champions league victory over Club Brugge owed more to the power of the French Franc than the skill of their team. Nothing however was proved, and UEFA seemed content to let the matter slide.

The disappointment of Europe was put to one side with a couple of trophies. The Premier League was retained with a victory at Airdrie. A game won without the services of Ally McCoist, who had broken his leg whilst playing for the

Scottish National team in Portugal. Ally was however present as the team did their lap of honour, though not actually in person, the players brought out a life size cardboard cut out of the striker. The cardboard stand-in was like Ally in every way, bar one, the replica Ranger never uttered a single word!

The last game of the season was the Scottish Cup Final at Parkhead. A huge Rangers support made the journey, and all in good voice. One of the most popular chants being a version of the 2 Unlimited song, "No limits", it was belted out to remind any watching Celtic supporters of the continuing emptiness of their trophy cabinet.

"no, no,
no, no, no, no,
no, no, no, no,
no, no ... there's no trophies!"

In fact there was a trophy at Parkhead. The Scottish Cup was within the building, but after ninety minutes of football it departed, along with the Rangers team to go back to Ibrox, Rangers beating Aberdeen 2–1 to claim the treble. This season's League Championship had made it five in a row. Five was nice, but Celtic had won nine in a row in the 60s–70s. Thoughts were now starting to drift towards that figure. Could Walter Smith's men possibly make it to nine as well?

The start of season 93/94 was dominated by a battle between Rangers and Dundee United for the services of Duncan Ferguson, though as time passed it seemed to become more of a personal struggle between the two respective chairmen; David Murray and Jim McLean. Dundee United resisted all overtures until the Ibrox side came in with a record breaking bid of £4.4m; too good an offer to turn down and Ferguson became a Ranger. It was, however, an extraordinary amount of money to pay for a youngster.

Ferguson was a decent, big bustling centre-forward, the kind of player that most teams desire. Rangers certainly did, and that's why they already had Mark Hateley in their line up!

The domestic season started with only three wins from ten league games, it wasn't great, but over the season recoverable. The same could not be said for the Champions League campaign. Walter Smith's men had been drawn against Levski Sofia, a reasonable side, but surely, given Rangers European pedigree, easily beatable. Sadly, it seemed not!

Rangers made heavy weather of the first leg at Ibrox, but a 3–1 lead looked sufficient to see them into the next round. However, a careless and late second goal was lost, a goal that placed the tie on a knife edge.

The second leg went well. With a composed and calculated performance the Scottish champions were drawing 1–1 going into stoppage time, and in total control of their own destiny. Watching at home, I screamed at the television, "Hold onto the ball, go to the corner flag ... run the clock down". It seemed to be a patently elementary and obvious plan. Not so apparently, Rangers pushed forward, bizarrely looking for a winner, and managed to lose possession ... Levski counter attacked and once in sight of goal, thundered a long range shot into the back of Ally Maxwell's net. Rangers had contrived to lose a goal, and consequently the tie, with the very last kick of the ball, snatching defeat from the jaws of victory. It was a truly shocking and naïve way to tumble out of Europe.

The disappointment of the European exit was quickly put into perspective when I received news that an old friend John Niven had been taken ill. John was a gentle giant of a man who travelled everywhere and anywhere with Rangers. He had contracted pleurisy whilst in Sofia; the long bus journey home from Bulgaria hadn't helped his condition, and on his arrival back in Edinburgh had to be rushed to hospital.

Despite all the efforts of the doctors, John died. At the age of just thirty-three, it was a real tragedy, I had lost a good friend, and Rangers a great supporter. It's traditional at times like this to say he was a good man, liked by all – well in this case it was 100% true, John was a good man, and he was liked by all. I genuinely don't think I ever heard anyone hold a bad word against him. At his funeral it was significant that amongst the flowers and tributes, were contributions from Hibs, Hearts and Celtic supporters. Rangers were represented by David Murray and John Greig. In his memory, and as a fitting tribute, my supporters' club, the Edinburgh Loyal, was renamed The John Niven Loyal.

Rangers weren't playing well this season, and they weren't helped by a string of injuries, a problem we were going to have to get used to. By October there were nine first-team players unfit. It became a running joke, rather than increase the capacity of Ibrox, we should build an extension onto the treatment room. It wasn't funny though, all teams have knocks and niggles, but to have so many players out at one time seemed, frankly, to be negligent. Questions were asked about the way training was structured, and just how competent were the club's medical staff? The fact that Rangers did not have their own training centre was also a matter of concern. They were buying players for millions of pounds, paying them a small fortune in wages, yet, at the same time, training on public parks, renting cricket grounds, and transporting players to and from Ibrox by mini bus. For a multimillion-pound business, and professional sports club, Rangers could at times appear very amateurish.

It wasn't just the superstars at Ibrox that were hitting the treatment table. I'd been playing five-a-sides for many years, pretty regularly and pretty poorly. To be honest I've never been much of a footballer. But my performance, even by my low standards had been deteriorating, from poor to downright dismal, with a foot injury giving me problems. I soldiered on for a few months, but eventually it got just too sore and I had to seek medical advice. During my consultation the doctor seemed to get the impression that I was some sort of semi-professional. When I told him that I had a couple of games coming up he offered me a cortisone injection, just to see me through the next few weeks. I thought, why not? It's what real football players get, so I agreed to the treatment – it made me feel kind of important for some strange reason.

There were two distinct moments when I knew that I'd made a bad decision. The first was when the doctor pulled out, and loaded up the syringe ... the needle on it was absolutely enormous. The second moment, and most fearful, was when he said,

"If you want to yell out, feel free ... this might be a little painful".

I'd like to say I took it like a man, but, when the needle went into my foot, and hit bone, I squealed and wailed like a hysterical schoolgirl. It was unbelievably sore. On the positive side my foot felt great, and I could continue my rather undistinguished five-a-side career.

In October, Rangers and Hibs contested the League Cup final. A close fought game was poised at 1–1 and looked to be heading for extra time. Worryingly, Hibs were playing well and looked perfectly capable of lifting the trophy. With that came the frightful thought of a journey home, sharing the M8 motorway with bus loads of jubilant Hibees. Not a pleasant prospect! Fortunately I had nothing to worry about. Cometh the hour, cometh the man, Ally McCoist, only just recovering from his broken leg, was introduced to the fray. With nine minutes remaining, the ball was lofted into the Hibs penalty box. McCoist took the ball on his chest, but surrounded by five defenders there was no danger – no danger 'til he leant back, and in one swift movement hooked an overhead kick into the corner of the net. The striker wheeled away to receive the adulation of his adoring fans. Job complete; cup winning goal scored. He wasn't known as Super Ally for nothing!

The journey home brought an unexpected moment of schadenfreude. The John Niven Loyal had just reached the Maybury junction on the Edinburgh city limits. Parked at the side of the road, was an open topped bus, festooned with green and white balloons, a banner fluttering forlornly from the top deck read 'Congratulations Hibs, League Cup winners'. Clearly no one had bothered to call the driver and let him know the bad news … we did!

The season continued with Rangers playing very inconsistently, unable to string any more than two wins in a row. The burgeoning injury situation was now taking its toll and if Celtic wanted to halt the run of successive championships, this was surely was the time to do it. Their chance came at Parkhead, in the New Year fixture. Celtic were unbeaten and performing well under new manager Lou Macari, they were very confident of knocking the blue half of Glasgow off top spot. That confidence didn't last too long. Rangers were a goal up in sixty seconds, the lead was doubled in the third minute and after twenty it was up to three.

With the Teddy Bears in delirium, the Celtic support all but imploded. A fan, clad in green and white, invaded the park and attempted to assault Ally Maxwell. A curious choice of target, as Maxwell's somewhat erratic goalkeeping was probably Celtic's only chance of getting back into the game! At half time, angry protests erupted in the main stand, with various missiles being launched at Celtic's board of directors. The natives were undoubtedly revolting!

Celtic pulled a goal back just after half time, but the mood of their support wasn't helped when that goal was ironically cheered by the ebullient Rangers fans, who were enjoying a fine days entertainment. Back in the early 70s, I'd watched Celtic toy with my team at Hampden. Well, now it was payback time, and I savoured every moment of the eventual 4–2 victory.

Rangers were seven points clear at the top of the table, and cruising towards six-in-a-row. A win over closest challengers, Motherwell, would clinch the title. Rangers lost that game at Fir Park and the championship party was put on hold – and to be honest I wasn't overly disappointed, it was an away game, and I wasn't there. Winning the league was a mere formality, and I wanted to be there to see it. A few weeks later I watched Rangers play Hibs at Easter Road, once again a win would clinch the title, and once again they lost. A point in the next game at Kilmarnock was all that was arithmetically required, and then a real championship party could commence.

Rangers went to Kilmarnock, and lost 1–0. With Motherwell also dropping points, the league was officially won, but it was the flattest and most subdued title winning party ever. The following week, Rangers drew 0–0 with Dundee in a dreary game at Ibrox, and were presented with the Premier League trophy. It had however been a quite wretched end to the season, only two points won from a possible fifteen and no way to prepare for a Scottish Cup final, when Rangers would be striving for an unprecedented 'double treble'.

The season concluded with that Scottish Cup final against Dundee United, and to be honest it wasn't all that hard to predict the outcome. Rangers had stumbled over the league winning line, and looked to have already packed their bags for the summer. Dundee United, who'd finished joint sixth, seized their opportunity and won the trophy with a 1–0 victory. Their winning goal perfectly summed up the end of season form. A bad pass back and a fluffed goalkeeper's kick presented Craig Brewster with an open goal, a gift wrapped chance he didn't miss.

The result was bad enough, but the cup final had one last sting in its tail. I stayed behind, as always, to watch the cup presentation, and to applaud my team, though to be perfectly honest, I wasn't sure they really deserved it. As Dundee

United paraded the trophy to their supporters, the Hampden PA blasted out 'Dignity' by Deacon Blue, presumably because singer Rickie Ross was from the city of Dundee. I'd been to see the band a couple of times in concert and loved that particular song, but from that moment onwards its opening bars would forever remind me of celebrating Dundee United fans. The song had sadly been ruined. Still, after losing their previous seven finals, I couldn't begrudge the United fans their moment of glory. What on earth was coming over me? Was I becoming magnanimous in my old age!

What should have been a great end to the season had seen Rangers clinch the championship, without winning. The League trophy had been presented without a win or a goal scored. The Scottish Cup was meekly surrendered in the same manner. Something had to be done, Rangers needed some spark, some inspiration … some magic in their team.

Chapter 13:
Premier Leagues and Procurator Fiscals

Season 94/95 started with Rangers hosting their own four-team tournament at Ibrox. Once again, recognising that pre-season friendlies were generally dull and lifeless, I turned down the prospect of a game against Manchester United, and went instead to watch the youth team play a testimonial at Ashfield Juniors. On this occasion, I possibly made the wrong choice, as the game at Ibrox was a feisty affair with some hard tackles, Alex Ferguson losing his rag, and Eric Cantona copping a red card. My game was a little duller in comparison, but on the plus side had only cost an entry fee of £1. It did, however, have its own memorable moment. Midway through the second half a Rangers player was brought down in the penalty box. Injured in the process, he had to be replaced. As the substitute ran onto the park, he announced that he was going to take the resultant penalty kick.

John McGregor, the Rangers coach, retorted "Oh no, you're not!"

Paying no heed the player ran into the penalty box. With John McGregor going apoplectic on the touchline, the youngster placed the ball on the spot. Once again McGregor bellowed that the boy was not to take the kick, and once again he was ignored – the impetuousness of youth won out. The boy took a few steps forward and confidently struck the penalty ... sending the ball high over the crossbar He was promptly hooked having been on the park for less than a minute. The remainder of his Rangers career, I suspect, lasted just about as long.

In avoiding the Ibrox tournament, I missed the debut of Brian Laudrup. Last season Rangers had looked somewhat pedestrian and uninspired. Brian Laudrup would magically change all that. In the early 1960s Rangers supporters were privileged to watch Jim Baxter in his prime. Now, in the 1990s, a new generation were to witness their own genius at work. That may sound a little extravagant in praise of the Dane, but at times words could not do justice to his performance and influence on the Rangers side.

The domestic season started well, with Brian Laudrup majestic, everything was looking rosy – and then the roof fell in! Rangers crashed out of Europe, losing 1–0 at home to AEK Athens. Three days later, Celtic came calling, and went back to Parkhead with all three points, comprehensively winning 2–0. The following Wednesday Falkirk knocked them out the League Cup. In eight days Rangers had played three home games, and lost the lot, tumbled out of two competitions and fallen behind in the League race. It wasn't good, and didn't get much better in the days that followed. The newspapers, the local media – Radio Clyde in particular – piled into the Ibrox men. Everyone had their two penneth, with advice, criticism and by the sound of it, downright joy at Rangers' apparent demise. If that wasn't bad enough cracks were starting to appear from within Ibrox.

Basile Boli, another new signing, had gone home to France during an international break, and whilst there given a none too complimentary interview to a local magazine. He apparently had a lot to get off his chest, and he went about it with gusto – little of it turned out to be very complimentary. To sum up the bold Basile's comments; 'Rangers et Walter Smith sont merde.' The comments were of course put down to a bad translation, the standard 'get out of jail card' used by all foreign players when their comments are reported back in Scotland. It would be fair to say though, that from that moment on, Boli's days at Ibrox were numbered.

Rangers were, of course, too good a team to just roll over and surrender their crown as Champions. Falkirk were beaten at Brockville, Walter Smith's men went back to the top of the Premier League, and with no one putting up a discernable challenge, they romped their way to another league title, to seven in a row.

It was a championship that restored a little cheer to a support, still reeling from the death of former favourite Davie Cooper. The ex-Rangers winger had collapsed and died of a brain haemorrhage at the tragically young age of 39. Cooper had been without doubt a wonderful player, and it had been a privilege to watch him play, it's just a shame he'd spent much of his career in a sub-standard team. That fact hadn't seemed to bother the man though. He was once quoted as saying, "I played for the team I loved". What better epitaph could there be for a Blue Nose.

The dust had only just settled on 'seven in a row' when rumours started to circulate that Rangers were interested in signing Paul Gascoigne, rumours that were treated with more than a little scepticism. Gascoigne was after all a genuine world class player. Why on Earth would he want to come to Scotland? As time passed the rumours became more and more credible, then sensationally, on a glorious July afternoon, a peroxide blonde Paul Gascoigne was paraded outside Ibrox as Rangers player. The £4m signing was a huge gamble given Gascoigne's well publicised injury and behaviour problems, but it was also a signal of intent. The club were heading onwards and upwards!

As part of the build up to season 95/96, Rangers once again organised their own four-team tournament, 'The Ibrox International Challenge'. Paul Gascoigne made his debut in the first game, scoring against Steaua Bucharest. I wasn't there to witness it though; I was a hundred miles away in Belfast watching the reserves play a friendly against Linfield. This wasn't my first time in Northern Ireland, I had of course made a flying visit in 1984 as part of my escape from Dublin, this time I wanted a more relaxed visit. It somehow didn't quite work out that way.

Arriving early, I booked into my hotel which was in the Sandy Row district of the city. I knew that there was a Rangers supporters' club in the area, and, as the song said, "King Billy's on the wall … over at Sandy Row", so it had to be a pretty sound place for a Blue Nose to stay!

The football part of the day wasn't that impressive or memorable, honours even in an unremarkable 2–2 draw. After a few beers I left the ground and decided to walk back to my hotel. I was in no rush, and thought it would be a way of passing the time, maybe stop off for a pint or two en-route. There were however a couple of major flaws in my plan. Firstly, I wasn't exactly sure of the direction to go. Secondly, and more importantly, I'd forgotten that Belfast has its own peculiar demography. I set off; strolling in what I thought was the correct direction and after a while reached Donegal Road. I was sure I just had to head down that road to reach my goal, so that's what I did. Unfortunately I turned to the left, and not to the right. Walking, daydreaming, too much beer in me, I found myself in a housing scheme, and looking round it clearly wasn't Sandy Row.

It was local election time in Belfast and there were posters on every other lamp post, and worryingly, they all seemed to be green, and promoting Sinn Fein. I looked round and saw another, a silhouette of a gunman on it, with the slogan 'sniper at work' – this wasn't good ... this wasn't good at all! I didn't know where I was, but I did know that it was no place for a guy wearing an Edinburgh Loyal polo shirt (thankfully under my jacket) and carrying a Union Flag (thankfully at the bottom of my carrier bag). It transpired that I'd managed to wander into some Republican housing estate just off the Falls Road. Now normally when lost, I'd go into a pub, have a quick pint and ask for directions. But, going into one of those cornershop bars and saying "give me a pint of lager please, and could you direct me to Loyalist Sandy Row", seemed, just a little foolhardy. The times were undoubtedly changing in Belfast, but I guessed that the Northern Ireland peace process, still in its embryonic stage, was not quite ready yet for this type of cultural exchange.

So I just walked, and walked, trying to look inconspicuous, terrified that I'd be spotted and sussed. Silently cursing myself for being such an idiot! Eventually I spotted a large Union Flag fluttering far away in the distance; I casually picked up my pace and discretely as possible, made a bee-line for it. After a time the landscape changed and the Irish tri-colour was replaced by the much friendlier Red Hand of Ulster. When I finally walked a pavement painted red, white and blue, I knew I was home and dry. The rest of my evening was spent in the Sandy Row Rangers Club, safe and secure, but still shaking!

A week after my Belfast adventures, I found myself in the more sedate surroundings of Creamery Park. It may have been a run of the mill testimonial, the reserves taking on Bathgate Thistle, but it was still a big game. This was the day that Graeme attended his first Rangers game. In 1963, thirty odd years ago, my father had introduced his son to The Rangers. Now I was doing the same for my son. It was a special moment. Graeme seemed to enjoy his day out, though I'm not sure how much of that involved the actual football. He watched some of the first half action, but as a three year old his attention span was a little short, so we wandered round the ground, kicking a ball that we had brought. He then discovered a big pile of grass clippings; those clippings proved to be a bigger attraction than the football and kept him amused for the remainder of the day. A shame really as he missed most of the goals in a good 7–3 victory!

I'm pleased to say that in the following days Graeme spoke about the football and asked when he could go again. We did go again, and as the season progressed we would attend more and more reserve and youth team games together. Those games were increasingly being held in and around West Lothian, in places like Linlithgow, Livingston and Bathgate, very handy as Jacqui and I had recently moved into the area. Our home in Edinburgh had been a good one, but it was just too small to accommodate our growing family. We sold the flat in Edinburgh and with the proceeds bought a three bedroom house in East Calder. With a front and back garden it was the perfect move.

Rangers had managed to qualify for the Champions League group stages, though sadly without the success of season 92/93. The Scottish champions were, quite simply, out of their depth, finishing bottom of the group without a win to their name, only three points gathered from a possible eighteen. The two games against Juventus were particularly brutal. The Italians, who would eventually win the competition, trounced Rangers 4–1 and 4–0. I watched the away tie on TV, with a mixture of horror and anguish as Juventus totally outplayed Walter Smith's men. As the game progressed the home side raced to a three goal lead, and frankly it was a lead that looked like growing and growing. It reached a point where I simply couldn't take any more, and with a heavy heart I switched the television off. If that action was intended to take away the pain, it didn't work. My television screen may have gone blank, but the game was still in progress, and somehow, not knowing what was happening was far worse than knowing. I felt guilty for deserting my team in their hour of need, so with a stiff drink to hand, I settled back down in front of the television, just in time to see Juventus score again.

Scottish football went a little crazy at the tail end of 1995. The Glasgow Procurator Fiscal decided that the city had become so crime-free that the police could now spend their time and resources investigating incidents on the football field. The SFA and referees also decided to enforce the laws of the game to the nth degree. I was trying not to become paranoid, but it wasn't easy as everyone seemed to be concentrating their attention onto Rangers.

On November 11th, Rangers and Aberdeen played out a rather bad tempered 1–1 draw at Ibrox. After the game, it was announced that, on the direction of the Procurator Fiscal's office, the police would be investigating certain on-field incidents, particularly those involving Paul Gascoigne. The Glasgow Police did just that and interviewed, under caution, Paul Gascoigne, John Brown and Alan McLaren. Billy Dodds, as a token Aberdeen player in my opinion, was also interviewed. Interestingly, on the very day of that tempestuous game, a few miles away another incident was occurring. At Airdrie, the Dumbarton goalkeeper was double red carded, one of the cards being for a headbutt on an opponent. Curiously the Lanarkshire Procurator Fiscal did not deem this worthy of investigation. I wonder why?

The Police eventually submitted their extensive report to the Fiscal, and in a show of common sense, no charges were brought forward. The Rangers support gave a collective sigh of relief, and then gasped in astonishment as it was announced that the SFA was looking into another incident involving Paul Gascoigne. They were considering charging the player with 'bringing the game into disrepute'. What had the maverick Geordie done now?

Back in October, Rangers played Hearts at Ibrox. During the match Paul Gascoigne playfully patted Alan Laurence on his bottom. A member of the public spotted this heinous act on television, and reported it. He was, by all accounts, outraged. Rather than tell the bloke to grow up, and go away, the SFA decided to conduct an investigation. It was frankly absurd, and for once the club stepped in to defend their player. Treating the charge with the contempt it deserved, Donald Finlay QC, the Rangers vice-chairman made a statement.

"We should be enquiring why a Hearts player had his backside on Mr Gascoigne's hand, which might do more to bring the game into disrepute."

The matter was thankfully and sensibly dropped, and football could take centre stage again. Celtic were now winning regularly, and were, for the first time in many years mounting a serious challenge. The spectre of Rangers winning 'nine in a row' was obviously spurring them on.

With the crucial New Year Old Firm game looming, Rangers needed a moral boosting win to set them up, and they got it with a terrific 7–0 victory over Hibs. There were talking points a-plenty from the game, but once again the madness of officialdom took centre stage. During the match the referee dropped his yellow card. Paul Gascoigne spotted it, picked it up and ran over to return it. Being Paul Gascoigne, however, he had to do it in his own inimitable style. He approached the official and flashed the card at him, jokingly booking him. It was an entertaining moment, which the referee soon halted; he took the card and promptly flashed it back at Gascoigne, booking him! The referee, suffering from a humour bypass, sadly wasn't joking. It was the culmination of a quite stupid few months which had seen Rangers under attack from all quarters.

The Old Firm game duly arrived, and with it the twenty-fifth anniversary of the Ibrox Disaster. To his credit, Fergus McCann, the Celtic owner had organised a minute's silence in recognition of the anniversary. McCann had clearly let his heart rule his head on this matter, hoping that the occasion would bring the city of Glasgow together, for at least a few moments; he thought that the Celtic support would respect the silence. If however, he had known his history, he would have realised that there was little chance of that happening. As the referee's whistle sounded, the jeering and abuse started. Broadcast live to the nation on Sky television, there was no hiding it. Fergus McCann, a decent man, tried his best to quell the abuse, and failed miserably. The Sun newspaper reported the event:

'McCann was clearly embarrassed as he pleaded for silence ... 'The Parkhead chief, who first asked "please be silent" was forced to insist: "25 years ago 66 people tragically died in this fixture. Now I would ask you to show respect. Please stand in silence." He could have been speaking in a foreign language for all the difference his pleas made as the heartless chanting and jeering went on.'

I wasn't at the game. Not having Sky television, I had to listen to the game on the radio, anger building up inside me as I heard the abuse. Once again, I could only wonder as to why the Celtic support lay claim to that title of 'greatest fans in the world'.

The league's final Old Firm game of the season came in March, and was critical for both sides. The general consensus was that whichever team won it would go onto lift the Championship. Inevitably I suppose, with pressure on both sides, it ended in a 1–1 draw, a result that favoured Rangers who still had a narrow lead at the top of the table. I wasn't at the game; domestic matters had intervened. Jacqui was pregnant again and well into her eighth month. On the day of the match she was having stomach pains and although it was still early we thought it may be the start of her labour. Big game or not, I realised that my place was by her side, and not in an Ibrox stand. I did of course listen to the game on the radio, happy until the eighty-seventh minute when Celtic equalised. No change at the top of the Premier League and no change at home, the labour pairs proved to be a false alarm.

We were now into April and well past the expected delivery date. It was April 7th 1996 to be precise, the same day as the Scottish Cup semi final, Celtic vs Rangers. Once again I knew that I couldn't attend and passed my ticket onto a suitably grateful workmate. As the game kicked off, I sat at Jacqui's bedside, thirty-five miles away in Livingston's St Johns hospital, waiting for nature to take its course. It was a nervous time for both of us, with the problems of Graeme's birth still fresh in our minds. The midwife was aware of that and continually assured us that everything was fine. At one point she addressed me, as I paced anxiously up and down the room;

"There is nothing whatsoever to worry about Mr Whitelaw", she said. "Everything is coming along nicely"

On hearing this, Jacqui raised herself up a little, hair matted and with sweat on her brow, she bellowed, "He's not worried about this; he's worried about the bloody football!" Jacqui I'm afraid, knew me only too well, I had a little radio stashed away in my pocket, an earpiece keeping me updated with the news from Hampden. It had all been going so well. Rangers were in complete control, with goals from Ally McCoist and Brian Laudrup. Then, with a few minutes remaining Pierre Van Hooijdonk pulled a goal back for Celtic, hence the nervous pacing. I was banished to the corridor in disgrace, returning a little later, after the final whistle, looking a little shamefaced, but inwardly relieved that my team had held on to their lead and made it to the final!

The baby hung on as well, not making his appearance 'til the next day. With no distractions, I was available to give my full and total support; this time present at the birth, all dressed in hospital green, a somewhat unusual colour scheme for me! It was a quite amazing experience to see the birth of my second son, but being of the squeamish nature, I didn't see absolutely everything. I wouldn't have missed it though for anything. Our new son was named Dale, by Graeme, who liked that name for some reason. I added the middle name Gordon. It was a traditional family name and had a nice Rangers ring to it as well, Dale Gordon having played with the club a few years previously.

Rangers kept winning and the League title was dutifully won on April 28th against Aberdeen. However, for a while it looked as though the visitors were going to be party poopers. They took the lead. Paul Gascoigne equalised, but Aberdeen clung on desperately trying to deny us the required three points. With ten minutes remaining Gazza took charge. Winning the ball inside his own half, he powered past half the Aberdeen team, weaving his way to goal before lashing a shot into the net. When Rangers won a last minute penalty there was only ever going to be one taker. Gascoigne stepped up, and he scored, claiming a hat trick that sent Ibrox into ecstasy.

One man not celebrating that day was Scottish journalist Gerry McNee, a man perplexingly known as 'the voice of football'. McNee had conducted a season-long vendetta against Paul Gascoigne, using his Sunday Mail column to snipe, criticise and whine. McNee's apparent hatred of the player even stretching to the fact that he wouldn't even refer to him by name; Gascoigne was simply known as, 'the number eight'. One can only guess at McNee's mood when the team emerged from the Ibrox tunnel, ready to pick up the Championship trophy. Each player wearing a t-shirt with the number eight emblazoned on it. This was, of course, in reference to the fact that we'd just achieved eight in a row. I like to think though that part of it was a 'get it right up you' to the journalist. On a side issue, Rangers should have told McNee that he was not welcome at their stadium. The club really needed to stand up for itself and its players.

Twenty-four hours later another League championship was clinched, this time the Youth League. The Rangers youngsters travelled to Alloa Athletic, and won 14–1, marking my biggest win to date as a supporter. The game also featured possibly the world's most pointless red card. The youths were leading 11–1 with about ten minutes to go, when they scored to make it a round dozen. The goal, however, looked suspiciously offside. One of the Alloa players wasn't happy and he vigorously protested. On and on he moaned, 'til he received a yellow card. Still not happy, he complained again and again. Standing a few feet away, I heard the referee plead with the youngster, begging him to walk away and just accept the decision.

"Do you really want a red card?" the referee asked.

It seemed that the player did, and he launched into one last tirade. His reward was a second yellow and consequently that red card. Stupid!

The trophy tally increased a week later when Rangers lifted the Scottish Cup, beating Hearts 5-1 in the final. Gordon Durie had the distinction of becoming only the fourth player in history to score a hat trick in a final, yet wasn't named man of the match. Brian Laudrup trumped him, once again producing a footballing master class; he set up all three of Durie's goals, and still had time to score twice himself. It was a quite breathtaking display from a quite magnificent player.

The season was at an end, eight in a row had been achieved. The minor matter of nine in a row now beckoned.

Rangers Vs Ajax. European Super Cup 1973

Champions 1974

From the scrapbook 1973, last minute Alfie Conn. Rangers 2, Celtic 1

Altered Images 1983

Local newspaper is perhaps a little harsh on Rangers' new signing Robert Prytz. Sweden 1983

Davie Cooper, me… and that Einsiedeln shirt. Switzerland 1984

The final whistle at Pittodrie 1987. Champions at last

*It might only be a pre-season friendly... but Mr Souness really,
really wanted to win it. Switzerland 1987*

Tottenham 1986 and those terracing fences

An East Calder trio- with a Rangers Treble,
1999

You just didn't mess with the nine in a row team. Ian Ferguson
Vs Mike Galloway… no contest!

Thirty years of Punk Rock. John, Joe and Phil. The Zips 2008

Everyone has a Manchester memory… this is mine

Chapter 14:
Mission Accomplished

The league campaign, and the quest for nine in a row, started at Ibrox with a rather nervous 1–0 victory over Raith Rovers, though with Celtic drawing their first game, it was a promising start. I was to scribble into my diary that night: 'Two points up, thirty five games to go – only one hundred and four points required!' It was clearly going to be a long, long season.

During 'the barren years', I used to manage sixty-odd games a season, so it was ironic that on the brink of a major milestone in the club's history, I was to see fewer and fewer first team games. We had a new mouth to feed and money was tight. To help pay the bills, more and more overtime had to be worked and that meant missing some home games, as well as those away from home. I did however manage to maintain my season's quota. Weary from looking after a demanding Dale, Jacqui wanted some peace and quiet, and being the dutiful husband I decided to help her out. So once or twice a week, I'd take Graeme out for an evening's excursion, giving Jacqui her period of rest and relaxation. As luck would have it, the reserves and youths played their games midweek – I wasn't going to look a gift horse in the mouth and as a result Graeme and I became fully paid up members of The Reserve Team Loyal, attending over forty reserve and youth team games; small team games as we called them.

One of the bonuses of attending reserve games was that Graeme got a chance to see many of the first team players in action; either keeping themselves match fit, or more often than not, simply recovering from injury. It was the injury crisis at Ibrox that just wouldn't go away. In August, we watched the reserves draw 3–3 with Dunfermline, a game that became the Paul Gascoigne show. He managed to score a fine goal, hit the bar with a free kick, miss a penalty, then round it all off with a booking – just another day at the office for Gazza.

The push for the big nine was going well. Maximum points had been gathered from four games, when Hearts made a visit to Ibrox. Rangers were well on their way to five successive victories, leading 2–0, when Hearts lost the plot, and in a flurry of red cards they were reduced to seven men. With nine in a row at stake, this seemed to me an ideal opportunity to rack up our goal difference. It could after all be important at the season's end. However, Richard Gough disagreed, and gave clear instructions that the team should go easy, and just play out time with no further scoring. It was I suppose, the sporting and honourable action, though I have to wonder what would have happened if the boot had been on the other foot. Would Hearts have been quite so understanding? One man who clearly agreed with me was Ally McCoist; he came on as a late substitute and promptly rattled the ball into the Jambo's net. He hadn't scored over two hundred and fifty Rangers goals by passing up golden opportunities like this! I just wished that he'd gone onto score a few more. No disrespect to Hearts, but I wanted the goal difference boosted.

October saw me become a TV star, though 'stardom' is perhaps stretching it just a little. I'd been asked, along with a couple of others, to represent the Rangers fanzine, *Follow Follow*, in a nationwide TV quiz, our opponents being Liverpool's *Through the Wind and Rain*. The quiz may have been broadcast nationwide, but it wasn't seen by too many of the viewing public, hosted as it was by L!VE TV, a somewhat low budget and tacky satellite station. Their status in the broadcasting world could be gauged by the calibre of their staff and programme content. On current affairs they had 'The News Bunny', a man dressed as a giant rabbit, whose job was to mime out the events of the day; whether good or bad, joyous or tragic. Their weather reporter was just as bizarre; a dwarf who bounced up and down on a trampoline, leaping higher and higher the further north his forecast took him. Clearly the quiz was never going to rival *Mastermind*, particularly when you consider that the station's flagship sports programme was the classy *Topless Darts*!

In keeping with the layout of the television station, the rules of the quiz were somewhat convoluted and meant that despite answering the majority of the questions correctly, we controversially lost 2–1 to the Scousers. There was a chance to claim a last gasp equaliser when presented with the question: Name the three members of The Jam; I splashed in with the answer:

"It's Paul Weller, Bruce Foxton and … and … and the other one"

Unfortunately I couldn't quite get 'the other one' off the tip of my tongue, and out we went, falling at the first hurdle. How embarrassing for an old punk rocker to forget old Rick what's his name!

Still attending the small team games, Graeme and I went to Bathgate to see the reserves play Motherwell. As often happened, it was a game used to re-introduce a player after injury, this time Ally McCoist's turn. It was a cold and drizzly day, and the crowd; about hundred or so, were huddled under the terracing cover – all bar one. That hardy soul, well wrapped up in an old raincoat, and clutching a big umbrella shuffled his way round to the far side. Standing in the rain, the guy proceeded to give Ally McCoist absolute dogs' abuse, his every touch was jeered, a barrage of insults hurled at him. It was a bit harsh I thought, McCoist wasn't having a great game, but he was after all only getting some match practice. He certainly didn't deserve this level of attention.

Ally tried his best to ignore the ridicule, but was clearly rattled and eventually he reacted. To our astonishment he vaulted the pitch side fence and raced over to confront his tormenter. As the referee ran over to calm things down, McCoist came back onto the field laughing, as did the referee. Watching from the other side of the ground, we wondered what was going on – all became clear. The raincoat-clad spectator made his way around the ground, and revealed his true identity – it was Paul Gascoigne. He'd travelled all the way from Glasgow that afternoon with the express intention of winding up Super Ally. With his mission accomplished, he wandered away, chuckling contentedly.

On Sunday 2nd November, Rangers drew 2-2 with lowly Raith Rovers, Celtic on the same afternoon beat Aberdeen. The leadership of the Premier League changed hands, Celtic were top, only on goal difference, but top, and it gave the league table a somewhat uncomfortable look – if only we'd battered a few more goals past that seven-a-side Hearts team!

Fortunately the natural order was quickly restored when the men in blue travelled to Parkhead and won a quite remarkable game. Brian Laudrup gave Rangers a first half lead; he pounced onto a slip in the Celtic defence, burst through on goal and lashed a shot into the corner of the net. Celtic pushed forward remorselessly, desperate to draw level, but were repelled time after time by captain, Richard Gough, who was quite magnificent. When the Celtic forwards managed to get past the big defender they faced a goalkeeper playing at the top of his game. Andy Goram, irresistible, just wasn't going to be beaten.

The second half followed a similar pattern, except Rangers were now picking off their opponents with lightening counter attacks, and creating their own chances, and what chances! Time after time they were one on one with the Celtic keeper, and time after time those opportunities were squandered. Gascoigne even managed to miss a penalty. The men in blue mounted yet another counter attack. Jorg Albertz raced into the Celtic half. Onwards he ran, into their penalty box. Drawing the Celtic keeper from his goal line he casually rolled a perfectly weighted pass to Peter Van Vossen. With the ball at his feet, the Dutchman was presented with an open goal, and a chance to kill off the game. The Rangers support massed at that end of the ground leapt to their feet, poised and ready to acclaim the inevitable goal. A virtual silence engulfed Parkhead as Van Vossen steadied himself, took aim, and carefully guided his shot over the bar – and not *just* over the bar, but miles over it. Along with thousands of others I stood, hands on my head, unable to quite grasp what I had just witnessed. As we slowly slumped to our seats, the Celtic support, only a few feet away leapt to express their joy and to acclaim that never to be forgotten miss. Gnawing away at me was that old phrase; you have to take your chances!

With a mere five minutes remaining, my worst fears looked to be coming true when Celtic were awarded a penalty; and no doubt about the decision, Richard Gough for once just a little late in his tackle. Celtic's Pierre Van Hooijdonk stepped forward and blasted the penalty to his left. Andy Goram, as I said, just wasn't going to be beaten, and he wasn't. He dived to turn the ball away, then, in typically Goram style, he expressed his delight – with a clenched fist and a few carefully chosen expletives! At the other end of the ground the massed ranks of the Rangers support were roaring their own approval, giving it back in big style to a clearly distraught Celtic support. It had been a pulsating match, with the added drama of a pitch invasion, not for once by an irate supporter, but from a fox that had somehow gained entry to the ground. It did a couple of circuits of the pitch before disappearing, as quickly as Celtic's title challenge.

In the Premier League, with teams meeting four times a season an Old Firm game is never too far away and this season was no different. In January the big two met again. As always it was an important game, but by general consensus it was 'the last chance saloon' for Celtic. For them, it was a must-win game. I travelled to Ibrox on the John Niven Loyal, confident. Well, I was 'til the team news came through on the bus radio. Rangers had problems, big problems; a flu bug had ravaged the squad. Richard Gough and Brian Laudrup, heroes at Parkhead, were out of the game. Another half dozen would play, but were severely under the weather. At seven o'clock I'd quite happily have taken a draw. I really should have more faith!

Calling on all their reserves of strength and determination, Rangers produced a quite courageous performance. A goal up, then pegged back, Rangers went into the last ten minutes running on empty, but resolute in their desire to win the points. Some careless defending gave new signing Eric Bo Andersen a glimpse of goal. A glimpse was all he required and the home side were 2-1 in front. There were only five minutes left, but the drama was far from over. Celtic hit back and looked to have equalised through Jorge Cadette. The goal however was chalked off, much to the dismay of a Celtic support who howled their disapproval. Indeed they still protest about the validity of the decision – well into the next century! Another Bo Andersen goal then sealed the result in Rangers favour. It was a huge step on the road to nine.

This game sent the conspiracy theorists into an absolute frenzy. Every referee's decision 'til the end of the season was analysed with a fine toothcomb. The Celtic support, even more paranoid than usual (and that's saying something) were searching for any glimpse of bias towards the Ibrox men.

Paul Gascoigne was proving to be a very important player in this most crucial of seasons, particularly with the seemingly never-ending injury crisis still taking its toll. With injuries in mind, it was surprising when Rangers agreed to go over to Holland to play in a meaningless six-a-side tournament – taking over a squad of first team players was surely just asking for trouble. It therefore came as no great surprise when the inevitable news broke. "Gascoigne injured in Amsterdam!" The influential player had picked up ankle ligament damage, an injury that would see him miss the next dozen games. During that period, the Ibrox men would drop ten points, allow Celtic back into the title race, and tumble out of the Scottish Cup. You just couldn't make it up!

The Scottish Cup defeat came at Parkhead, and was a disappointment on the park, and directly responsible for a bit of a personal disaster at home. With no ticket, and no Sky TV, I had to tune into the game on the radio. Full of beer and nervous energy I listened in the kitchen, doing the dishes and tidying up, just trying to keep busy. It wasn't a happy night, gloomy after going a goal down, my mood wasn't improved when Celtic were awarded a penalty. Another goal so early in the game would almost certainly kill off Rangers' challenge. As Paulo Di Canio stepped up to take the kick, I stood, anxiously gripping a cupboard door handle, hoping and praying that the Italian would miss – he didn't – the roar coming out of the radio told its own sad story. As the commentator confirmed the bad news, I vented my frustration on the closest thing to hand, tugging angrily at that handle. The door ripped from its hinges and then, to my horror, with a creak and a groan the entire cupboard assembly slipped and tumbled from the wall. As Rangers were crashing out of the Scottish Cup, dishes, plates and glasses were smashing onto my kitchen floor. It would be fair to say, I'd had better evenings.

I've always found it strange that Celtic supporters refer to the Daily Record as the Daily Ranger, as though that paper is some kind of Ibrox mouthpiece. Over the years I've found little to substantiate that claim. In fact the Record, along with the Sunday Mail seemed in my experience to revel in Ranger baiting. This was never more clearly demonstrated than in a March '97 edition of the Sunday Mail. I was flicking through the paper, when my eyes were drawn to an advertisement:

"Looking for something different to commemorate an anniversary or birthday? Then why not order a superb framed copy of the front page from Scotland's champion, the Sunday Mail"

One of the front pages they used as an example was the edition from Sunday 3rd January 1971. The headline on that front page, a front page to be used remember, to commemorate a birthday or anniversary was emblazoned with:

"66 KILLED IN IBROX DISASTER. POLICE NAME THE DEAD"

The picture on that front page showed the covered bodies of dead supporters lying on the Ibrox turf. I couldn't believe my eyes. Did the Sunday Mail really think that anyone would want this particular front cover to celebrate a birthday? How could a newspaper be so crass and insensitive and how on earth had this got through their editorial control, if of course they had any? As far as I could see there were only two options:

1. The Sunday Mail was totally and utterly incompetent as a newspaper in assessing and understanding its readership.

2. There was a bad bastard at the Sunday Mail who thought this was a good way to have a dig at Rangers and their support.

I could see no other explanation, and either way, the Sunday Mail came out with no credibility whatsoever. I called the paper that morning but was fobbed off and told to try again on Tuesday, when "someone" would be available. I did just that, only to be told that they couldn't comment. I should submit my complaint in writing – submit it in writing? I'd done that on the very day the paper had been issued!

I called Ibrox on the Monday morning to draw their attention to the matter. No one was available to speak to me, but I was assured that a club representative would call me back. Sadly, no one did. An angry letter was also despatched to the club.

The Sunday Mail eventually replied:

"The editor has carefully considered your letter and has decided to withdraw the advertisement. Please accept our apologies."

Rangers also got back to me, John Greig replying to my letter to the club.

"I have written to the editor of the Sunday Mail expressing our view on the matter and I completely agree with you that the terrible disaster affects many people and we could do without being reminded of that day in this manner"

The advertisement was indeed removed and the sorry episode closed, but it still left a bad taste in my mouth. The Sunday Mail/Daily Record is pro-Rangers? Don't make me laugh!

The final Old Firm game of the season was only four days away and for once it probably justified the oft given tag, 'match of the century'. With the more difficult title run in, Rangers just had to take something from the game, but to do that they needed some inspiration; something to revive the old fighting spirit. Walter Smith, in a surprise move, delivered just that. In a masterstroke he brought Mark Hateley back to the club. The big striker may have been older and not quite the player as he had once been, but he was a winner, and very experienced in the ways of the Old Firm. His impact could be measured from his very first interview at Glasgow Airport. He was asked what it was like to be coming back to Ibrox.

Mark replied, "I'm not coming back. I'm coming home." He was indeed coming home and he knew exactly what was required.

In keeping with the season so far, the Old Firm game was a frenzied affair with Rangers certainly up for the challenge, none more so than Hateley, who turned the clock back with a typically robust performance. Both sides had chances, and as so often happens, the game turned on a few minutes of action. With the first half drawing to a close, a Celtic free kick rattled the crossbar. Two minutes later a Jorg Albertz free kick was turned goalwards by Ian Durrant, Brian Laudrup following up scrambled the ball over the line to give Rangers the lead. It was an untidy, but nonetheless most welcome goal.

The second half grew increasingly frantic as the clock ticked ever onwards, ever closer to nine in a row. Tension mounted, the tackles flew in, and inevitably it all kicked off with a brawl outside the Celtic penalty box. Players squared up, and some punches were thrown. The referee intervened and much to our dismay issued a red card to Mark Hateley. Two Celtic players followed him into the book, but only as yellow cards. Referee Hugh Dallas deemed that no further disciplinary action was necessary, though quite how he missed Jackie McNamara's left hook into Mark Hateley's face is a bit of a mystery, particularly in a season when match officials were allegedly 'helping the Rangers cause'. The game then continued with Rangers a man short, clinging onto their single goal advantage. The numerical discrepancy lasted for about ten minutes until Celtic were also reduced to ten men. Malky Mackay was sent off for cynically hauling Brian Laudrup to the ground, and not for the first time it has to be said. Though to be fair, sometimes that was the only way to stop the Danish danger man.

The contest ended with a Rangers victory and the spectacle of Celtic's Paulo Di Canio seemingly at war with everyone and anyone in blue, be it supporters in the stand, or the team on the park. He was clearly not a happy man and had to be dragged from the field after trying, rather unwisely, to pick a fight with Ian Ferguson. Rangers celebrated their win with a mini huddle before being shepherded off the park by the match officials who were looking more than a little concerned. With Celtic supporters spilling onto the field, crowd trouble looked a distinct possibility. Not that there was any prospect of disorder from the away end, singing and dancing was in order there, particularly when a flag emblazoned with 'Champions 1997' was unveiled.

The game may have been over, but its stormy climax sparked angry comments and recriminations that would rumble on and on. Rangers were deemed to have been very unsporting in doing that mini huddle, or 'mock huddle' as the newspapers insisted on calling it. Curiously only ten days before, Celtic, in the aftermath of their Scottish Cup victory had done a full-scale huddle in the centre circle at Parkhead, triumphant in their victory. That action however had been portrayed as 'a great display of team spirit' by the very same newspapers. It seemed to me, our only crime was the temerity to win at Parkhead. In the days that followed Rangers were attacked from all quarters for their apparent unsporting actions, Tommy Burns, the Celtic manager, being particularly vitriolic.

"Blame Rangers," he cried, "Celtic are different class – Celtic accept defeat in dignity". I must have been watching a different game!

Nine in a row was now in the bag and Rangers marched on to their date with destiny, at home to Motherwell on May 5th. Nine points clear with only three games remaining; a single point was all that was required. A huge crowd gathered at Ibrox that day, with thousands more outside clamouring for tickets. Everything was set for the mother of all title parties. Unfortunately no one had given the script to Motherwell; who had their own agenda, fighting for their Premier League survival. The game ended in a 2–0 victory for the visitors and with it came the realisation the ninth title may now be in some jeopardy. Six points up, with two games left, two difficult away games, Celtic, with two games at Parkhead, could feasibly pull level – unlikely, but uncomfortably possible.

It's said, if you fall off a horse, its best to get right back on again, Rangers did the football equivalent by playing their next game a mere forty-eight hours after the Motherwell disappointment. That game was against Dundee United, a team that had recently won at Ibrox. It wouldn't be easy. Supporters lucky enough to have tickets headed for Tannadice, and thankfully I was one of them, I'd come too far along the nine in a row road to miss out at this late stage. I travelled, however, with a growing sense of foreboding, my glass has always been half empty, and I had visions of two consecutive defeats and a Celtic title triumph on goal difference. If only we had scored more goals against seven-man Hearts!

The game kicked off with tension thick in the air, nerves all around the ground jangling. On eleven minutes a cross ball was swung into the Dundee United penalty box. Brain Laudrup connected and bulleted a header into the net. The roar was deafening, the stands were shaking and my fears were lifting. Deep down I knew that this time there would be no mistake. This time we were really going to do it. Rangers came close to a second goal, a goal that would really have lifted the roof, Charlie Miller smacked a shot off the crossbar, Paul Gascoigne struck the post, but the score stubbornly remained at 1–0. As the clock, oh so slowly, reached ninety minutes we knew, we knew the time had come, and a chant started to echo round the ground; a four word song, sung louder and louder.

"... nine in a row ... nine in a row ... nine in a row ... nine in a row ..."

At last the final whistle sounded and celebrations could start for real. I stood and cheered, and hugged the total stranger next to me, but then sat down as I waited for the trophy presentation, soaking up the atmosphere, overcome by emotion. Looking round I could see a few supporters of my vintage doing the same. We'd endured Celtic's triumph in the '70s and now we had our own moment to savour. The Premier League trophy was presented to captain, Richard Gough, he hadn't played that night, but thoroughly deserved the honour of receiving this most special of prizes, having participated in each of the nine championships. The look on Gough's face as he lifted the cup told its own story and would forever embody that never to be forgotten evening.

I watched the game highlights on video that night. Over and over, sipping a few celebratory beers, and eventually crashed out on the living room floor with the game on its fourth or fifth loop. I didn't make it into work the next day – I really don't think anyone expected me to.

The season's final, and now meaningless game was at Tynecastle. As the team bus travelled eastwards along the M8, I travelled in the opposite direction, westwards, to Scotland's newest and biggest open air cinema, Ibrox. Rangers were showing the game on the big screens, to an all-ticket 30,000 crowd. The game was lost 3–1, and let's be honest, no one cared! Over at Ibrox we waited patiently for the return of the victorious Rangers. At Tynecastle, the travelling support were dashing back to their cars and buses, ready to break every known speed limit, desperate to join us in the Stadium. No such problem for the team, they boarded a helicopter to make the homeward journey. For the first time, but most certainly not the last, the Rangers support gazed skywards, searching for the sight of a championship helicopter. Eventually the fans and the team were re-united, and the celebrations could begin in earnest.

The first team's season might be over but the youth team still had a couple of fixtures left to fulfil; a routine league game and then the Youth Cup Final. Graeme and I went over to Bathgate for the league game against Cowdenbeath and got into the ground just in time to see the ball boys running out. This was an unusual sight, as ball boys up 'til now, had never been used in youth team games. The Cowdenbeath team then took the field and it slowly became apparent that the ball boys were in actual fact here to play football. It transpired that Rangers, in preparation for the cup final, had fielded one of their younger age groups, possibly the 15s in this Under 18s game. The Cowdenbeath players, big bruising Fifers towered over their youthful opponents and it came as no surprise that the junior 'gers were steamrollered 7–0. The game produced two new milestones in my Rangers supporting life. The seven-goal defeat was the heaviest I'd ever endured, and the attendance at the game, a grand total of nine, was the smallest I'd ever been part off.

Two days later Rangers lost the Youth Cup final to Celtic. It was ironic that in a season where Celtic and their supporters had complained bitterly about refereeing decisions, their winning goal came from a disputed last minute penalty. Driving home from the game I reflected on the season, and the lack of silverwear, only two trophies. It had in all honesty been a big disappointment.

Only joking!

Chapter 15:
A Bridge Too Far

Season 97/98 had an extremely early start, with the reserves heading off to Northern Ireland, two games to be played in the first week of July. My journey started with a 4am alarm call, a drive to Stranraer and the Seacat hydrofoil directly into Belfast. By mid-morning I was getting rather peckish but resisted the temptation to eat on the boat, preferring to wait so that I could fulfil a long held ambition – to sample an Ulster Fry. I'd first heard about this somewhat monumental breakfast when watching Coronation Street. One of the characters, Jim McDonald, used to wax lyrical about his mother's fry up, and ever since I'd wanted to sample one, just to see what all the fuss was about. I wasn't to be disappointed; down the Newtonards Road I had a meal that kept me satisfied 'til well after the conclusion of that evening's game with Crusaders. The platter of sausages, bacon, eggs, mushrooms, tomatoes and beans, topped off with potato and soda scones was never going to win a healthy eating award, but washed down with a strong cup of tea was tremendous, and well worth the wait.

Growing up as a Rangers supporter, going regularly to Ibrox, it was impossible not to have heard of the Ulster 36th

Division, whether in story or in song, the achievements of
that fine body of men during the Battle of the Somme was the
stuff of legend. In an attempt to learn some more I visited the
Somme Heritage Centre, a museum set up to commemorate
the sacrifices made by the men and women of the province
during the First World War. It was an enlightening and
thought provoking experience, and one that nicely set up
Saturday's game against Ballyclare Comrades, a team founded
by three veterans of the Great War. The match at Dixon Park
was won 2–1, with both goals coming from a teenage Barry
Ferguson. Also prominent in blue was a young Italian by the
name of Rino Gattuso. Little did I know that I was watching a
future Champions League and World Cup winner – though
sadly not in the blue of Rangers!

Another Italian joining the club was Marco Negri. He
arrived as an unknown quantity – exploded into Scottish
football with an avalanche of goals, burnt brightly and then
extinguished as suddenly as he arrived. A man, who appeared
to have the world at his feet, yet lived his life under a
permanent cloud, a scowl drawn across his face.

The quest for ten in a row started encouragingly, with
Marco Negri scoring at a quite remarkable rate, nineteen
goals in his first eight league games. Rangers were two points
clear at the top of the table and looking good. Off the park,
however, there were signs that all may not be well – rumours
circulated that Paul Gascoigne was available for transfer.
Stories surfaced that Walter Smith would be resigning as
manager at the end of the season.

In October I ventured deep into enemy territory, to
Barrowfield, the Celtic training ground for an Old Firm
youth game. What I witnessed was a quite breathtaking game
of football, a seven goal thriller, which included a penalty (for
Celtic) and a red card (to Rangers). The match also contained
an incident which perhaps went some way to explaining the
long-running Ibrox injury curse. There were eighty minutes

or so on the clock. Michael Rae, the Rangers keeper, made a good blocking save but was injured in the process. He continued to play after receiving treatment from the physio, but was clearly in some distress. Hobbling at the edge of his penalty box, he called over to the touchline and informed them that his leg was just too painful, he couldn't continue.

"I can't put any weight on it" he yelled.

The reply from the touchline simply beggared belief, "well stand on one leg then."

I thought it was some kind of joke, I hoped it was some kind of joke, but amazingly it wasn't, and that's what the keeper did. He hopped about, trying to repel the remaining Celtic attacks. Sure, Rangers were 4-3 down, and yes, they were down to ten men, and okay, they had used all their available substitutes, but it was only a youth team game and the result wasn't *that* important. Was it really worth risking the long-term fitness of the keeper by keeping him on the park for those final few minutes? More importantly it posed questions about the medical prowess at Ibrox. If this was how players were treated in the full public view of a game, what on earth was happening behind closed doors at training?

That day, Friday 31st October 1997, was my wedding anniversary. Jacqui and I had been married for ten years. We'd managed ten in a row, a portent hopefully that Rangers would do the same. Another omen towards ten in a row came the very next day when Marco Negri bagged a hat trick against Kilmarnock; he'd now scored in ten successive league games. I was willing to clutch at any straw that pointed to a tenth title!

With speculation mounting, the rumours regarding Walter Smith were confirmed; the manager would indeed be leaving at the end of the season. To be honest I wasn't exactly heartbroken at the news. It seemed like the correct decision as both Rangers and Walter were looking just a little jaded. In football parlance, Walter had probably taken the team as far as he could. The club needed some fresh blood and some new ideas to push them onto the next level, hopefully to success in Europe. The timing of the announcement, however, was more than a little strange, and coming mid-season created a distinct feeling of uncertainty around the club.

The press inevitably went into a frenzy; suggestions for Walter's successor were produced from here, there and everywhere, Terry Venables, Sven Goran Eriksson, good grief, even Kenny Dalglish! However, there was no further news from inside Ibrox. In this case the proverb 'no news is good news' just didn't seem to apply. Speculation and uncertainty mounted, team performance dipped, and in the weeks that followed, only ten points were gathered from a possible eighteen: only two wins from six games.

One of those games was a 1–1 draw at Parkhead. This was a rearranged fixture, originally scheduled for Monday 1st September, but hastily postponed following the death of Diana, Princess of Wales. Some said the game had been cancelled out of respect, others thought it was to prevent disruption of the inevitable minute's silence. To be honest, given the antipathy of the Celtic support towards the Royal Family the latter seemed most likely, and broadcasted live on Sky TV, would have been a huge embarrassment to Scottish football. Either way the postponement certainly favoured the Parkhead club who were struggling at the time, with only one win from their first three league games.

On the face of it, a draw at Parkhead wasn't such a bad result, the point after all maintained Rangers' lead at the top of the table, but Celtic certainly took more from the game, netting their equaliser in the dying seconds of the game. The manner in which Celtic fought back would give them an impetus for the rest of the season; indeed they would only lose one of their next eighteen games. For the men in blue it was a shattering blow. To recover, we needed some big performances; players like Brian Laudrup needed to step up to the plate, to help turn a series of draws into victories.

Since becoming a Ranger, Brian Laudrup had been an incredibly influential player, at times winning games almost single-handedly. This season, however, his performances had been lacklustre to say the least. In the final year of his contract, many put this lack of form down to a desire to leave the club, and perhaps there was something in that. Laudrup had never been a player to linger too long in one place; he was now in his fourth year at Ibrox so perhaps it was time for him to move on. On the other hand, Laudrup had been hindered by a series of niggling injuries. Between September and January the Dane only managed to complete three out of fourteen games, completely missing five of them. It then emerged that he'd been playing with a fractured bone in his back. No wonder his performances had been poor! It wasn't just injuries that had given Laudrup problems; he'd suffered a strength sapping bout of chicken pox at the start of the season, an illness that sidelined him for over a month. After New Year, he would also be struck down with tonsillitis. It was a difficult time for the player, and something that should be considered by those who claim that he never tried a leg during the ten in a row season.

Despite some indifferent form, Rangers were still leading the title race and a win at Parkhead in January would have put them seven points clear, a huge advantage going into the final stage of the season. Unfortunately it was Celtic who claimed the points and the gap at the top of the table was reduced to a single point. A blow to the title hopes, but not a crippling blow – that came a week or so later when Marco Negri picked up an eye injury. It allegedly occurred after a squash game with Sergio Porrini, but rumours abounded with other theories as to its source, some involving off the park indiscretions. Whatever the cause, the injury had a devastating effect on the striker, and a player who had scored thirty league goals in the run up to New Year would score only three in the following five months. Those missing goals undoubtedly cost vital league points.

Saturday 31st January was the day, in my opinion, that our ten in a row dream died. Rangers were in Perth, attempting for the first time in this record breaking season to win three successive league games. They lost 2–0. It was a poor result and an even poorer performance, but they were still joint top of the table, so not a complete disaster. My pessimism was based on Walter Smith's post-match comments; he told the assembled press, "Half of that team don't have what it takes to win the championship". Perhaps he was playing mind games; perhaps he was trying to gee up his team for the final run in. Unfortunately, I felt, along with countless others, that he was simply telling an uncomfortable home truth. We just weren't good enough.

With progress on the park stalling, the board room were kick-started into action and an announcement was made – the manager for season 98/99 would be the PSV Eindhoven coach Dick Advocaat. It was an exciting appointment and met with general approval; Advocaat had tasted success at Eindhoven, winning them a championship. He'd also been the Dutch national manager, so had vast European and international experience. He looked to be the right man to lead Rangers to the next level.

With the season heading towards its climax, Rangers were boosted by some additions to their player pool. Not new signings though, rather the comeback of a couple of long-term and expensive injury victims.

Sebastian Rozental was first to make his reappearance. The Chilean striker, signed the previous season for £4m, had been crocked in his very first start for the club. His knee injury so serious that it necessitated treatment by an American specialist, thirteen months later he was ready to start again. A big crowd turned up for a reserve game at Ibrox, and witnessed a good performance from the player. A few weeks later he made another reserve appearance, scored a couple of goals, and was declared fit and ready for the first team. Seb played one full game, came on as a substitute three times and then aggravated his original injury; it looked like the medical staff had brought him back too soon. The next sighting of the unfortunate player was of him pushing an airport trolley; he was heading back to America for another operation. It would be six months before we would see him again.

Lorenzo Amoruso was next on the comeback trail. Signed from Fiorentina in July, he managed half of a pre-season game before succumbing to the Ibrox injury curse. Seven months later he turned out for the reserves at Bathgate. Lorenzo had gone from the Stadio Artemio Franchi in Florence, to the green grassy slopes of Creamery Park, though I'm quite sure that he was just glad to be kicking a ball again. The big Italian played well and looked like being a good addition to the squad, but then so he should, at the cost of four million pounds. Rozental and Amoruso, eight million pounds in transfer fees, wages to date of two million pounds, and between them they had played a couple of hours of football. Rangers were starting to look like a football club who had money to burn.

Going into March, Rangers were four points down in the league race, but with the final Old Firm game approaching they still had a chance to peg that back. It would, however, take a monumental effort, so it was rather surprising when they agreed to sell Paul Gascoigne to Crystal Palace. It was clear that Gascoigne was becoming increasingly injury prone and arguably past his best. His off the field activities were also questionable, so a sale probably made financial sense, but, with Brain Laudrup struggling with his own problems, it looked like a decision that would rip the creative heart from the team. It seemed to me that the club were running up the white flag and surrendering ten in a row.

The deal with Crystal Palace eventually fell through, and in its aftermath the club released a statement. In an attempt to pacify a disgruntled support they said that Paul Gascoigne is not for sale, he's still in the team plans, but, if someone wants to buy him, then they can – I was so glad they had cleared it all up! As March ended, the speculation over Paul Gascoigne was resolved once and for all when he was transferred to Middlesbrough for £4m. Good money, but the wrong decision in my opinion.

We were now into the business end of the season and an absolutely critical double header with Celtic loomed. It was win-or-bust time. Match #1 was a Scottish Cup semi-final at the technically neutral Parkhead. That game followed a well worn pattern; Celtic pounded Rangers in the first half but were unable to get past the formidable combination of Richard Gough and Andy Goram.

The second half belonged to Rangers. Attacking incessantly a goal seemed inevitable, as did the scorer – Rangers broke from deep in their own half; two passes took them to the edge of the Celtic penalty box. Jorg Albertz curled a cross to the far post and Ally McCoist did the rest. He flew in and bulleted a header into the net. Ally ran to the corner flag, and in front of a delirious support he fell to his knees, raw emotion written all over his face. He knew his days as a Ranger were drawing to a close, and he knew what this goal meant. The rest of his team mates seemed to understand and other than a few slaps on the back he was left to savour the occasion on his own. Richard Gough then approached, Ally turned to face him, and the players embraced. A couple of words were exchanged, two legends together in their own private moment, detached temporarily from the pandemonium that surrounded them – it was quite touching and intimate… in a manly football way!

The second Celtic game, a crucial league encounter went perfectly to plan, and brought another Rangers victory. All of a sudden the Ibrox men found themselves top of the table, level on points but with a goal difference advantage of one. With four games remaining, ten in a row was back on! Still looking for good luck omens, I was encouraged to see the reserves win their league title, beating nearest rivals Hearts 3–2; one championship would hopefully followed by another. Depressingly, however, a few days later we lost 1–0 to third bottom Aberdeen. A result that meant Rangers were playing catch up once again.

With two games remaining, Rangers were a point behind Celtic. At home to Kilmarnock they had a chance to pile some real pressure onto their title rivals who, on Sunday had a potential banana skin away to Dunfermline. Rangers lost 1–0 to an injury time goal and the realisation dawned that ten in a row was not going to happen. That was a bitter pill to swallow, but for me the real disappointment of the day came when thousands of supporters stood at the final whistle, turned their back on the team, and silently slipped away. This was the season's final home game; the last time Ibrox would see players like Laudrup, McCoist, Goram and Gough. It was Walter Smith's final game at the stadium. Every single supporter should have stood and applauded those heroes; no matter the circumstances, no matter the disappointment. Perhaps as a support we had become spoiled, with too many conditioned to unadulterated success. Those who left early just couldn't understand, or tolerate, failure – they should have been at Ibrox in the 80s! The majority, of course, did stay to acknowledge their team. I stood and applauded, recognising that we would most likely never experience another period of such dominance of the Scottish game.

The next day we were struck by feelings of what might have been as Celtic drew at Dunfermline. It gave us a glimmer of hope, but deep down we all knew that Celtic would undoubtedly win their final game. Fate was just being cruel, teasing us with a week of uncertainty – seven days of desperate hope.

I watched Rangers play Dundee United on a beam back at Ibrox, along with thirty thousand other supporters, hoping that the miracle would happen. Any optimism we had was crushed when Celtic scored an early goal – the dream was dying. A second Celtic goal was the final nail in Rangers' coffin and our ten in a row hopes were buried. All that was left to do now was to escape from Glasgow as quickly as possible, to avoid the celebrating Celts. Not a pretty sight at the best of times!

Graeme and I had recently been joined at the football by Dale, who at two years of age was being introduced to the family tradition. One of his early games was a youth team fixture at Bathgate, a game that got us a little closer to the action than anticipated. Strolling round the ground, we watched as play swung from one end to the other. Kilmarnock attacked. A cross ball was driven into the goalmouth and a defender stretched to block – what followed had a dreadful inevitability and seemed to happen in a painfully slow motion. The ball cannoned off of the defender's foot and flew just past the post. Dale unsuspectingly wandered forward, minding his own business, when whack! – The ball smacked off his face, sending him head over heels sprawling into the Bathgate turf. Play immediately stopped as Dale lay on the grass wailing; the players gathered to make sure he was okay, the defender, whose final touch had created the calamity, most apologetic. We were quickly joined by the Rangers physio who dashed round to give Dale some treatment on the touchline. Over the years I'd seen many players receive the magic sponge but never thought I'd see it administered to a spectator, let alone my own son!

Saturday 16th May 1998 was the date of the Scottish Cup Final, and Rangers last chance to lift a trophy. Sadly it wasn't to be. The game was defined by two controversial refereeing decisions. In the first minute Hearts took the lead from the penalty spot. The award given for a tackle that quite clearly occurred outside the penalty box. In the final minute Rangers were denied the same award when Ally McCoist was downed well inside the very same penalty area. The game ended in a 2–1 Hearts victory. The cup was Gorgie-bound and for Rangers, trophy-less for the first time in ten years, it was the end of a magnificent era.

The post-match period displayed the Rangers support at its very best; they rose to acclaim their heroes, no one leaving the ground this time. The team was applauded, those players leaving the club serenaded with their own personal tribute songs. It was a sad moment; it was a disappointing moment, yet also a moment of great pride. It was a support proud of a team that had given so much. What then followed was a demonstration of sportsmanship of the highest order. Rangers were cheered as they received their runners up medals; Hearts were applauded as they received their trophy – and still the support stayed inside the ground to acclaim their heroes. Hearts paraded the Scottish Cup in front of their understandably jubilant fans; it was, after all, their first major trophy in thirty-five years. Their lap of honour seemingly ended when they reached the supporters divide, and were faced by the massed ranks of the Teddy Bears. Abuse and derision may have been expected, but what the Hearts team received was further applause, warm applause as they continued their way round the park. I'd never be so pompous as to claim that the Rangers support, are 'the greatest fans in the world', but on that day, they'd have taken a lot of beating.

Leaving the ground, I glanced over at the ecstatic Jambos and thought of my old Granddad; he'd been a big Hearts fan and would undoubtedly have loved this moment. I had a wry smile and recalled his tales of those old and famous Hearts teams. It didn't exactly take away the pain of defeat, but it did provide just a sliver of a silver lining.

The season was over and Rangers were trophy-less, just as they had been when Graeme Souness and Walter Smith arrived, and maybe that's how it was meant to be – the football Gods saying, nine in a row, and no more.

One era had ended. Another was about to start.

Chapter 16:
A Shot of Advocaat

Dick Advocaat was now in charge, and he wasn't messing about. Walter Smith's team was systematically dismantled and a new one assembled, the signings came thick and fast – and they weren't coming cheap. Over £20m spent before July had ended.

Advocaat's new team were launched into their debut season with a UEFA Cup tie against Irish side Shelbourne. They kicked off on Wednesday 22nd July 1998 at 8pm and came dangerously close to being sunk without a trace an hour or so later. The Dublin part-timers shocked everyone by racing into a three-goal lead. Nightmare! I stood aghast, watching from the public bar of the Mid Calder Inn, scarcely believing my eyes. This wasn't part of the grand plan! Fortunately, Rangers got their act together, and inspired by a two-goal Gabrielle Amato fought back to win 5–3.

The new manager had a reputation as a bit of a disciplinarian, so I expect that the team got a good rollicking in their full time dressing room. But whatever Advocaat said to the players was nothing compared to the tongue-lashing I got when I eventually staggered home. Before leaving for the pub, I'd promised Jacqui that I wouldn't get pissed.

"This'll be an easy win," I assured her, "I'll have two pints, one in each half, and then straight home."

That genuinely was my plan. However, the cataclysmic first half put paid to that and I was ordering my third beer after just thirty minutes. By the time Amato scored to put Rangers 4–3 ahead, I was draining my sixth. Staying for a post-match couple was probably pushing my luck just a little too far, and it was the doghouse for me when I eventually made it home.

The manner in which Rangers lost those goals to Shelbourne had been quite shambolic, so it came as no surprise that Advocaat went on the hunt for some defensive cover, his primary target being Daniel Prodan. The Romanian was undoubtedly a class act but the signing wouldn't be without risk. Prodan had been out of action for four months with a serious knee injury, an injury that meant he missed not only the end of Athletico's domestic season but also Romania's subsequent World Cup ties. That information ought to have sent alarm bells jangling all over Ibrox. The last thing we needed was another injury-prone player.

Rangers were of course well aware of Prodan's problems, and put the player through a rigorous examination and fitness test – an examination the player apparently passed with flying colours. Contract negotiations commenced, a work permit was granted, and as July drew to a close, Prodan became a Rangers player. However, the way things subsequently worked out, it may have been more accurate to refer to him simply as a club employee.

The search for defenders continued, with Colin Hendry of Blackburn Rovers targeted. Hendry was captain of the Scottish national team, a powerful centre-half and a leader of men, but very expensively priced at £5.5m; an awful lot of money to spend on a thirty-two year old who would have little or no re-sale value when his contract ran out. Rangers made an opening bid of £2.5m; Blackburn Rovers responded with outrage and angrily declared that Hendry was not for sale. What then followed was a rather acrimonious squabble between the two clubs, with Chairman David Murray taking an increasingly dominant role in the transfer process. Murray seemed doggedly determined to get his man and this begged the question. Who *really* wanted the player at Ibrox? Was it manager Advocaat, or Chairman Murray? Either way, the battle was won and Colin Hendry became a Ranger, at the not inconsiderable cost of £4m.

The league campaign had a disappointing start with a 2–1 defeat at Tynecastle, but after five games Rangers were sitting top of the table, leading a host of clubs by two points. Advocaat's team were in fine form, scoring goals and winning regularly. Importantly, all the new faces were settling in, with Rod Wallace probably the pick of the bunch. Signed for free, he was playing well, happily banging in goals for fun. However, when I say all the new signings were settling in, I should have added the proviso – all bar one. The odd man out was Daniel Prodan who had yet to make his mark.

Prodan's knee injury, the one subject to that most stringent and rigorous medical examination, had flared up again, almost as soon as the player touched down in Scotland. Ruled out of the first twelve games of the season, it was September before he was deemed fit enough to start his Rangers career. His first game was a reserve fixture at Fir Park. Sitting in the main stand, I watched for five minutes and thought, *Prodan is either the slowest and most cumbersome defender in the whole world, or he's still crocked*. Sadly the latter was true, and an injury that had once been described as troublesome turned out to be career ending. Prodan, signed for £2.2m, would never play for the first team. He did, of course, remain at Ibrox to draw his considerable salary. Somewhere in the region of £5m wasted. Still it was only money!

Prodan was just the latest example of a malady that had been plaguing the club for some time. As Oscar Wilde might have said, to sign and lose one player with a serious injury may be regarded as a misfortune; to sign and lose a string of them just looked like carelessness. One had to wonder if players were being recruited with undisclosed and undetected injuries. Were Rangers being taken for mugs? Looking back a few years at some of the clubs other signings:

1990: Oleg Kuznetzov, two games, injured, out for a year
1991: Brian Reid, three games, injured, out for two years
1993: Duncan Ferguson, seven games, injured, out for seven months
1995: Stephen Wright, sixteen games, injured, out for three years
1997: Sebastian Rozental, two games, injured, out for a year
1997: Johanas Thern, two games, injured, out for two months
1997: Lorenzo Amoruso, one game, injured, out for eight months

Including Prodan, that made eight crocked new signings in eight years. Rangers were either the world's unluckiest club, or there was an underlying problem with their medical team. Or, did the problem lie elsewhere?

The team still trained on amateur cricket grounds, on muddy rugby pitches, or, if all else failed, amongst the empty Buckfast bottles of Bellahouston Park. In the winter months it became absurd, with the multi-million pound squad resembling a nomadic tribe touring the west of Scotland, searching for a football friendly oasis to practice on. It was no way for Scotland's biggest and best football club to operate. Something had to be done. Fortunately Dick Advocaat recognised the problem and persuaded David Murray to initiate plans for a custom built training complex. It would take three years to come to fruition and at the cost of £12m, it wouldn't come cheap (nothing associated with Rangers these days did). It would, hopefully, alleviate the never-ending injury and training problems. And, as a fringe benefit it might make them look like a modern, well-run club.

Without a training complex, Rangers had to play trial and bounce games at junior grounds, an example being a low key friendly against Bathgate Thistle. Dick Advocaat had arranged the game to give his fringe players some much needed match practice, one of those players being Sebastian Rozental who was making his latest comeback from injury. The Chilean striker lasted some twenty-five minutes, then, with Bathgate Thistle on the attack, he turned and simply walked, unprompted, off the pitch. His doleful expression as he trudged past the bemused Rangers dugout told its own sad story. It was later announced that Rozental had suffered a setback in his recovery programme; an announcement that came as absolutely no surprise to those of us who had attended the Bathgate fixture. Sadly Sebastian had to look out his airport trolley once again, in preparation for yet another transatlantic consultation with his American doctors.

Rangers and St. Johnstone made it through to the season's first Cup Final. These games are normally an immediate sell-out, with tickets difficult to pick up. This one, however, was different. It just hadn't captured the viewing public's imagination and as such, tickets were readily available. Disappointing, but it gave me the opportunity to get a one for Graeme. At six years of age, he was going to his first cup final.

As the big day approached, Graeme grew more and more excited. In contrast, I found it very difficult to raise any level of enthusiasm. In many ways I was envious of the St Johnstone support; this was their first cup final since 1969 and they were determined to enjoy the day, come what may. For ninety-nine percent of them, it was a totally new experience. Without being blasé, this would be my thirty-second major final. I'd been to so many good and exciting games and I just couldn't see this one living up to any of them. It all seemed so pointless and predictable; we would win at a canter, in a dull and boring game. I'd seen it all before.

I wasn't far wrong in my thinking. The game was disappointing, as grey and dreich as the Scottish weather, brightened only by a Rangers victory, though the scoreline of 2–1 was much closer than anyone outside Perth had predicted. I may have seen it all before, Graeme on the other hand hadn't and he was delighted with the result – going home happy, wearing his new scarf and tammy, waving his League Cup winners' flag, a flag carefully bought after the final whistle. Confident or not, I wasn't going to tempt fate by getting it before the game.

Advocaat's recruitment policy hadn't ended and as the year drew to a close, he added another couple of players to the squad, Neil McCann and goalkeeper Stephan Klos; the two players joining for a combined £2.5m. Considering the money spent already, this was practically bargain basement stuff! The Neil McCann signing was interesting and demonstrated just how far the Rangers support had travelled in only a few years. There was a time when the recruitment of a Roman Catholic, self-confessed Celtic fan from Greenock would have caused mass heart failure amongst the faithful at Ibrox but in 1998 his signing was met without a murmur. All that mattered, and rightly so, was ... Could he play? Could he score goals? And could he help win back the championship?

As the months passed, Rangers pulled away from the pack and into pole position for the SPL title. On Sunday 25th April 1999, they beat Aberdeen at Ibrox to go seven points clear, to within touching distance of the league flag. A win in their next game would be the clincher, and that created a problem, a big problem. In fact, a nightmare scenario, as the next game was at Parkhead with Celtic in opposition. It should be noted of course, this was only a problem for the authorities and those of a Celtic persuasion. To the average Blue Nose it was a prospect to savour. Tickets for the potential title decider were inevitably like gold dust and I didn't have one, so it was Sky TV in a friend's house for me.

The game was certainly not for the faint-hearted and contained enough incidents and talking points to keep the newspapers busy for the next few months, on both the back and front pages. It kicked off at 6.05pm and within sixty seconds two free kicks had been awarded. Referee Hugh Dallas was clearly going to be a busy man. Rangers drew first blood, with Neil McCann scoring in the twelfth minute. That was a figurative drawing of blood; later on the red stuff would literally be spilled. On the half hour, Dallas made his first major decision by sending off Celtic's Stephane Mahe, a decision not well-received by the Celtic support, nor by the player who protested vehemently and refused point-blank to leave the field of play, preferring to argue the toss with the match official. Growing angrier and angrier, he was eventually dragged away before he could get himself, and his team into any more bother. The atmosphere inside Parkhead was at fever pitch.

As half time approached Rangers won a free kick, this somewhat innocuous decision sparked off major rebellion amongst a section of the Celtic support and at least one of them gained access to the pitch and made a beeline for the referee. In Stephane Mahe style, he wanted to discuss the decision with Dallas. The interloper was fortunately apprehended before he could do any serious damage. The drama, however, had only just begun. A steward was hit by a missile and had to be led away by medics. The television cameras then panned round to capture a picture of the referee who was crouched over, blood streaming from a head wound, victim of another missile-throwing lunatic. Play was further held up as the referee received treatment and order, of sorts, was restored. If this was how the Celtic support reacted to a straightforward free kick, how on earth would they respond to a more serious decision? We were soon to find out!

Rangers took the free kick, the one awarded so long ago, and the ball swung into a crowded penalty box. Tony Vidmar tried to get onto the end of the cross but was obstructed and manhandled to the ground – penalty kick! The Celtic players inevitably protested, as did their supporters, and another of their number invaded the park. More coins rained down, and then, manic, even for an Old Firm game, a Celtic fan launched himself from the top tier of the stand, crashing onto his comrades below. Relatively unscathed, the bold bhoy was stretchered away, still protesting! The atmosphere was at boiling point.

When the dust had settled, Jorg Albertz slammed the penalty home to double his team's lead, and then wisely ran back into his own half with the minimum of celebration. Behind him more Celtic fans were spilling onto the park, more missiles were thrown. Parkhead was close to going nuclear!

The second half was almost sedate in comparison to the frantic first; it did although have its moments. On the hour mark, Stuart Kerr, the Celtic keeper, intentionally handled the ball outside his penalty box. This would normally be grounds for an instant red card, but referee Dallas decided to limit his punishment to yellow. Discretion was clearly his watchword now, and quite frankly, who could blame him! With twenty minutes remaining, Neil McCann raced onto a through ball, rounded the goalkeeper and tucked a shot low into the corner of the Celtic net. In an instant he answered all those questions we had previously asked of him:

Yes, he could play!

Yes, he could score!

And yes, he most certainly could help us win back the championship!

The game ended in acrimony – would it be any other way? Jorg Albertz was showered in loose change as he attempted to take a late corner. Rod Wallace was sent off. Vidar Reseth of Celtic quickly followed. Final score: Celtic 0, Rangers 3, and as the Rangers end bounced in joy, a little living room in East Calder was doing the very same!

The game may have been over but the drama most certainly wasn't. Rangers, in a repeat of their nine in a row victory at Parkhead did another huddle. You know the one; the mock huddle, producing near hysteria amongst the Celtic support that were still in the ground. With their celebrations over, the team were ushered from the pitch, under yet another hail of missiles, launched this time by the remaining occupants of the Main Stand. If referee Hugh Dallas thought his troubled day was over he was sadly mistaken. Later that night his bungalow windows were smashed. Football related? Could be!

Once again a Celtic game at Parkhead was under the spotlight, and once again it was dubbed "an Old Firm shame game", despite virtually all the contentious incidents being perpetrated by those wearing green, a colour not generally associated with the Rangers team, or their support.

The following week I watched Rangers draw 0–0 with Hearts A rotten game, but no one minded. The supporters were at Ibrox for an SPL championship party, and that's just what they got. The roar when Lorenzo Amoruso thrust the enormous trophy into the dark Glasgow sky was quite deafening. Queen's 'We Are The Champions' boomed from the tannoy, and everyone sang along, and as always got the tune horribly wrong when they reached the second part of the chorus.

*"We are the champions my friends,
And we'll keep on fighting to the end,
We are the champions,
We are the champions,
No time for Celtic,
'Cause we are the champions – of the world."*

Freddie Mercury may have been able to reach those high notes, despite many years of practice the Teddy Bears could not!

At the end of May, I went over to Bathgate for the final youth team game of the season, and the chance to see another trophy presentation. Unfortunately not this time to Rangers, but to the Celtic youngsters who only needed a draw to pip Aberdeen to the title. The Celtic support clearly wanted to witness at least one trophy in their so far barren season, and turned up in their thousands. That made watching the game somewhat uncomfortable for the Reserve Team Loyal as we were outnumbered by at least 100:1; twenty of us in a crowd of over two thousand. What followed though was as good a game as I'd ever seen. The young Rangers team battled and scrapped, determined to deprive Celtic their moment of glory, and they succeeded, winning 2–0. It was deeply, deeply satisfying.

The season may have been over, but there was still some football left for Graeme, Dale and I to enjoy. We travelled down to Newcastle for the Carling Masters, an indoor six a side tournament for ex-players. It would have been nice to see Rangers claim yet another trophy but it wasn't to be. Not that it mattered of course; this was after all just a fun event. The oldies lost their first two games to Newcastle and Sunderland, but gave us something to cheer with an 8–3 victory over Middlesbrough.

After that game we decided to head for home. The tournament wasn't over but it seemed like a good idea – for a couple of reasons; firstly to beat the inevitable long queue in the car park (being in Newcastle, I suppose we had now joined the Metro Loyal!), but secondly, and more importantly, to escape the wrath of a particularly large and obnoxious Geordie. The guy had been a total pain in the neck, bragging to all asunder, what a big Newcastle fan he was. He'd spent the afternoon largely ignoring the football, preferring instead to gather autographs on his tournament programme. As the Middlesbrough game ended he proudly proclaimed, to anyone within earshot, that he'd now got every single players signature – pride of place going to those of his 'Toon Army' heroes Peter Beardsley and Chris Waddle.

With his mission accomplished, he placed the programme under his seat and stood to cheer his team in their game against Sunderland. Dale also stood up, and chose that precise moment to drop his newly acquired extra large coke. The carton slipped from his fingers, tipped up and landed with a big splash, squarely on top of the big Geordie's prized programme. It was time to leave – and sharpish! As we drove away from the arena car park, I thought I heard a loud cry of anguish. Perhaps Sunderland had scored. Perhaps there was another reason – we certainly weren't going back to find out!

Chapter 17:
Oranjeboom or Bust

Advocaat's second season in charge started with a magnificent European victory over Parma. The current UEFA cup holders and one of the favourites for the Champions League had been dumped out of the competition by a team from Scotland. We'd hoped and prayed that Dick Advocaat could restore Rangers as a European force and he was now doing just that. The reward for beating Parma was entry to a Champions League group amongst teams from Spain, Holland and Germany. It was a tough draw, but one to relish.

Rangers would ultimately fail in their attempt to reach the knock-out stage of the competition, but unlike previous attempts, this time they put up a real fight and came within a whisker of qualification. Two defeats by Valencia were disappointing. Two victories over PSV Eindhoven were tremendous. The two games against Bayern Munich were frustrating in the extreme. At Ibrox, Rangers dictated the game and were leading the Bundesliga champions 1–0 with seconds remaining. Bayern then equalised with a wickedly deflected free kick. How typically German!

The return game in Munich, the last game in the group, became a shoot-out for qualification. The Scottish champions just required a draw. Bayern had to win, and did just that, though the men in blue gave them one hell of a fright. Dominating for long stages, Rangers had seventeen attempts at goal, hit the woodwork three times and had a shot cleared off the line. The German side, with Teutonic efficiency, won 1–0 with a goal from the penalty spot. The result was of course a disappointment, but the real tragedy of the evening came with a crippling injury to Michael Mols. The Dutchman had been in outstanding form since signing from Utrecht; nine goals in nine league games only told part of the story. It was his style of play that enthralled the support; the man had the knack of doing the unexpected, almost Laudrup-esque in his touch, control and movement. With Mols in their side, Rangers looked to be a match for anyone.

Rangers had caught Bayern on the counter attack. Oliver Kahn, the Bayern keeper charged off his line to intercept and hooked the ball away from Rod Wallace. His clearance spun wide towards Mols on the touchline. Kahn, recognising the danger kept on going and made, to be fair, a good sliding tackle on the Rangers striker, eliminating any danger. A worldly wise striker, a nasty striker if you like, would have jumped and then landed on top of keeper, studs and all. Michael, unfortunately, was a nice guy and tried to ride the tackle, not wanting to injure Kahn. In doing so, he landed awkwardly and twisted his knee. Damaged cruciate ligaments would tragically rule the player out for the remainder of the season.

One striker out, but two others were on the comeback trail, Marco Negri and Sebastian Rozental. They both took part in a reserve game at Love Street, with contrasting fortunes. Rozental was keen and active, looking to link up with his team mates, desperate to impress. Negri on the other hand, was, well, moody and malingering; he went through the motions but clearly had absolutely no interest in the proceedings. Midway through the game, he approached the dugout and asked to be substituted. He had, apparently, a sore ankle. The request denied, he flopped onto the touchline and pathetically whimpered, making no attempt to rejoin play. John McGregor, the reserve team coach, looked exasperated and eventually barked out the order – just get him off! He then stood stony faced as Negri theatrically hobbled past. The moody blue would only play two more games, and then he was off.

Another man in the Ibrox departure lounge was Colin Hendry, less than two years after signing for the club. He'd only made one start in this season and had clearly become surplus to requirement. Interestingly though, in the same period, between September and March, Hendry captained his country on no fewer than six occasions including two European championship playoff games against England. He was a key figure for Scotland, yet not required by Rangers. Those statistics went a long way to answering the question so many had asked; who had really wanted the player at Ibrox? On this evidence the finger pointed firmly at Chairman David Murray. Colin Hendry, signed for £4.4m, was sold eighteen months later for £700k. Rangers may have been top of the Scottish Premier League, but in terms of financial management they were, without doubt second division!

On Saturday 15th April 2000, Rangers won at Dundee United and advanced to within a point of the Championship. The first opportunity to claim that point was the following week at McDiarmid Park; I'd missed last season's title decider and didn't intend on missing another, so a plan was hatched. On the Monday morning I drove to Perth with the intention of purchasing a couple of match tickets. They would obviously be for the St Johnstone end, but that didn't really matter. At least Graeme and I would get in. On arrival at McDiarmid Park I was greeted by a long queue snaking its way into the car park. Clearly my plan wasn't quite as clever and unique as I'd first thought! I joined the line and eventually reached the ticket office. In front of me stood a chap dressed in a wax jacket, wearing a deerstalker hat, quite clearly a member of the local farming community. He requested two tickets and was asked in return if the tickets were for St Johnstone supporters.

Looking exasperated, he snapped, "of course they are!"

At the neighbouring ticket booth another customer asked for fifty tickets. When presented with the same qualifying question, he replied, in a decidedly west of Scotland accent, that yes, they were all for Saints fans.

"No problem," smiled the girl behind the counter, "that will be seven hundred and fifty pounds please".

The farmer looked on incredulously as the 'St Johnstone fan' pulled out an envelope packed full of bank notes and handed over the cash. I got my two tickets and left – with the distinct impression that I may not be the only Blue Nose in that home-only section!

McDiarmid Park was bouncing on the day of the game. Host to a singing and dancing fest, with each stand trying to out-noise the other in their praise of the champions. Not everyone was happy though; I did spot one elderly farmer type who was complaining bitterly about all these Glaswegians in his stand. Oh well, you can't please everyone!

The season ended with a Scottish Cup victory, in front of a Hampden Park swathed in brilliant orange. Mounting a colourful tribute to Dick Advocaat, the Teddy Bears had abandoned their traditional red, white and blue to go Dutch for the day, oranje colours worn by ninety percent of the support. I'd like to say how tremendous it was to be part of that display, but unfortunately I can't. I didn't get a ticket; the first final I'd missed since that Drybrough cup victory over Celtic, way back in 1979.

Five domestic trophies out of six, mounting a decent challenge in Europe, the Advocaat era was ticking over very nicely. At the other end of the city, Celtic were languishing twenty-one points behind Rangers, and scrambling to appoint their fifth manager in as many years – the good times looked set to roll on and on.

Season 2000/2001 started well with four league wins out of four, then calamity. Rangers travelled to Parkhead to take on Martin O'Neil's Celtic and lost 6–2. It was a day of unmitigated disaster with absolutely nothing whatsoever going right for the men in blue. The scene was set less than a minute into the game, when a blatantly offside Chris Sutton opened the scoring. After seven minutes it was two, after eleven it was three.

Rangers had gone double Dutch with their latest big money signings and those two newcomers had a particularly horrific afternoon. Fernando Ricksen was ripped apart by the painfully average Bobby Petta, and had to be substituted after twenty-three minutes. It was an act of mercy – to protect him and the shell shocked support from any more misery. Bert Konterman fared little better. For long spells he looked like a startled rabbit caught in Henrik Larsson's headlights. It wasn't good, it wasn't pretty, and it didn't bode well for the future. Dark clouds were gathering on the horizon.

A week later, Rangers drew 1–1 at Dens Park, whilst at Parkhead, Celtic, aided and abetted by a hotly disputed penalty, beat Hibs. The Champions suddenly found themselves in third place, five points behind a rejuvenated Celtic. Rangers recovered with a 1–0 victory against Hearts, but worryingly the fickle hand of football fortune was now favouring the men in green and white. Celtic won 2–1 at Dunfermline with the help of yet another contentious penalty award. Where were the Masonic Rangers-supporting Celtic-hating referees now I wonder? Neil Cameron in the Evening

Times summed it up perfectly in his report from the Dunfermline–Celtic game:

'Paul Lambert went crashing down inside the box under a challenge from Ian Ferguson, but the original contact, such as it was, was made outside the area. These are decisions referees have to make in a split second, but they are paid to do so and I have to say Mr Young gets more than his fair share wrong. And it would be nice to think those paranoid Celtic fans finally get it into their heads that the men in black don't have it in for them. Young was terrible, with some of his decisions just beggaring belief, but they were bad for both sides, and his most significant came when Lambert was awarded that penalty.'

Cameron was of course right; referees are fair and honest men, but they are human and sometimes make outrageously bad decisions! In football, the better team, the winning team, will always appear to get the majority of the decisions. It's not bias or favouritism, it's simply because those teams are in possession and attack more than their opponents. Fortune tends to favour the brave. The unpalatable fact was that Celtic were rapidly becoming the countries biggest, strongest and best team.

An awful October brought little joy. Rangers lost three league games out of four. The final defeat was a 3–0 drubbing by Kilmarnock at Ibrox; a game in which Rangers managed only one shot on target, that coming in the ninety-third minute. It really wasn't good enough. Rangers had now slumped to fourth; twelve points behind Celtic and worryingly ten behind Hibs in second.

Desperate times call for desperate measures. In November, Rangers astonished the football world, and most of their supporters, by splashing out £12.5m for the Chelsea striker Torre Andre Flo, in the process smashing the Scottish record transfer fee by a whopping £6m. Flo was a highly rated player. But was he really worth that kind of money? More pertinently, could we afford that kind of money? The transfer fee took this season's spending to a mind-blowing £27m. Expenditure was far outstripping income; the club's debt was billowing.

Although no one wanted to admit it, the league title had already gone. The football battle was now with Hibs for second place. That position did not come with a trophy, but it did offer a gateway to the Champions League millions. Money was increasingly important to Rangers – that runners-up place just had to be achieved.

Personal matters then intervened and football, for me, faded into insignificance. My mother, always a very strong and active woman, was struck down with Legionnaires' disease following a Swiss holiday. She was admitted to Glasgow's Royal Infirmary and despite the very best of treatment, she died. She'd been in fine form before her holiday, as loud and brash as ever, full of life, and then she was gone. It was so sudden, so unfair, and left a huge void in my life. My mother had always been there for me; she'd done so much and asked for little in return. There was so much that I should have said, so much I wanted to say, and it was now too late.

On January 2nd 2001, I went over to Ibrox for a service in memory of the victims of the 1971 disaster, so hard to believe that thirty years had passed since that tragic event, where had the time gone? Inside the ground, I took a seat in the East enclosure, in almost the exact spot where I had stood all those years before, and as the service progressed my mind wandered back to memories of that fateful day. I remembered travelling with my dad, the excitement of my first Old Firm game, the roar that greeted Colin Stein's equaliser; then thoughts of returning home to my distraught and frightened mother. I shed a tear that afternoon, as did many others, remembering those who went to a football game – and didn't come home.

Rangers faced a critical week in their increasingly depressing season with a double-header against the old enemy; a League cup semi-final quickly followed by an SPL game. The semi-final gave Rangers a chance to restore the old order, and scupper at least one of Celtic's trophy aspirations. It wasn't to be. Celtic won 3–1 in a game dominated by some curious refereeing decisions. Henrick Larsson gave Scott Wilson a dunt, with no foul awarded he took advantage to score. Later on, the same Celtic forward went dramatically sprawling in the penalty box. With most of the Hampden Park spectators searching for the mystery sniper, the referee awarded a spot kick! Still, decisions even themselves out, so we looked forward to a change of fortune at Parkhead four days later. Unfortunately it was more of the same. Celtic won by a single goal. Fernando Ricksen was sent off and Rangers were denied what looked like a stonewall penalty when Tore Andre Flo was tugged back whilst running through on goal.

The next day I went over to Almondvale for a reserve team fixture. Rangers dominated for seventy minutes. Leading 1–0, they looked comfortable – and then they conceded three goals inside five minutes to lose 3–1. Unbelievably, it was Celtic yet again; three defeats in six days. This was becoming hard to take. To cap off a quite miserable week, I had my attention drawn to GQ magazine, not a publication, it has to be said, that I generally perused. In it was an interview with the singer Rod Stewart, during which he said:

'To all you blue-nosed bastards out there, Celtic Football Club will win the Scottish league this year.'

As if the situation wasn't bad enough, now we had to listen to an over the hill, wrinkly old Englishman pontificating inanely over the state of the Scottish game!

Championship aspirations had long evaporated, but there was still time for some success, if Rangers could claim the Scottish cup.

No chance!

Advocaat's toiling team went to Tannadice and lost 1–0 to a Dundee United side who were second-bottom of the league, and trailing their Glasgow opponents by a massive forty-five points. A team, assembled at a cost of £32m, tumbled from the Scottish Cup without a whimper. So toothless were they, that Paul Gallacher, the Dundee United keeper, wasn't asked to make a single save. It was pitiful. It was woeful, and performances like this could not be allowed to continue. Yet, Rangers just stumbled on. Rumours started to surface regarding splits, cliques and disputes in the dressing room. A conflict was developing, if you believed the talk, between the Dutchmen and the rest of the squad.

The next two home league games were surrendered by two goals to nil. Scorelines that might have had serious implications for the Champions League slot were it not for the fact that Hibs had chosen this particular stage of the season to self destruct. They only managed to win one of their final eleven games. Second place was at least secure, but that achievement owed more to Hibs ineptitude than it did to the endeavours of the men in blue.

The league title had long been lost by the time of the final Old Firm game. I went to Ibrox optimistically hoping for a moral boosting victory – something, anything, to restore some pride to what had been a quite appalling season. I didn't get my wish, far from it. Celtic destroyed us 3–0 and their supporters whooped it up big style in the Broomloan Road stand. Balloons thrown, piss-taking banners unfurled, they partied for the entire ninety minutes. By the end of the match they were ironically cheering for a sorry Rangers side; the ridicule so bad that I actually hoped that my team *wouldn't* score a last gasp goal – I really didn't want to see them celebrating any more than they already were. It had been a thoroughly dismal and depressing afternoon.

Another day brought another game, with the Reserves heading up to Aberdeen for an Under 21 League title decider. Pittodrie has never been the most welcoming of places for a Blue Nose, and this reserve game was no different. Sensing a trophy, the locals turned out in force, with a good seven thousand inside the ground. It felt like six thousand nine hundred and eighty-eight Aberdonians, and a dozen or so from the Reserve Team Loyal. Outnumbered and behind enemy lines, we had decided to go undercover, no colours and no cheering to identify ourselves. That was the plan, and it worked well, 'til Peter MacDonald opened the scoring and we all spontaneously leapt to our feet to acclaim his strike – Cover blown!

The Red Ultras in the Beach End quickly turned their attention towards our little corner of the Main Stand. On their feet and pointing menacingly, they blasted out a rousing chorus of "who let the huns out". It wasn't good, but took a more serious turn when I realised that everyone in my group was wearing dark jackets ... well all bar me. My fawn jacket singled me out from the rest, and I couldn't help but think all the chants and threats were personally directed in my direction. Would I become their target at the game's end? But, in for a penny, in for a pound, we cheered our team onto a 3–1 victory and the Championship. A late penalty miss by Aberdeen certainly helped our cause, both on and off the park. It seemed to dishearten the more vociferous of their support and they sloped away, leaving us free to celebrate with the team as they made their way to the players' tunnel.

A quick and safe exit was then achieved, though in my case perhaps just a little too quick. On the road home I was double flashed by a Grampian Gatso speed camera. Captured doing 70mph in a 50mph zone – the three points won by Rangers would soon be matched by three points on my driving licence!

Rangers met Hibs at Ibrox on the final day of the season. The game started with an impeccably observed minute's silence for the Celtic legend Bobby Murdoch, and ended with a welcome 4–0 victory. It also marked the departure of a couple of the fan's favourites, Jorg Albertz and Tugay. Interestingly, both players left with tellingly barbed comments.

From Tugay: 'the players don't like each other, the dressing room is split 50:50.'

Albertz was much more specific: 'there are too many Dutchmen at Ibrox!'

From the outside it was impossible to say whether the Dutch colony were the cause of any problem. But one couldn't help but see parallels with the Dutch national team, who were renowned for two things – their ability to play wonderful football and their tendency to squabble and fall out when times became tough. Rangers had enjoyed the former, were they now suffering from the latter? It was a problem that clearly had to be addressed. Dick Advocaat had to act, but as a Dutchman himself, did he see the problem? Was he part of the problem?

Rangers were a shambles. No trophies on the park and an absolute car crash off of it. This year they had lost £17m and were £50m in debt. Was this kind of financial performance sustainable? Could the club maintain this level of debt? David Murray certainly thought so, he commented in the end of year results:

"As Chairman, I am responsible for the overall direction of the club and as such I must plan for long-term stability in addition to meeting our short-term aspirations. I am confident that we are in good shape, both on and off the park, to meet the challenges of the future and ensure the continuing success of the club."

I have to say that I wasn't totally convinced.

Chapter 18:
There's Only One Neil McCann

It was around this time that my football horizon started to broaden and I became involved in the youth game. It started inevitably enough with Graeme who was now eight years old. He enjoyed football and loved going to the small team games, but he wanted to play as well. To encourage him, I took him along to a local football club, Livi Star, who had a well established and thriving soccer school.

The coaching session lasted a couple of hours and gave the youngsters a good, but relaxed, insight into organised football. Graeme enjoyed it, wanted more and ended up going every week. Most parents just dropped their kids off and left; using the soccer school, I suspect, as an un-official baby-sitting service. I preferred to stay and watch; to see how Graeme was developing. As the weeks passed I offered to help out, mainly chasing after balls and setting up the odd training routine – nothing too technical! Gradually though I became more involved, progressing to some very basic coaching. I've never been much of a footballer, but even I could keep a step or two ahead of a six, seven or eight year old – well most of the time!

The competitive stuff started for Rangers at the end of July, and went rather well. Maribor from Slovenia were beaten 3–0 away from home in a Champions' League qualifier, Aberdeen then thumped by the same score line in an SPL game at Pittodrie. It was a super start, with new signing Christian Nerlinger playing a prominent role, scoring in both games. The German unfortunately only lasted one more match. Crocked in the Maribor return, he hit the treatment table and missed the next forty-five games, and he wasn't alone, up to eight of his first team colleagues were also incapacitated. What was it with injuries and Rangers?

The season's good start floundered as early as the first day in August. A goalless draw at Ibrox against newly promoted Livingston meant catch up in the SPL after only two games. A similar 0–0 draw with Fenerbache in the Champions League left group stage qualification, and all that went with it, hanging by a thread – a thread that snapped a fortnight later with a 2–1 defeat in Istanbul. With pressure starting to mount, Dick Advocaat issued a curious statement. He said that he knew the reason for the crippling and mounting injury crisis – but he wasn't going to tell anyone what it was! He did, however, have an answer to the problem; one that he was only too willing to share. It was nothing new or revolutionary though, just the same old story – Rangers needed to spend money.

David Murray quickly responded. In the *Evening Times* he stated, 'There is money set aside and we are going to strengthen, there is no doubt about that, and if we do, then we will have to spend more than the whole of the Scottish football league put together.' He continued, 'If we have a problem and this injury situation gets worse, I will not think twice about buying a £6.5m Michael Ball, or another £6m player if required.'

Just a thought, but might it not have been better to investigate the cause of all these injuries, rather than just throw more money at the problem. Was the chairman really willing to push an already debt-ridden and loss-making club further into the red, just to alleviate an injury crisis?

The Michael Ball that Murray referred to in his somewhat bombastic statement was an Everton full back, and a player that Rangers were interested in signing. There was, however, just one tiny area of concern. Michael Ball was known to be injury prone, and was in fact suffering from what was euphemistically called, "a troublesome knee." Were Rangers mad? Had they forgotten Daniel Prodan already?

My involvement in youth football was now gathering pace. Livi Star had entered an Under 9s team into the West Lothian Soccer Sevens. One of the club coaches took me aside and explained that they really wanted to enter a second team, one that Graeme would undoubtedly be part of, but they didn't have anyone to take charge of the proposed side. It didn't take a genius to work out where this conversation was heading! The inevitable outcome was that I became coach of my own Livi Star team – with only three weeks 'til the season's start.

The big day dawned and we all gathered at a local Sports Centre, ready to take on the world, starting with BFC Linlithgow. Hoping to quell any last minute nerves, I told my squad to just go out and enjoy themselves. Don't worry about making any mistakes – and don't be nervous.

"We're not nervous!" they all bellowed enthusiastically.

I wish I could have said the same. I'd been up half the night fretting about my team selection and strategies, and by kick off time my stomach was positively churning. Strategies at Under 9s? I had a lot to learn about youth football!

The referee started the game and everyone immediately abandoned their positions and charged after the ball – so much for my carefully planned formation! BFC went a goal up and I started to worry. Was my manager's jacket on a shoogly nail already? But, all's well that ends well; we recovered to win 9–2. Winning isn't everything at Soccer Sevens. It's all about progress and development. But I'll tell you what – winning that day was great!

September brought the first Old Firm game of the season; Rangers played well, dominated the game for long spells, but lost 2–0. Back in the 1990s, Walter Smith's team used to do that sort of thing to Celtic; the boot was now, regrettably, firmly on the other foot. A fact confirmed by Celtic's Stilian Petrov. Post-match he said, "it's very easy for us to win these games." Comments like that were not helping Dick Advocaat.

My career as a manager at Under 9s, on the other hand, was going pretty well. We were winning some, losing some, but improving all the time and most importantly, everyone seemed to be enjoying their football. In October we played Livi Hearts, and what should have been a run of the mill game got, just a little, out of hand. There was some history between the two clubs, all adult related, and absolutely nothing whatsoever to do with the kids. But they picked up on it, and the game, on both sides, was systematically built up into a grudge match.

On the day it was a super game of football between two fully committed teams. Livi Star opened the scoring; Livi Hearts equalised and then took the lead. The score fluctuated one way, and then the other, until it stood at 4–4. With a minute remaining, Livi Star attacked. Graeme latched onto a pass and drove a shot into the back of the net. It was a fantastic moment and our touchline celebrated wildly. The coach in me was shouting encouragement to his team. The dad in me was regrettably making an arse of himself, leaping up and down, roaring approval at his son's goal. In hindsight it was a rather unedifying spectacle.

The final whistle sounded to load cheers, and a 5–4 Livi Star victory. At this point I made the schoolboy error of turning my back on the field of play. Rather than shake hands and come back to our side of the park (as would have been normal) my team had formed themselves into a line and embarked on a flying Jurgen Klinsmann style celebration, sliding along the wet turf right up to the opposition sideline. They then compounded the insult by leaping to their feet and singing "Championees" to a very disgruntled home team. I dashed over and tried to calm the situation down with some conciliatory handshakes and apologetic words but to no avail, and later that evening I received a phone call summoning me to a club meeting, and a prospective hearing with the league association's disciplinary committee. Unsporting behaviour and running an unruly team was alleged. Heaven's sake! A few weeks as a coach, and I was already up before the beaks at Hampden!

Fortunately a few grovelling letters managed to smooth the troubled waters and the matter was dropped. A valuable lesson had been learned though – always keep your eye on the little rascals! This football lark was obviously a learning curve for everyone, coaches as well as players.

November brought the second Old Firm game of the season. Once again Rangers played well, and once again they lost. It wasn't as though the Ibrox men were playing particularly badly, it just seemed that Martin O'Neil had the hex on Dick Advocaat. In a championship battle between the Glasgow giants, success in the Old Firm games is key, and Martin O'Neil was undoubtedly winning that battle hands down. He'd now claimed six wins out of seven – the writing was on the wall for the Dutchman.

Rangers squandered more points in a 0–0 draw at Dens Park. Even the most optimistic Blue Nose now had to concede that the league title had gone; we trailed Celtic by twelve points, a Celtic team who were unbeaten, having only dropped two points from a possible forty-eight. The draw with Dundee also marked Michael Ball's final game of the season, in fact his last 'til the start of season 2003/2004.

The player had been signed back in August with a very apparent and well-publicised knee problem. He'd managed a grand total of eleven games – and would now be out of action for some twenty months. So, what was the problem? Surprise, surprise! That troublesome knee injury had resurfaced. The Smiths had been one of my favourite bands in the 1980s. As I read the news on Ball's injury, I could almost hear Morrissey mournfully lament:

Stop me, oh, please stop me
Stop me if you think that you've heard this one before.

Doing some research at the Mitchell library, I stumbled across a book, *The Advocaat Years* by Ronnie Esplin and Alex Anderson. Flicking through it I noticed a comment attributed to David Murray. When talking about the injury problems at Ibrox, he referred to a certain Romanian defender. 'Prodan was a big, big mistake because he didn't get a proper medical.'

I had to read that sentence over and over. It was unbelievable! I'd always assumed that Daniel Prodan had been given a thorough examination, but no! In their desperation to sign the player, Rangers had discarded the most basic and obvious of precautions; a proper medical. Though, on second thoughts, it was unhappily only too believable! One wonders how many others, Kuznetzov, Rozenthal, Amoruso et al. had gone through the same shoddy process. Michael Ball had surely been given a stringent medical. This time Rangers were just unlucky. Yes?

I was training one Tuesday with my Livi Star team. On that particular evening the other coaches were running late, so I'd to take charge of both teams. To keep twelve youngsters in check was difficult; to control twenty-four of them was well nigh impossible. In an attempt to buy some time, I sent them off on a jog round the field. Most were cooperating. One lad, however, was lagging and lingering, not really putting in any effort. I went over to have a word, to try and gee him up, and as he was wearing a Rangers strip, I applied a little psychology. On his back was the name, McCann. So, I told him that the winger always warmed up, and he should really do the same. Quick as a flash the youngster retorted ... oh no he doesn't, he's injured so he doesn't have to warm up.

Irritatingly the kid was correct. Neil McCann was indeed injured. Getting annoyed, I changed my tack and told him that he didn't really want to be like McCann, as the player was useless. His every cross ball hit the first defender and he was a waste of space (I had a bit of a downer on McCann at the time for some reason). The boy took great exception to those comments and wandered away, muttering that he was going to tell his dad about what I had said. I thought no more about it 'til one of the other players came over. Laughing, he asked me if I knew who the boy's dad was. When I said no, he laughed even louder, and then gleefully informed me ... it's Neil McCann!

"Away you go", I told him, "and don't be so silly".

As the training session ended, I glanced over at the gathering parents and recognised one of the faces. To my absolute horror it was Neil McCann of Rangers FC. I couldn't believe my eyes. Mortified, I had two choices, go over and face the music, or beat a hasty retreat. I chose the latter!

Speculation had been rife for months regarding Dick Advocaat's future at Ibrox. His Rangers side were slipping further and further behind O'Neil's Celtic, with no indication that a recovery was imminent, or even possible. Indeed Rangers were nervously looking over their shoulder, trying to fend off a Livingston side who were vying for second place. No disrespect intended, but Livingston! What was going on?

December brought the inevitable change. Dick Advocaat was moved 'upstairs', to a newly created post of Director of Football, and Alex McLeish, the Hibernian manager brought in. It has to be said that the appointment of McLeish was not met with universal approval. The majority of supporters realised that a change of management was necessary, but some wanted a bigger, more glamorous name. Others feared he wasn't up to the task. A few just didn't like his previous association with Aberdeen. Personally, I was reasonably happy with the selection. McLeish had been a good manager at Motherwell and Hibs, and at both clubs he'd developed teams that had played some attractive football. Not only that, he was a boyhood Rangers fan, so understood the club and its support. He was a safe, if unspectacular appointment.

February brought Alex McLeish's first real test as manager, a League Cup semi-final against Celtic. Could he break Martin O'Neil's stranglehold on the fixture? As it turned out he could, with some help from a most unlikely source – the much-maligned Bert Konterman.

Konterman was a real enigma. Signed for £4m, he'd played for Feyenoord in the Champions league and been capped twelve times for Holland, so he was clearly no duffer – yet at Rangers he often looked like a man who had never seen a football before, let alone played the game. It was regrettable, but Konterman's rather unkind nickname of 'Bertie Bombscare' had been well earned.

That evening at Hampden, Bert's name was loudly and ironically cheered by the Celtic support as the teams were read out. How they laughed at his inclusion in the Rangers side. What followed was a typically full-bloodied Old Firm clash, with play swinging from one end of the pitch to the other. Tied at 1–1 the teams entered extra time with the dreaded prospect of penalty kicks looming. Then the ball dropped to the Rangers #15. He took aim, and from thirty yards sent an unstoppable shot screaming into the back of the net. Konterman had just scored a wonder goal – not too much laughter now from the green and white brigade! It was undoubtedly Bertie's finest moment in blue, but it didn't disguise the fact that he really wasn't very good!

The SPL was clearly a lost cause, but McLeish did have the chance to claim some silverware with two cup finals approaching. The first of these resulted in a League Cup victory over Ayr United. The second final would be a stiffer test, against Celtic. That day didn't have the best of starts; I'd been out the night before for a few drinks with the Livi Star coaches and overindulged just a little. No, overindulged a whole lot. I woke up with a raging hangover, feeling so queasy that I actually considered not going to the game. Serious indeed! But, operating on autopilot, I managed to crawl out of bed and make it down to Mid Calder and catch the Tap Shop bus, sleeping all the way to Glasgow. Bus parked, I went for a hair of the dog, a kill or cure pint – it nearly killed me! I curled up in the pub, and once again fell asleep, until a none too gentle prod in the ribs indicated it was time to set off for Hampden.

Because of my poor condition I couldn't really enjoy the game, which was a shame because it was a wonderful football match. A goal down Rangers equalised, 2–1 down they drew level. At 2–2, the clock was about to hit the ninety minutes, extra time was calling. Then, in a last gasp attack, Rangers pushed forward. Neil McCann swung over a tempting curling cross, Peter Lovenkrands read his intentions and made the perfect back post run. He met the cross and bulleted a header downwards. Sitting directly in line, I saw the ball bounce and thought, for one awful moment, that it was going to clear the crossbar – it didn't. The ball looped over the despairing arms of the Celtic keeper, teasingly hung in the air for a moment or two and then dipped into the net. With my head spinning I leapt to my feet and somehow joined in with the bedlam that had engulfed half of Hampden. Seconds later the final whistle sounded to signal victory. Just as well, because I really don't think I could have survived another half hour.

The season had ended on an undoubted high, with genuine grounds for optimism. That was on the park. Off the park however the situation was starting to look more than a little murky, financially, the club was in a mess.

The Scotsman brought the thoughts of Hugh Adam to the fore. Adam, an ex-Rangers director, had recently disposed of his 59,000 shares in the club. In his opinion, 'they were heading towards worthlessness, thanks to the unsatisfactory business methods of David Murray.' In the newspaper article, Glenn Gibbons wrote:

'Hugh Adam has impressive credentials, having been chairman and managing director of Rangers Development and Rangers Pools since 1971, raising millions which built the modern Ibrox. Not given to sensationalism, Adam observed almost matter-of-factly that, if Rangers continue on their present track, their ultimate destination will be bankruptcy. That's the logical conclusion to a strategy that incurs serious loss year on year. In the past five years – and it's all there in the last annual report – Rangers have lost eighty million pounds.'

It was a gloomy prognosis, yet the noises coming out of Ibrox were still upbeat. The problems couldn't be as serious as Adam had predicted. Could they?

The youth football season also drew to a close, concluding with a Livi Star disco and presentation evening. With awards for the players and a few beers for the parents, it was a very pleasant way to end an enjoyable year. To add some glitz and glamour to the event, a mystery celebratory was invited to hand out the trophies. The identity of that celebrity was only too predictable ... it was of course Neil McCann. Perhaps the young McCann hadn't grassed on me after that training session. Perhaps he had, and his dad was too polite to bring the subject up. But either way, nothing was said, and I kept it that way!

If Neil happens to read this, my apologies – you were a fine player, and the majority of your cross balls were excellent. Especially that one in the Scottish cup final!

Chapter 19:
Winners and Losers

Friendly matches are always a prelude to any new football year, but it's not just professional sides who indulge in pre-season friendlies; my Livi Star team also had a new football year to prepare for. One of our build up games was against Kirkliston FC, a good and well respected team from the Edinburgh league. It was a game, and an evening that didn't quite run to plan. Just as I was setting off, my pre-booked referee phoned to call off. He was most apologetic, but just couldn't manage the fixture. This gave me a big problem because with only an hour until kick off there was no chance of getting a replacement. I asked pitch side, if any of the parents fancied taking on the task, but knew deep down that there was no chance of that happening. I was correct, and that left only one option – to do the job myself. Not something I was looking forward to.

Feeling very nervous, and extremely self-conscious I blew my whistle to start proceedings. The bigger and stronger Kirkliston immediately won possession, broke upfield and scored. They scored again and again. My team were in total disarray and badly needed some guidance, but as referee, I felt morally unable to help. It just didn't seem right to assist them from the middle of the park. The first half ended with a score line that depressingly read: Livi Star 0 Kirkliston 6.

At half time I temporarily became coach again and gave my shell-shocked team a quick pep talk, whatever I said seemed to work because they came storming back. An early goal was scored, and with confidence boosted, they slowly but surely chipped away at the deficit, until with seconds remaining the score stood at 6–5. Livi Star then won a corner. There was just enough time to take it, just enough time to create one last chance. Dare I hope for a morale boosting equaliser?

A cross was swung into the goalmouth and cleared, a shot then powerfully driven back in. It looked a goal all the way, 'til an arm was raised, and a hand pushed the ball over the bar. I inwardly groaned, and wondered what on earth had possessed one of my guys to do that, the ball had clearly been deflected by an orange clad arm. That fact of course didn't prevent my entire team appealing for a penalty, as did their mums and dads. I shook my head and quite properly awarded a free kick to the visitors, the team wearing blue. Waving away the persistent and vociferous protests, I then blew for full time.

Post-match, I shook hands with the Kirkliston players, one of whom winced as I clasped his hand. On asking if he was okay, the boy replied, "Yes, but it was really sore when I punched that shot over the bar". My heart sank as the realization hit me – It had been a penalty after all!

The match, if nothing else, gave me an insight into the trials and tribulations of being a referee; making split second judgements just wasn't as easy as it looked from the sidelines. To this day, I still maintain a Livi Star player handled the ball, but I'm clearly in a minority of one! I'd made a huge mistake, but it happens. Referees are only human and sometimes they make the most outrageous, but honest howlers. It's something that supporters, whether at youth club, or SPL level should try to appreciate.

Rangers' finances were now coming under scrutiny, something David Murray could no longer ignore. He'd taken a break from the day-to day running of the club, but still enjoyed his spot in the limelight. In September's Daily Record:

'David Murray, last night admitted the club had boobed by paying over the odds for misfit striker Tore Andre Flo. Murray, now honorary chairman, had to write off £7m in wages and transfer fees for the Norwegian – a disaster that contributed to the Ibrox clubs whopping £19m trading loss in the financial year up to June 30.'

The financial management at Ibrox was truly appalling! Incidentally, to call Flo a misfit was grossly unfair. It wasn't his fault that Rangers had given Chelsea the ludicrous sum of £12.5m for his services, nor was it his fault that they were willing to pay him millionaires' wages. Flo scored thirty-eight goals in seventy-two appearances, hardly the strike rate of a failure.

At Livi Star I didn't have transfer fees or wages to worry about. Players occasionally moved between clubs, generally though within the strict association guidelines ... but not always! I tried to run my team fairly, allowing everyone equal time on the park. Moving players into different positions whenever possible to give them a chance to learn and appreciate all aspects of the game. This would allow them to develop skills that would be beneficial in the years to come. Most parents recognised the long term strategy and were supportive. Some however didn't and weren't. One dad was particularly indignant that his talented offspring wasn't playing as the star striker every week ... "why are you playing him in defence/midfield, when he's the best player in the team? He should be up front scoring goals." Another dad was even more critical. He approached me one day, and asked if his boy could be moved into the other Livi Star team. "No offence, but your team's rubbish. My boy's far too good for it!" Charming!

Those two blue-eyed boys went AWOL for a couple of training sessions, and then a game. I wondered where they were, but it wasn't unusual for players to go missing for a few days so I wasn't overly concerned. Unfortunately moves were afoot behind my back, and as so often happens in youth football, the guy who does the coaching and the hard work is last to know when trouble is brewing. I got a phone call the next week from a friend, who informed me that a couple of my lads were now playing with another team; something that was strictly illegal whilst registered with Livi Star. It wasn't too hard to guess who the culprits were, their identity quickly confirmed by a few phone calls. The parents then admitted that their sons had moved on. One mother rather sheepishly said, "Sorry, we meant to tell you!" At the end of the day, it was no big deal, if players want to move, they can move. It would have been nice though, if the parents had been just a little more honest and open.

A few weeks later we played Murieston FC, a team that had just acquired a couple of new recruits! Tension was thick in the air that morning as we lined up to face each other. The pre-match team talk clearly superfluous as my young side were already fired up and determined to put one over on their old teammates. My sideline was also animated; mums, dads, uncles and aunties had all come down to lend their support, all willing Livi Star onto victory. They weren't to be disappointed. Playing some terrific football, my galvanised team won 5–3. Jubilation on our side of the park!

Mindful of our spot of bother at Livi Hearts the previous year, I kept a close eye on my players, and supporters, to ensure that there were no post-match shenanigans. All that was then left to do was to enjoy the ritual handshakes, and gloat, just a little, at the scowls adorning a few particular parents' faces. In the interest of fairness, I suppose I should add that Murieston beat us 8–1 in the return fixture, but, as far as I'm concerned, we won the game that counted!

The winter break saw the first sign that the belt may be tightening at Ibrox. Alex McLeish wanted to strengthen his squad, and targeted defender Daniel Eggen. The last Norwegian to play for the club had cost £12.5m, this one was on offer for £200k – and the Ibrox club wouldn't pay, or perhaps couldn't pay! In August 2001, David Murray boasted that Rangers were going to 'spend more than the whole of the Scottish football league put together.' Sixteen months later, the club were quibbling over a paltry £200,000, it was an indication that trying times were ahead.

The league championship race marched relentlessly on, and come the season's final day, it couldn't have been closer.

Rangers	Played 37	Points 94	Goal difference 68
Celtic	Played 37	Points 94	Goal difference 68

Sunday 25th May 2003 was showdown time; Rangers at home to Dunfermline, Celtic away to Kilmarnock. The Ibrox men had scored one more goal, so only needed to win, and equal, at least, the score line from Rugby Park. Sounded so simple!

A day of drama ebbed and flowed, Rangers got the early goal they craved, but were quickly pegged back by a Dunfermline equaliser that most certainly wasn't part of the script. Rangers went 2–1 ahead, but at that very instant, Celtic were scoring at Kilmarnock. The league race was still on. At half time both teams remained tied together at the top, Rangers just edging it by virtue of that extra goal. That position soon changed, Alan Thompson netted a penalty kick at Rugby Park, and Celtic moved to the top of the SPL. For ten agonisingly long minutes, they were champions-elect. Then Rangers scored, to regain the coveted top spot. The Ibrox men maintained that position but it was nerve-wracking stuff, with Celtic ready at any moment to pounce and deny them the championship. When the Rangers game ended, there was an uneasy few seconds until the final score from Kilmarnock filtered through. The news of a 4–0 Celtic victory confirmed that Rangers were champions – let the party begin!

Rangers received the SPL trophy to loud cheers and embarked on a well-deserved lap of honour, at one point doing the flying Jurgen Klinsmann slide, a move of course made famous by my little Livi Star team! That brought about the day's most poignant, yet comical moment. A few minutes after the slide, Lorenzo Amoruso noticed that his winner's medal was no longer on its Bank of Scotland ribbon. It had fallen off somewhere, most likely during that victory slide. The big man left his celebrating teammates and returned to the Govan Stand, where he had last seen it and forlornly searched through all the ticker tape and confetti that littered the pitch. It was hard not to smile as he hunted for it. Looking totally crestfallen, he glanced at the ribbon every so often, hoping beyond hope that the medal had somehow re-appeared. It hadn't of course, and remained lost somewhere on the Ibrox turf.

Meanwhile, down at Rugby Park the atmosphere was not quite so jovial. The Celtic support was downcast, and more than a little irked at the goal celebrations from the home support. The Kilmarnock fans had been enthusiastically cheering every Rangers strike as though their own team had scored – good on them! Celtic striker, Chris Sutton, then expressed the feelings of his teammates. Referring to Dunfermline FC, he said.

"We all suspected they might lie down and it looks like that is exactly what's happened."

It was an outrageous statement from a sore loser. One has to wonder, if Dunfermline had decided to lie down, what on earth were they playing at when they equalized at Ibrox, giving us all the fright of our lives? Rangers, already League Cup holders, were now only one game away from a treble. What a turnaround from Dick Advocaat's final eighteen months!

Rangers beat Dundee in the Scottish cup final, and won the treble, though it was a tired and weary performance – too many hangovers perhaps from an elongated championship party. The game's only goal was scored fittingly by Lorenzo Amoruso who was playing his final game for the club. Stringent economies were now kicking in, and contracts were not being renewed. Arthur Numan, Neil McCann, Claudio Caniggia and Bert Konterman had also played their final games. Barry Ferguson would soon be joining them. It was particularly painful to see Lorenzo depart. He'd been the most frustrating of players to watch. At times brilliant, yet also sloppy and frighteningly casual. There was never any doubt however about his commitment to the cause, amply demonstrated by his tears at the end of the game. Amoruso was the last player to climb the Hampden steps and had his moment of glory, emotionally milking the applause as he waved the trophy to his support. It was a moment the big man richly deserved.

The season was over, triumphant for sure. But what did the future hold? Players were leaving. Would adequate replacements be brought in? What was more important now, the balance sheet or the league table?

The new season was quickly upon us, and Graeme wanted to be part of it. He wanted the season ticket that I'd promised so long ago. I tried to explain that getting two seats together at Ibrox wasn't all that easy, but he didn't understand. Not that I understood either. We had, after all, been on the waiting list for over four years, and in all that time we'd heard nothing from the club, no news regarding the availability of tickets, nothing. I was starting to wonder if the waiting list was just a figment of my imagination!

When Rangers announced a public sale of season tickets I decided to give them a call. Knowing that the guy next to me in the Govan Stand was thinking of giving up his ticket I asked if that seat was available, and to my delight it was. Absolutely perfect! All I had to do now was to book it in Graeme's name. A simple enough task you would have thought. My conversation with the ticket office went something like this:

"Can I buy a season ticket for Govan Front G81?"

"Yes, you can sir."

"Excellent. Here's my credit card number."

"Sorry sir, the ticket office is too busy to accept telephone bookings. You'll have to wait till next week."

Wait till next week! That was no use to me! I tried to explain the situation. I needed the ticket so that my son could sit next to me. If I waited till the following week, that particular seat would almost certainly be gone.

"Can't we please do the booking by phone?"

"No sir. But if you come over to Ibrox we can do it for you!"

"I'm working in Edinburgh. It's not that easy to get to Glasgow – can't we please do it by phone?"

"No sir."

"So you'll accept my credit card if I travel all the way to Glasgow in person, but you won't take it over the phone?"

"That's correct sir."

"So, what if I was calling from England or Northern Ireland? Would I still have to travel all the way to Ibrox?"

"Yes sir."

"Don't you think that's just stupid?"

"Sorry sir, I don't make the rules. Can I be of any further help?"

I gave a big sigh, and pondered my options. There was no way the seat would still be available in a week's time. I had no alternative.

"Okay then, I'll come over this afternoon. Could you put that seat on hold for me please?"

"No sir. Can I be of any further help?"

"Can't I pay for it now, and then come over and pick it up – please?"

"No sir. Can I be of any further help?"

At the end of my tether I ended the call. Let's face it, was there any real point in continuing? I arranged a half day from work and set off for Ibrox. Rangers were a team deeply in debt and desperate for finance. I was a fan, a customer if you like. I had a credit card and wanted to give them money – a few hundred pounds that they doggedly refused to accept. At times like this I despaired for the way that my club was being run.

I drove the fifty miles from Crewe Toll in Edinburgh to Ibrox, and joined the queue at the ticket office. When my turn eventually arrived I was given the almost inevitable news that the seat I desperately wanted had already been sold. The girl behind the counter then cheerfully informed me – if I'd been in touch sooner I would have got it. It wasn't her fault, but at that precise moment I could quite happily have throttled her! Fortunately there were two adjoining seats available elsewhere in the stadium, so Graeme and I got our season tickets. You know, it's just as well I was a fan and a loyal supporter, because as a customer I was severely hacked off.

Alex McLeish managed to bring in some new players to replenish his severely depleted squad, but it was hardly an awe-inspiring list, mostly Bosmans and free transfers. When Dick Advocaat arrived at Ibrox he quickly spent £30m building a new team. Alex McLeish was now doing the self same thing, but he'd been allocated less that £1m to complete the task. If big 'Eck was going to retain the championship, he'd have to do it the hard way.

Saturday 4th October 2003 brought derby day on two separate fronts. At 9.30am, my Livi Star team kicked off against old rivals Livi Hearts. We hadn't enjoyed the best of starts to the season, only winning two of our first eight games, so I wasn't overly confident about this one. Oh, ye of little faith! My team turned on the style, played some terrific football, and won by five goals to nil. It was just one of those days when absolutely everything went right. The relationship between the two teams was still a little fractious so the post match pleasantries were short and to the point. Their coach came over and we exchanged the most cursory of handshakes. He walked away, then, clearly irritated, turned back and exclaimed, "You only won because the ball was too soft and the grass was too long!" My comments in return didn't exactly improve his mood, "Well it was your game, it was your ball, and it was your grass!" It would be a while before we would become bosom buddies! That, sadly, was as good as the day got. Graeme and I dashed over to Ibrox for the lunchtime Old Firm clash, and watched as a not very good Celtic beat Rangers 1–0. They didn't have to be good, because the men in blue were simply awful.

An appalling October saw seven points dropped from a possible nine. With the league title slipping away Rangers needed their players to be focussed, to be fully committed and dedicated. Unfortunately, for many modern footballers the concept of commitment and dedication are unknown qualities – take Fernando Ricksen as an example.

Fernando had always been a volatile player on the park, regularly picking up yellow and red cards. That was one thing. He did however have an off the field reputation as well, one that he seemed strangely determined to live up to. Ricksen had been out celebrating last season's championship win. On the road home he thought it a good idea to bawl obscenities through a neighbours letter box, the neighbour being Celtic's midfielder Alan Thompson. It was a prank worthy of a bored teenager, but not the action surely of an international footballer. More serious was the evening he crashed his car into a lamp post, whilst twice the drink-driving limit. Pretending not to speak English didn't fool the police who were quickly in attendance, and a driving ban inevitably followed.

In October he was fined £5,000 at Paisley Sherriff Court for letting off fireworks in his back garden. Not normally a criminal offence, but unfortunately his display had been timed for two o'clock in the morning! When a neighbour understandably complained, Ricksen verbally and physically assaulted him. He got a £2,000 fine for that!

In an attempt to redeem himself, Fernando appeared in the Daily Record pledging his undying love for girlfriend Graciela, he vowed to settle down and stay out of the limelight. A few days later the reformed character was spotted out on the town, canoodling with the glamour model Jordan. Showing true professionalism, he was later quoted as saying, "I'm Fernando Ricksen, and I can do what I want!" One really has to wonder what the late, great Bill Struth would have made of the wayward Dutchman. A swift kick up the backside, and a one way ticket back to Holland, would, I suspect, be the very minimum of his actions.

The winter transfer window saw a welcome addition to the first team squad when Gavin Rae joined from Dundee. There was no reason for the bank manager to worry though, as the fee was an unbelievably cheap £250k. In administration,

Dundee were legally obliged to accept the first half-decent offer that they received. Rangers' finances weren't in great shape, but thankfully my club wasn't in a position where they *had* to sell players, and it was re-assuring to know that despite their current troubles, they'd never be in such an awful predicament. Would they?

Gavin Rae made his debut at Parkhead in January, lasted thirty minutes and was taken off with a pulled hamstring. He'd been a regular in his Dundee side and clocked up over two hundred games in five years – half an hour with Rangers and he was crocked! The game was lost 3–0. Another defeat, and another Old Firm game, without a goal being scored.

Rangers won their next league game, to at least give the pretence of an SPL challenge. The victory, however, was marred by some prolonged and vindictive abuse directed towards defender Bob Malcolm, but not from the Motherwell fans, regrettably it came from a large section of the home support. Bob may not have been the best player in the world, and he certainly wasn't having a great game, but he was a true blue and always gave 100% to the cause. He really didn't deserve the ridicule he was receiving. After an hour he was substituted, to sarcastic applause and derisory cheers.

It seems to be a trait amongst football fans – of all teams I hasten to add, not just Rangers – when times are hard, a scapegoat is required, and the victim is generally a young Scot, not the overpaid foreigner. A player is performing poorly, he is jeered by his own supporters. His confidence drops and his performance deteriorates, he gets jeered even more – it's a curious way of supporting your team!

A nightmare season was finally over, and it ended with Rangers finding a new and ingenious method of losing money. The signings of two players, Capucho and Emerson simply hadn't worked and the club wanted shot of them, but unfortunately it wasn't quite that simple. The pair were on long, lucrative contracts and understandably didn't want to give them up; a compromise had to be reached, and was. The two players left as free agents, their wallets padded by what amounted to a big fat redundancy cheque. Rangers were crashing out money to sign players, giving them a hefty weekly wage, and now paying them to leave! It's said that a fool and his money are soon parted, that idiom also applies to football clubs.

The Brazilian Emerson made an interesting comment as he departed. Clearly miffed at being paid off he claimed that he had been made a scapegoat for "Rangers' season of misery" – because he'd been signed by David Murray and not by Alex McLeish. In his words, "I was bought by the owner of the club". It begged the question. Just who was making the football decisions at Ibrox?

Chapter 20:
I'm a Believer

S tarved of football, and gagging for some action, I suspended my self-imposed ban on pre-season friendlies and went to the curtain raiser against Tottenham. A good decision as it turned out, because it was a fine game, exciting and competitive – if only all friendlies were the same! Rangers won 2–0, and picked up their first silverware of the season, the Walter Tull memorial trophy.

Walter Tull was a name unknown to me, but the more I read about him, the more I understood why he had been commemorated in this particular game. The grandson of a West Indian slave, he was one of the first black men to play professional football in Great Britain. In 1909, he signed for Tottenham Hotspur, before moving onto Northampton Town. When the Great War started, he enlisted and joined the Footballers' Battalion of the Middlesex Regiment. Recognised for his leadership skills, Tull was quickly promoted to sergeant and fought with distinction on the Somme in 1916. Breaking all conventional boundaries, he then became the first black man to be commissioned as an officer in the British Army, despite the Manual of Military

Law specifically excluding "any negro, or person of colour from being an officer."

Planning for the future, Walter decided that when the war was finally over, he would move to Glasgow and join Rangers. Tragically that was never to happen. Mentioned in despatches for gallantry and coolness under fire, he was killed in action on 25th March 1918. Tull was held in such esteem, that several of his men risked their own lives, and attempted, under heavy machine-gun fire, to retrieve his lifeless body from no-man's land. Those efforts were sadly un-successful. He is now remembered, along with thousands of other lost soldiers, on the Arras Memorial in the Faubourg d'Amiens Cemetery in France. Many modern footballers are lauded as superstars and role models. Not one of them could hold a candle to Walter Daniel Tull, a true hero.

The youth football season had also started, with one major development; Livi Star were no longer playing soccer sevens. Teams in Scotland move to the eleven a side game at Under 13s, and that's where we now were. To accommodate the change, the two Livi Star teams merged to form one big squad, a group of players hopefully good enough to challenge for league titles and trophies. The merged side was led by Derek Watson; Derek was a football man through and through, and a damned fine coach. He'd taken a previous Livi Star team from soccer sevens to eleven a side, so was the perfect man lead us at Under 13s.

We went into the season quietly confident of doing well, and initial results tended to back up that confidence. After five games, we were joint top of the table, level with Fauldhouse, both teams boasting an impressive 100% winning record. A closer look at results should, however, have sent us a warning. We were winning games 3–2 and 3–0; they were beating the same teams 13–2 and 13–0.

Sunday 29th August 2004 was a big football day for both of my teams. Livi Star were playing Fauldhouse, Rangers playing Celtic. It didn't go well.

Livi Star lost 5–2 to a Fauldhouse team who were simply bigger, stronger and better than we were. Sadly, even at this early stage, it was quite clear where the West Lothian Under 13s league title was heading, and it wasn't to Livingston. A couple of hours later Celtic won by a single goal at Parkhead. Rangers had now lost a soul-destroying seven Old Firm games on the trot.

By September the knives were out for Alex McLeish, his team had slipped to fourth, and points-wise they were closer to Dunfermline at the bottom of the table than they were to Celtic at the top. As always, injuries weren't helping. Alex Rae, a close season signing, managed five games before crocking his knee.

Already out of Europe's Premier Competition, Rangers had been decanted into the UEFA cup, and found themselves playing on the island of Madeira, a small dot somewhere in the Atlantic Ocean. They really couldn't have gotten much further from the Champions League if they'd tried! Watched by a bunch of curious holidaymakers and the usual band of intrepid supporters, Rangers lost 1–0 to the unknown CS Maritimo. It was a defeat that stoked even greater pressure onto McLeish. The manager's job now depended on winning the return leg, and somehow getting back into the league title race. On current form, that seemed most unlikely.

Rangers bounced back with a victory over Inverness, but the performance was far from impressive. The three points also came at a cost when new signing, Dragan Mladenovic, was stretchered off with – surprise, surprise, a knee injury. Five games into his Ibrox career, he would be forced to sit out the next three months.

Then came the Maritimo return. On a night of high drama Rangers led 1–0 after ninety minutes. Extra time produced no further goals and the game went to penalties. Alex McLeish could only watch, and wait, his destiny hanging in the balance. An agonising string of penalties were scored, and missed, until Gregory Vignal slammed the ball home to give Rangers victory. McLeish still had a job, and Graeme, after fifteen long months as a season ticket holder, actually had something to cheer about!

On a personal note, October brought the sad news that the DJ John Peel had died. Up until 1976 my musical tastes had been pretty mainstream and exceedingly boring. Listening to the Sex Pistols and the Clash changed all that, but it was John Peel who really opened my ears to a whole new world of music. Peel was unlike any other Radio One DJ; his programmes were refreshingly free of corny jokes, inane jingles and pointless competitions. He simply got on with playing music. When he spoke, it was about life in general, football and beer. He was just a normal, regular bloke doing a job he loved. West Indian soca, Jamaican dub reggae, industrial punk and 50s US soul. Throw in some Captain Beefheart, and a sprinkling of Scots poet Ivor Cutler and you had a typical John Peel show. It was two hours of chaotic creativity, sometimes unlistenable, but always un-missable.

I'll never forget the night he played, and lauded, the Zips debut single. I don't know how the guys in the band felt, but I was ecstatic to know that he'd enjoyed their music, and broadcast it live to the nation. Although I never met the man, he seemed, somehow, to be a personal friend, and his death came as a huge shock. The fact that thousands round the world felt the exact same way is testament to how special he was.

Rangers were on a roll, performances were improving and a new found confidence seemed to be sweeping over the team. Then, good grief, the unthinkable happened! Rangers actually managed to win an Old Firm game! Celtic came to Ibrox on league cup business, confident of an eighth straight victory, and for a long time it looked as though they were going to get it. Rangers dominated the game, but fell behind to a John Hartson goal. It was the same old story, then, with five minutes remaining Dado Pršo equalised. With no further scoring the game went into extra time, and was decided by a quite wonderful Shota Adverladze goal. The Rangers support erupted in joy, sensing victory over their old rivals. And no one celebrated more than the occupant of Govan Front D197; Graeme was, at long last, watching Rangers beat Celtic.

Old Firm wins were now like corporation busses, you wait ages for one, then two come along at once! Rangers 2, Celtic 0: the gap at the top of the table was suddenly down to a single tantalising point.

I was still pretty much a home game supporter. Graeme and Dale were older now; twelve and eight years old. They were easier to look after, but getting more and more expensive to maintain! Regrettably, the family budget wouldn't stretch to away games. There was though the odd exception to that rule, and this season Graeme and I made the trip up to Tayside for the New Year's Day fixture with Dundee United. It was a horrible winter's day, bitterly cold, with a biting wind swirling slushy sleet around the ground. Sitting in Row A of the Fair Play Stand, we were open to the elements; soaked to the skin, freezing cold, and completely and utterly miserable. The things we do for our team!

Dundee United took the lead on eleven minutes and held it all the way to the end of the ninetieth. With the game going into injury time, Rangers mounted one last attack. Desperate for an equaliser, everyone pushed forward, including the goalkeeper. With the seconds ticking away a cross ball was swung into the six-yard box. Stephan Klos emerged from a ruck of players and, in a glorious moment, bulleted a header into the Dundee United net. Graeme and I went absolutely bonkers! Delirious, of course, that we'd just witnessed a last gasp equaliser, but ecstatic that it had been scored by the popular goalie. It was superb – except the Rangers keeper hadn't scored! When we got back to the car we were informed by Radio Scotland that the goal had actually come from the shoulder of Hamed Namouchi! Oh well!

The winter transfer window saw the departure of Jean-Alain Boumsong. Signed for nothing in July, sold five months later £8m, it was clearly a great deal for Rangers PLC. However, for Rangers FC it was a victory for finances over football, and sign of mounting monetary problems. Though, as it turned out, Boumsong's departure wasn't as damaging as first feared. Marvin Andrews stepped up to the mark, replaced the Frenchman and formed a strong defensive partnership with loan signing Soti Kyrgiakos.

Big Marvin was proving to be quite a remarkable character, a tower of strength both on and off the park. He'd suffered a pelvic injury whilst with Raith Rovers. An injury so serious that doctors advised that surgery was the only option if he wanted to continue his playing career. In pain and suffering from depression, Marvin attended his local Zion Praise International Church and spoke to its minister. That man, Pastor Joe Nwokoye, told him that with faith and prayer, the injury could be cured without surgery. They prayed, and sure enough, the career-threatening injury miraculously disappeared. In gratitude, Marvin dedicated himself to God. He studied the bible, became a born-again Christian, and graduated to the role of assistant Pastor. At the church, Marvin, guided by Pastor Joe, then helped in their faith-healing mission.

As January drew to a close, Rangers' championship aspirations took a potentially fatal blow when goalkeeper Stephan Klos suffered cruciate ligament damage. It was possibly a chance for Marvin Andrews to demonstrate first-hand his new healing prowess and cure the German. He didn't get the chance. The medical team didn't fancy that option, and sent Klos away for an operation. A cruciate injury clearly wasn't fixable by faith!

The games continued thick and fast, Rangers went to Dens Park and won by a couple of goals. It was a good result, but tempered by an injury to Marvin Andrews. It didn't look too serious at the time, but appearances can be deceptive. On Monday morning the injury was revealed to be cruciate ligament damage. The big centre-half's season was over, and an operation loomed. Or perhaps Marvin could, with Pastor Joe's help, rectify the problem by faith! I had of course only been joking about Marvin curing himself. I'd every respect for his beliefs, *but come on*; a cruciate injury would need more than just blind faith! Marvin Andrews begged to differ, and stated quite confidently that God was on his side, and the Lord Jesus Christ would provide a cure. He firmly believed, and because of that, there would be no operation!

Neither medics, nor God for that matter, could get Marvin Andrews ready for Rangers' next game, the League Cup final against Motherwell. A game dedicated to the memory of Davie Cooper, the tricky winger who had of course played with distinction for both teams. Rangers produced a performance worthy of Super Cooper that afternoon, and beat Motherwell 5–1. Whilst it was great to see a trophy being claimed, the day's highlight, for me, was the display from fullback Maurice Ross. He scored the opening goal, played very well, and thoroughly deserved, in my opinion, to be named Man of the Match.

I was pleased because Maurice, for some reason, had taken over Bob Malcolm's role as the fans' whipping boy. His every performance scrutinised for mistakes, his every error pounced upon and loudly criticised. I really couldn't understand it. I'd watched Maurice's career progress through the years, from the youths, to the reserves and into the first team. He'd developed well as a player, and pleasingly, always took time to chat with Graeme and me as we watched the small team games. He was a nice guy and didn't deserve the rough ride that he was getting! At this crucial time of the season, we really needed to get behind the team and encourage them, not mump and moan at certain individuals.

Nearly two weeks had passed since Marvin Andrews' injury, and he still hadn't agreed to an operation. He quite firmly believed that God would cure the problem. The football club, on the other hand, firmly disagreed with that prognosis. They were frustrated by Marvin's intransigence, and just couldn't understand why he wouldn't accept the inevitable and go under the surgeon's knife. Exasperated, their patience exhausted, Rangers issued an ultimatum to the player. Go home and reflect on your situation. It's an operation, or your time at Ibrox is over!

Marvin did just that. He went home, he reflected, and he returned to give his answer. God would cure the injury, there would be no surgery! Though in a concession to medical science, Marvin did allow a leg brace to be fitted to support his knee – God was allowed just a little help in the healing process! The club and player were in a standoff.

Rangers' UEFA cup run ended in December. For Livi Star, a European adventure was about to begin. We were off to play in the Jægerspris football tournament. Flying to Denmark, our outward journey was relatively uneventful, bar an extremely heavy Ryanair landing. The pilot seemed grimly determined to get us back onto terra firma as quickly as possible and he positively smacked the aircraft onto the runway. It bounced back up into the air, then hopped, skipped and jumped to an eventual halt. Our players, with youthful bravado gave a big cheer, whilst at the same time, one of the Livi Star coaches cowered in his seat, grimly gripping his seat armrest, absolutely terrified. A bus ride then took us to the town of Jægerspris, twenty-odd miles outside Copenhagen. We were welcomed by our hosts, and treated to a big spread of sandwiches and refreshments; juice for the players, beer for the coaches and parents. A much needed drink, I can tell you, after that airport experience!

Friday was our first proper day in Denmark. We spent the morning wandering around Copenhagen, taking in a few of the tourist traps. McDonalds and ice cream for the players, a few bottles of Carlsberg for the coaches – it seemed a shame not to sample the local delicacies! Our visit to the capital city had a somewhat surreal climax. We'd gone to the Royal Palace for the Changing of the Guard. Waiting for the ceremony to commence, I heard, in the distance, the unmistakable sound of a flute band – I had to be imagining it; this was Copenhagen after all, not Harthill. But the sound just got louder and louder. Then, round the corner marched a fife and drum band, escorted by rifle-bearing soldiers, all clad in a very smart blue and black uniform. The traditional Changing of the Guard, complete with flute band, was in full swing. It was a fine foot-tapping moment – even if the tunes weren't exactly familiar.

Back in Jægerspris, I had a chance to look over the facilities available to the football club, and what a contrast to those in Scotland. The town had a single school which catered for everyone, from six up to sixteen. They had four football parks, three grass and one astro-turf, a couple of soccer sevens pitches and the traditional five-a-side courts. Inside the school was an enormous gym hall that was used by the local handball league, and for winter football training. These facilities were replicated all over Denmark, and indeed Scandinavia. Is it any wonder these countries produce a string of good, well-rounded footballers?

The first game of the tournament was that afternoon, our opponents being Frederikssund, the best team, apparently, in the district. We went into half time a goal up and looking comfortable. Unfortunately the effects of travel fatigue, the McDonalds and ice cream all kicked in, and we lost 4–1.

Jægerspris had a clubhouse and that allowed for a few refreshments. With the players settled down for the night, the Livi Star coaches and parent helpers all retreated for a few beers with the locals. Fortunately their English was much better than our Danish, and a good night was enjoyed by all. Round about midnight the Danes had to leave, but that didn't mean the party was over. On his way out, the club president kindly told us to make ourselves at home – and presented me with the key to the bar.

"Help yourself," he said, "just lock up when you are done!"

Now, there was a time when that would have been an open invitation to binge, but I was sensible now. We only had another one... or three!

Saturday brought the second game of the tournament, when we played our hosts Jægerspris IK. Fully rested, we put up a much better performance and ran out 4–1 victors. Very pleasing, and from a personal point of view it was great to see Graeme net one of the goals. To be honest though, the fully rested comment only applied to the Livi Star team. Their coaches and supporters were looking more than a little bleary-eyed. Perhaps we'd enjoyed that free bar just a little too much.

The tournament's final game was on Sunday. Livi Star played their best football of the weekend and beat Skibby IK, 5–1. The most memorable moment came, not from the result, or any of the goals, but from a simple second-half substitution. Ready to replace a few players, we called over to the referee, but were ignored. Play raged on, and no matter how loudly we shouted, the referee just blanked us. I was going blue in the face, getting more and more exasperated, 'til one of the Skibby officials approached. He explained in broken English, pointing to his ears, that the referee was deaf and couldn't hear us. A simple wave of the touchline flag gathered the referee's attention, and allowed a rather embarrassed Livi Star coach to make the substitutions. Oops!

Back home in Scotland, the news wasn't good. Dundee United, anchored at the bottom of the league table, and fifty-six points adrift of Rangers, came to Ibrox and won by a single goal. It was a shocking result, and one that might just derail our league title aspirations. Jim Traynor, writing in the Daily Record, certainly thought so. In his match report he wrote, "Put the SPL trophy in a big green box and tie it up with a big green ribbon."

That was a tad premature, I thought. There were after all seven games to go, one of them being an Old Firm clash at Ibrox. There was still time for recovery, but the forthcoming Celtic game was clearly vital, and Rangers needed all their best players fit and ready, which leads us neatly back to Marvin Andrews. The big man still hadn't had his surgery. He was adamant that God was helping him, and unbelievably it looked as though he could be right. Confounding all conventional medical opinion, he'd restarted training and playing bounce games. Rangers needed a powerful player on the field for the Celtic game, someone who could counter the strength of Sutton and Hartson, and Marvin, if fit, was the very fellow.

Alex McLeish wanted his big centre-half on the park, but the club was worried about the ramifications of fielding a player with a clearly defined medical problem. There were all sorts of legal and compensation issues if the injury was aggravated. A compromise was reached when Rangers asked Andrews to sign a release document; absolving the club of any liability should the worst happen. Marvin quite happily agreed. With a big smile he said God was his insurance. He was quite clearly driving his manager to distraction, but you just couldn't help but admire the big man's consummate faith and belief.

The crunch Celtic game arrived with Marvin Andrews' name on the team sheet. Six weeks after receiving a career-threatening injury, he was playing in a bruising Old Firm clash. Andrews did all that was asked of him, and lasted over eighty minutes, taken off through fatigue, rather than injury. His efforts were in vain though, as Celtic won 2–1. As the dust settled, and the ground emptied, a rather amateurish banner was unfurled at the front of the Broomload Road Stand. It read: 'Five points clear. We won the league at Ibrox.' Irritating, but to be honest it was hard to disagree. That night I wrote two words in my diary, 'League over.'

With the defeat came the inevitable clamour for Alex McLeish to be sacked. For many in the Rangers support, there is no half way house. If the manager isn't a total success, then he's a dismal failure, full stop. McLeish had failed to deliver the league title, therefore he had to go! That was the perceived logic.

Meanwhile, at the other end of the city, the Celtic support were gleefully counting their chickens. With the league title in the bag, they got the calculators and calendars out, and deduced that their championship party would be at Tynecastle on Sunday 15th May. Parading the league trophy in front of the Jambos was going to be a moment to savour. Heart of Midlothian, the spoilsports, immediately stepped into the debate, and announced, come what may, there would be no trophy presentation at their ground; it just wasn't going to happen. Cue much indignation from an outraged Celtic support, but Hearts were adamant. And good for them!

On Saturday 30th April, the trophy presentation debate became somewhat superfluous when Celtic surprisingly lost at home to Hibs. The next day, Rangers won at Pittodrie, and the gap between the two clubs was reduced to a couple of points. I was to scribble in my diary, 'It's possible!' All we could do was win our final three games and hope, just hope, that Celtic would slip up somewhere. It was an unlikely scenario, but, as Big Marvin was fond of saying – keep believing!

Both teams won their next two fixtures and a final day cliffhanger was set up – with Celtic overwhelming favourites. All they had to do was win their last game at Motherwell. Rangers had to go to Easter Road, beat Hibs, and hope for some kind of miracle. Keep believing!

Judgement day arrived, with me at home, watching on TV. With simultaneously live broadcasts, I flicked from channel to channel, trying to gauge how the games were progressing. After half an hour that exercise became somewhat futile when Chris Sutton scored for Celtic; it was all over, the league title was gone.

I retreated upstairs, in a bit of a mood, to do the week's ironing. A curious action I suppose, but I had to do something to expel my nervous energy. Listening to the radio, I perked up a little when Nacho Novo scored. Rangers were leading 1–0, doing their bit, but with Celtic in control at Fir Park, it was all so superfluous. There was no way they'd let this one slip. Still, at least the ironing was getting done.

At about a quarter to four everything changed. My radio commentary was suddenly interrupted with dramatic news from Fir Park – Motherwell had scored a last-minute equaliser! The ironing was swiftly abandoned, and I dashed downstairs in an attempt to catch the last few moments on TV. My good lady wife was watching a film, and wasn't best pleased when I suddenly burst into the living room babbling that I needed to get the football on. Wrestling the remote control from her, I frantically pressed the buttons trying to find the appropriate TV channel, stopping quickly to view the pictures coming in from Easter Road. Rangers were still winning, and their support in the Dunbar Road end was bouncing in delirium. I flicked the remote again, and arrived at Fir Park, just in time to see Motherwell attack. Scott McDonald burst through a stretched Celtic defence; he cut inside and looped a shot into the net. Terry Butcher, the Motherwell manager leapt in joy, as I did, nearly crashing my head off the living room ceiling. Motherwell were wining 2–1!

I paced up and down, staring intently at the television. My heart was thumping; all sorts of crazy thoughts running through my head. What if Hibs equalised? What if Celtic fought back and scored two late goals? This was absurd pessimism, even by my bizarre standards, as both games were now deep into stoppage time. The Setanta broadcast cut to Easter Road and showed the celebrating Teddy Bears. Their game was over. Meanwhile, back at Fir Park, referee Hugh Dallas walked towards the Motherwell keeper, took the ball from him, and blew the final whistle on season 04/05. Rangers, unbelievably, sensationally, were champions!

I watched the title celebrations, breathless and stunned, unable to quite take in what I had just seen. Then smiled, as the television cameras settled on Marvin Andrews. He was on his knees, gazing upwards, with his arms outstretched. Wearing a white T-shirt, emblazoned with the slogan: 'The things that are impossible with men are possible with God.' Big Marvin truly did believe!

It's probably my biggest football regret, not being at Easter Road that day. I could, however, do the next best thing and get over to Ibrox. Graeme, Dale and I jumped in the car and set off, hoping to be part of a premier party. The journey through was magnificent, with the M8 choc-a-block with cars and busses festooned with scarves and flags, all heading to the stadium with the same idea.

Unfortunately, the Ibrox experience was a bit of a damp squib. The team arrived and took the SPL trophy to the centre circle where they were acclaimed by a good thirty thousand. They then embarked on a lap of honour, starting at the Copland Road. The celebrations had barely begun when the inevitable pitch invader encroached onto the park. The trick with these people is to repel the first one vigorously, deterring any others. Unfortunately the stewarding at the ground was very light, the Rock Steady Crew were too inexperienced, unable or un-willing to apprehend the interloper. The one pitch invader became two, became ten, and pretty soon the park was swarming with them. The team inevitably left for the safety of the main stand, intending to return when order was restored. Unfortunately that state was never fully achieved and the party was over. It was all so disappointing, especially for Dale who was really looking forward to seeing the trophy close up. And he was right to be disappointed. The evening was ultimately spoiled by some kids who didn't know any better, some adults who should have known better – and a lot of pissed-up neds who just didn't give a damn.

But, no matter, it had been a wonderful day, to be forever known as Helicopter Sunday, in commemoration of the helicopter that suddenly changed direction and delivered the SPL trophy to Easter Road. The Celtic supporters for some reason prefer to call it Black Sunday – I can't imagine why!

The football year was over, and I looked ahead to the next. What would that bring? Alex McLeish didn't do normal seasons; it seemed to be all or nothing. Which way was the Rangers rollercoaster now heading?

Chapter 21:
Greeks, Goalies and an Outgoing Manager

Alex McLeish's fifth season in charge at Ibrox started in much the same manner as all the others – with the question of finance to the fore. The first team squad needed some fresh faces, but there was no money available.

One player who did arrive was the Marseille captain, Brahim Hemdani. Signed on a Bosman, there was no transfer fee, so no immediate impact on the balance sheet, a document just as important these days as the league table. Hemdani made his debut in a friendly against Ipswich Town, and in time-honoured fashion was crocked, an existing groin injury aggravated. The highly rated Algerian would be ruled out of action for three months and miss the next fourteen games. Another new signing; another long-term injury! Just why did this continually happen? Time to stick on another Smiths record!

Well, I'm afraid,
It doesn't make me smile,
I wish I could laugh,
But that joke isn't funny anymore.

Rangers' PR was no laughing matter either. For a number of years the club had been systematically attacked by certain individuals in the media. Perhaps I was becoming paranoid, but these attacks seemed to be organised, and on the increase. A classic example coming in an April 2002 edition of the Sunday Herald. Sanjeev Kohli, Scottish comedian, journalist, and Celtic fan, wrote a piece commenting on the absence of Asians in British professional football. Midway through the article he developed the theme onto racism in Scotland, and made a quite preposterous statement:

'Mark Walters arrived at Ibrox and was showered with exotic fruit by his own team's supporters.'

Not only was that just not true, it was a barefaced lie, and Sanjeev Kohli must have known that. He must have known that the barrage of fruit came at Parkhead, not Ibrox, and from a set of supporters much closer to his own heart. But why let the facts get in the way of a good story? Rangers should have stepped in and demanded a full retraction and apology. Regrettably they did neither, and a completely fabricated slur on the club was allowed to grow arms and legs.

In August 2005, David Murray finally took some action and issued a bold statement in which he condemned the anti-Rangers stories.

'From the beginning of the 2004/05 campaign until virtually the final kick we were constantly criticised in certain sections of the press and media on a variety of topics and a lot of it was very personal and, I believe unnecessary ... I know this is an issue which infuriates Rangers supporters and I have a suggestion for them today which I hope they will consider ...

the answer is simple. If you do not like what certain journalists are writing then stop buying their newspapers ... Yes, we can make a difference. Stop buying newspapers who, in your opinion, unjustly attack us and maybe the perpetrators will think twice. They know who they are.'

This was barnstorming stuff from the chairman, and a radical departure from his normally conservative attitude to the press. A sign, perhaps, that he'd finally acknowledged the problem, and was at last going to stand up and defend the football club – then I re-read the statement in its entirety, and one line jumped out.

'I also bore the brunt of critical attacks.'

Ah, was Mr Murray concerned about the long running snipes at the football club, or the more recent personal attacks on him? Was I being overly cynical in thinking it was more likely to be the latter?

Unfair or vindictive criticism was one thing, but sometimes Rangers just set itself up for ridicule. The transfer window of 2005 being just such an example, the machinations of this period just emphasised the current state of the club – shambolic!

Dragan Mladenovic had his contract abruptly torn up, he'd been with the club for just over a year, and managed only eight games. Compensated for his remaining three years, the Serbian left Ibrox a very wealthy man. His ex-employers were, in turn, a couple of million pounds out of pocket. Rangers short of money – I wonder why?

Michael Ball's tortured career at Ibrox also ended. He'd spent most of the previous season on the sidelines; injury free, but unavailable for selection because Rangers couldn't afford to trigger an extra £500k transfer payment to Everton. Incredibly, the full-back had been paid an absolute fortune – to not play football! Ball left to join PSV Eindhoven, primarily to get him off the wage bill.

Then there was the curious case of Filippio Maniero, a free transfer from Torino. Bespectacled, he was driven to Ibrox on transfer deadline day, looking more like a bewildered librarian than a top class striker. And that's probably because he wasn't a top class striker! Maniero had plied his trade with eleven different clubs over fifteen years, never staying for more than a year or two. His time at Ibrox was especially short, a mere ten weeks. He didn't play for the first team, he didn't claim a place on the substitutes bench. – in fact, he was very often not even in the country. Maniero left in November to join the mighty Nuova Piovese in one of Italy's lowly regional leagues. A player supposedly of Rangers quality had moved from the Scottish champions to the Italian equivalent of Glasgow Green football.

Back in the world of youth football, the transfer window was open as well, and saw both Graeme and I moving onto pastures new. We'd enjoyed our time at Livi Star, but felt that a change of club would benefit both of us, a case of re-charging the batteries, and taking on a fresh challenge. We joined a newly formed team, Uphall Diamonds – no transfer fee involved! It proved to be a seamless transition. The Diamonds were a friendly bunch, coached by Craig Morrice, a fellow Blue Nose, helped by his wife Gloria, an Ulster girl, who did the secretarial work – I felt at home right away!

Starting from scratch, the initial months were difficult. The team was trying to gel, whilst playing sides that had been established for four or five years. Wins were difficult to come by and when they did, they frustratingly didn't last for too long. To explain, Kirkliston were beaten on a Tuesday evening – the very next day they folded, and the three points we'd fought so hard for were taken away. A few weeks later, a ten-man Diamonds defeated Lothian Juniors 3–1, the next day they too folded, and once again the spoils were gone. It was almost as though the shame in losing to our team was too much to bear! As September drew to a close we'd played nine games and gathered just a single point. We were statistically the worst team in West Lothian.

Away from the football I had a pleasant and most unexpected surprise. Dale had shown himself to be a promising musician, learning to play both acoustic and, very loudly, rock guitar. He'd heard of a shop on Glasgow's Cathcart Road, Southside Music, which stocked good and reasonably priced guitars, and he wanted to take a look. It was my job to get him there, so off we went; the budding rock star excited, his dad resigned to the fact that this trip was almost certainly going to cost a lot more than just petrol money. I really could be an old skinflint at times! We found the shop, and Dale spent a happy hour or so, browsing and trying out the various instruments. Keeping out of the way, I chatted to the sales assistant, and then, out of the corner of my eye spotted a small poster pinned onto a notice board.

'The Zips – playing near you soon'

It couldn't be, could it? Was this the same band I'd known and loved all those years ago? Could they possibly have reformed? Could they?

With baited breath, I asked about the poster and was given the news that I desperately wanted to hear; yes, The Zips had indeed reformed, and not only that, they would be playing in Edinburgh very soon. It was a happy car that made its return to East Calder, Dale in the back seat contentedly strumming his brand new Yamaha Pacifica. Me up front, driving, trying to recall tunes that had lain dormant for a quarter of a century!

Regrettably, The Zips' gig clashed with a League Cup tie at Ibrox, but I'm afraid there was never any doubt where I was going to be that night. Wild horses couldn't have dragged me away from Whistlebinkies bar. Sharing a few beers, I had a nostalgic chat with the band, and then they took to the stage. Sure they were older than I remembered, waistlines just a little wider, hair speckled with grey, but they still thrashed out some wonderful stuff – the band could still cut it! I was transported, for a few hours anyway, back to the 1970s, and loved every second of it.

Four guys – three chords – two-minute buzz bombs – one hell of a night!

The football season wasn't going well, and the pressure was mounting on Alex McLeish. What he needed was a few good results, what he didn't need was a goalkeeping crisis … but that's just what he got. Rangers went to bottom of the table Livingston; they raced into a two-goal lead, but were soon pegged back. The Livi fight back helped in no small way by a quite appalling error from Ronald Waterreus. Ten days later, the keeper made another astonishing blunder to gift Artmedia Bratislava a Champions League goal.

McLeish had a dilemma. With a League Cup tie at Parkhead looming, what was he going to do about the goalkeeping situation? Waterreus was having a torrid time between the sticks and looked devoid of confidence. Waiting in the wings was Stephan Klos – he'd recovered from his injury, but was he ready to step back into the firing line? The manager pondered, and then announced that Klos would be his keeper.

Restoring Klos was without doubt a gamble as the German quite clearly wasn't match fit. How could he be? He hadn't played a game of football, of any sort, since July; over three months without facing a ball in anger. Normally players make their recuperation from injury with at least a few games in the reserves. Men like Ally McCoist, Paul Gascoigne and George Albertz had all done it in the past, so why hadn't Stephan Klos? One explanation doing the rounds was that he'd simply refused to play for the second XI, but that surely couldn't be true. The keeper wasn't deciding when and where he could play … was he?

Then again, perhaps he was. Alex McLeish made a statement in which he said, 'Klos felt he wouldn't get a lot out of reserve football.' I could only surmise that the goalkeeper was dictating the situation, and I for one couldn't understand it. Surely it would only be beneficial to take part in a few genuine games of football. Training every day was fine, but training sessions are structured, and by their nature predictable. Reserve games would have allowed Klos to at least hone his match concentration, always an important attribute for a keeper. Time, I suppose, would tell if 'Der Goalie' was ready.

Klos made his return against Aberdeen, and received a hero's welcome from an Ibrox crowd who were clearly one hundred percent behind their favourite. Encouragingly he kept a clean sheet, though in truth he had very little to do. Unfortunately neither did his opposite number and the game fizzled out as a 0–0 draw.

Parkhead followed, and was a night of abject misery for everyone associated with Rangers, particularly their keeper. In the twenty-sixth minute Shaun Maloney took a pot shot at goal. It was well hit, it was on target, it swerved – and would, in my opinion, have been meat and drink for a fully match-fit Stephan Klos. The ball hit the back of the net to give Celtic a 1–0 lead. With eight minutes remaining the keeper attempted to block a low Nakamura cross. He seemed, however, more concerned about a potential collision with Bobo Balde, and somehow managed to spill the ball into his own net. Celtic were 2–0 ahead, their place in the semi-final assured.

On a very poor evening, Rangers' plight was summed up by the actions of Soti Kyrgiakos. Yellow-carded in the first half, he was well aware that he was walking an Old Firm tightrope. The defender was then penalised for a second half foul – he disagreed with the decision – and in a childish act of petulance sarcastically applauded the referee. For rank stupidity he was shown a second yellow, and the follow up red. The Greek tragedy left the park laughing, still applauding the officials as he sauntered towards the tunnel. I'm so glad that someone in blue found it funny! The Daily Record summed up his actions perfectly; 'what a buffoon!'

First trophy of the season gone, languishing in fourth place, twelve points adrift of the leaders – it wasn't good. Speculation mounted that David Murray was searching for a replacement manager. The next couple of games would clearly be crucial, and the last place Rangers wanted to go was back to Parkhead, but that's where fate had placed them, with Alex McLeish having another goalkeeping quandary. Persist with Klos or restore Waterreus? He returned to the Dutchman and consequently had to face the wrath of an absolutely fuming Stephan Klos. The under pressure manager really needed a good performance from his team, and his goalkeeper. His team lost 3–0, and Waterreus blundered, allowing a tame Aiden McGeady shot to slither into the net.

Defeat at Easter Road. Winless for eight games, this was now statistically the worst Rangers team in history, and didn't the press just love informing us of that fact! Just to reinforce that unwelcome tag, the men in blue went to Falkirk and chucked away a two-goal lead. The run of failure now stretched to nine. How times change, I could remember when we'd celebrated nine-in-a-row!

Murray announced that he would stand by Alex McLeish, but everyone knew it was only until he could find a replacement. Fuel was then thrown onto the managerial fire when it was revealed that a man by the name of Le Guen was in talks with the club. No-one at Ibrox would comment on the speculation, but it was certainly no secret. So, where did this leave McLeish? It was hard, in all honesty, not to conclude that he was a dead man walking.

Domestically abysmal, Rangers then took to the European stage and showing some rare spirit and commitment, battled back from a goal down to claim a 1–1 draw against an admittedly under-strength Inter Milan. It meant that the worst Rangers team in history had progressed to the last sixteen of the Champions league. With the football club now on a temporary high, the Chairman emerged at his bombastic best and regaled the press with some truly outrageous statements.

'Alex [McLeish] is now in a safer position than ninety percent of the managers in British football … We are probably one of the best fiscally run clubs in British football.'

This was an Alex McLeish who was virtually on his final written warning. Every man and his dog knew that McLeish was finished; it was simply a matter of time. And as for Rangers being one of the best fiscally run clubs in British football. Words failed me! You know, there were times you just had to admire the gall of the chairman!

Beware of Greeks bearing gifts, a well-known expression that doesn't seem to apply down Dunfermline-way. Rangers went to East End Park on Boxing Day and were leading 3–2 going into injury time. I was listening on the radio at home, praying that my team could hold on and collect an important three points. Having beaten Hearts the week before, this was an opportunity to put pressure on the Edinburgh side in the race for a Champions League slot. Dunfermline won a last gasp corner and rushed to take it, but were stopped in their tracks by a referee who intervened to warn Soti Kyrgiakos about his quite blatant holding and jersey pulling. Play then restarted, with the radio commentator somewhat incredulously describing the action.

'He's still doing it … just look at him … he's still doing it … he's going to give away a penalty!'

Kyrgiakos clasped a fist full of Andy Tod's jersey, and tugged. The referee, watching closely gave one shrill blast of his whistle and awarded an entirely predictable penalty kick. The game ended 3–3. Kyrgiakos, in my opinion, should have been shown the departure door after that fiasco. The man was a car crash of a defender, a total liability! The result left Rangers fifth, a depressing seventeen points behind Celtic, and a financially catastrophic thirteen behind Hearts.

The West Lothian youth football season continued apace, with Uphall Diamonds still searching for their first official victory. It's not as though the team was playing particularly badly, they just needed a little bit of luck to turn a string of defeats into a victory or two. January brought a game against Dykes FC. Two goals down with only ten minutes to play, it depressingly looked like more of the same, especially when the visitors broke free. A high and looping shot beat the keeper, hit the underside of the bar, bounced down onto the goal line, and back into play. This was the spot of good fortune that the Diamonds had been looking for. They countered, and in a sweeping move scored on the break. It could have been 3–0 and game over; instead it was 2–1 and game most definitely on! In a tremendous grand finale the home team scored again, and again: Uphall Diamonds 3, Dykes FC 2.

We had reached the turning point, and with confidence boosted the next four games were all won, including a memorable 2–0 triumph over runaway league leaders Blackburn United. Unfortunately there was no turning point for the Rangers, they just continued down the road of doom, gloom and despondency.

Hibs came to Ibrox on Scottish Cup business, and comprehensively won by three goals to nil. A week later, the season was truly in tatters. The men in blue went to Aberdeen and lost yet again. I listened to most of the game on the radio, but switched off with a few minutes to go when a chant of 'Easy! Easy!' bellowed from the Beech end. The Aberdeen fans were enjoying their moment of glory – I wasn't. The two-goal defeat at Pittodrie was the final straw and it was announced that Alex McLeish would be leaving at the end of the season. The man with virtually the safest job in British football was about to lose it! There was no official news on his replacement, but a few days later the Daily Record revealed that Paul Le Guen's wife was house hunting in the west of Scotland. In this case it was safe to say that deux plus deux most definitely equalled quatre.

The last game of the season brought a win over Hearts. A good three points, but not good enough to bring Champions League football to Ibrox, Hearts had finished second, piping their more illustrious Glasgow rivals by a single point. Let's not dwell on that crazy penalty given away in December. Financial ramifications would undoubtedly follow.

The Hearts game was Alex McLeish's last as manager. Not fully accepted when he arrived, there were those who never really took to him, and those who were pleased to see the back of him. But, on that final day, Ibrox rose and gave big 'Eck a rousing send-off. There was genuine affection and respect for a man who in his tenure had given us some truly memorable moments; the last minute Lovenkrands Scottish Cup final, the Dunfermline shootout league decider, and of course that never to be forgotten Helicopter Sunday.

There is a minority view that Alex McLeish's time at Ibrox was an overall failure. To those who subscribe to that theory, I would say that Dick Advocaat shopped at Harrods, spent millions, and delivered five trophies. Alex McLeish shopped at Poundstretchers, spent buttons, and delivered seven trophies. The big man had done okay in my book!

Chapter 22:
There May Be Trouble Ahead

Paul Le Guen arrived at Ibrox and made it quite clear that he expected his players to meet a certain standard. Discipline and physical fitness were his bywords; double training sessions would be the order of the day.

In July, the squad prepared to jet out to South Africa for a pre-season training camp. Rangers left Glasgow with twenty players – alas, only nineteen made it to the African continent. There had been an altercation on the outbound flight; someone guilty of unacceptable behaviour, and no guesses needed as to the culprit! It was of course Fernando Ricksen. Le Guen's disciplinary code kicked in and the wayward Dutchman was despatched post-haste back to the UK. The manager made no comment on Ricksen's indiscretions, other than to state that 'the players simply have to apply the rules that are laid down and there will be no problem … his conduct was a disgrace.'

The league season started well with some breathtaking football and a sparkling win over Motherwell at Fir Park. The only criticism that could be levelled was that a barrel load of chances had been missed. It wasn't a huge problem though;

the return of the suspended Kris Boyd and the imminent signing of Filip Šebo would undoubtedly sort that out.

Rangers' next game was played at a red, white and blue bedecked Ibrox. Behind each goal a card display majestically portrayed the Scottish saltire and French tricolour. With fraternité in the air, Paul Le Guen was enthusiastically welcomed to his new home. Viva la revolution – Allez les Bleus! So far so good, then the game started. Dundee United galloped into a two-goal lead, their forwards ruthlessly exploiting the defensive frailty of Karl Svensson. The new centre half looked hopelessly out of his depth and seemed worryingly fearful of the high ball. Not a good phobia for a defender to suffer from, particularly in Scotland, where 'route one' is very often plans A, B and C. The men in blue fought back to claim a point, but once again a cornucopia of chances had been squandered. If we were pinning our hopes on Filip Šebo being a goalscoring saviour, then we were to be sadly disappointed. The Slovakian came on as a second half substitute and promptly tripped over the ball. Graeme turned to me, shook his head, and showing wisdom far beyond his years said, 'Dad, he's a dud,' and Graeme was sadly correct. Šebo was, without question, a £1.8m dud!

These were exciting times at Ibrox, the fans were one hundred percent behind the new manager, but vocally they were just a little subdued. Something was missing – and that something was 'the Billy Boys.' For the first time in living memory the rousing anthem hadn't been aired. It wasn't through choice I hasten to add, the song had been placed on a blacklist; a favourite ditty for decades had been banned by the Rangers hierarchy. Other songs were under close scrutiny. What on earth was going on?

It all stemmed from the previous season's Champions League, and the ramifications of a game against Villareal. The Rangers fans had been charged with, and found guilty of, what UEFA euphemistically called 'discriminatory chanting'.

In this case the inference was that the chanting had been sectarian in nature. This was a serious matter, UEFA were determined to stamp out what they saw as offensive behaviour in football grounds – well, as serious as they could be without actually investigating the blatant racism that was commonplace in Italy and Spain. Football clubs such as Juventus and Real Madrid were far too big to be tackled, Rangers, on the other hand were just the right size to be used as an example.

The Ibrox club were fined £13,000 and warned as to their future conduct. A worrying development, as further indiscretions could involve sanctions such as ground closure and expulsion from UEFA competitions. The Rangers board felt they had to take action, and because 'The Billy Boys' had been specifically highlighted in the UEFA report, it was banned forthwith. It pains me to say this ... but the Rangers support, to a large degree, was its own worst enemy. They had been warned for years over the content of their songbook and done little to rectify the situation. This was, I'm afraid, the inevitable consequence of a head in the sand attitude – no one likes us, we don't care.

Perhaps we should have cared; perhaps we should have taken note of the growing campaign being mounted against the club. Virtually all the damming evidence supplied to UEFA came from inside Scotland, certain elements in our little country had seized the opportunity to stick the boot into Rangers, and, it has to be said, done their job extremely well. But it had been oh so preventable. The harsh facts are that Celtic, their support, and their friends in the media had long recognised the advantages of good, and aggressive PR. Rangers, and their support, quite spectacularly hadn't.

Rangers were in the process of rebuilding, and so were Uphall Diamonds. Last season's squad of sixteen had been boosted by eight trialists, making a total of twenty-four players – far too many to realistically run with. We would have to make a cut. This is always one of the harder parts of youth football, no matter how you try to pad it out, or waffle. The message essentially is ... sorry, but you're not good enough. We'd made the situation quite clear in the preceding months, so everyone was well aware that this moment was coming. Everyone had a chance to prove their worth, to stake their claim for a place in the final sixteen.

On D-day we took the unlucky players to one side and let them know, as sympathetically as possible, that they wouldn't be required. In doing so we offered to help them find a new club, a club better suited to their ability. What more could we do? Most of the boys took it philosophically, their parents understanding. Not all though – on hearing the news, one boy's father came storming over and let rip.

'You're all a bunch of fucking arseholes,' he yelled

'You don't have a clue about football,' he continued

'You can stick your team up your fucking arse!' was his final retort.

Charming!

Ironically, the irate father had rarely, if ever, come to see his boy train or play, and was in no position to pass judgement on our decision. As I said, it's one of the less pleasant aspects of the youth game, but one that every team inevitably has to go through at some stage or another. Thankfully the decisions we'd made were vindicated. The league campaign started, and win followed win. The Diamonds were playing well, and already contenders for promotion.

I may have been watching a team winning on a Saturday morning, but regrettably, Saturday afternoons weren't going too well. Rangers went to East End Park, to play bottom of the table Dunfermline, and dropped points in a 1–1 draw. Kris Boyd, sitting on the substitutes' bench, was clearly frustrated at the lack of firepower on display; he'd scored seventeen goals from fifteen league starts the previous season and saw himself as the solution to the goal drought, and he wasn't backwards in coming forward, 'Let me play and we will start winning!' Le Guen immediately hit back, and told Boyd to do his talking on the park, 'I expect my players to want to play. But anyone can speak. It is important that the best answer is on the pitch.

European football was so important to the finances of the club. Chief executive Martin Bain put it quite succinctly; to compensate financially for this season's lack of Champions League football, Paul Le Guen will have to take his team all the way to the UEFA cup final. I have to say, that made me smile. Rangers in a UEFA final? How likely was that!

Europe progress was made, thanks mainly to some wonderful goalkeeping by Alan McGregor who was replacing the injured Lionel Letizi. September had in fact been a particularly fruitful month for the young Scot, culminating in an award as SPL player of the month. With five clean sheets and a string of man of the match performances, McGregor was entitled to be pleased, and feel confident of retaining the #1 jersey. After all, hadn't Le Guen said, 'It is important that the best answer is on the pitch.'

With Letizi now nearing full fitness, the question of goalkeeping was on everyone's lips. Would Le Guen stand by his eminently sensible words and back the man on form; the man who'd done his talking on the pitch?

The answer to that question was no. Rangers met Inverness with Alan McGregor dropped to the substitutes' bench and Letizi back between the sticks. It wasn't a popular decision, particularly in the seventy-fifth minute when a low and eminently saveable shot was spilled by Letizi into the path of Graham Bayne who gleefully thumped the rebound into the back of the Rangers net. The returning keeper had been asked to make one save, and he'd failed miserably.

To say the natives were restless would be a gross understatement. Letizi's next touch was jeered, he was booed, and a chant for Alan McGregor reverberated around the ground. It wasn't an action I particularly approved of, as it was most unlikely to improve the situation. The keeper needed support, not derision, but deep inside I was as livid as the next man. The match ended with Inverness victorious by one fumble to nil.

Rumours of splits and feuds in the dressing room abounded, Boyd and McGregor were clearly unhappy, Barry Ferguson was reported to be at loggerheads with his boss – what Le Guen needed was some success on the park, something to silence his critics and reassure an increasingly concerned support. A League Cup quarter final at home to first division opponents looked as good a place as any to start, it didn't work out that way: Rangers 0, St Johnstone 2.

Results such as this are normally classed as a giant killing or a cup shock. Well, this was without doubt giant killing, but it was far from a shock. Not to me, nor I suspect to thousands of other fans. We could see it coming a mile away. Rangers were a team devoid of spirit; they were lacklustre and uninspired. The only surprise on the night was that the defeat wasn't heavier – and let's not kid ourselves here, the final score could easily have been three, or four, or more. We had been well and truly humped.

Three points were won at Dunfermline – Kris Boyd scored and Alan McGregor, replacing an injured Letizi, kept a clean sheet. Paul Le Guen, a stubborn man, finally conceded that McGregor was now the first choice keeper. On Boyd, however, he was not so yielding. When asked about the striker, he remained silent and walked out of the post-match press conference! And then there was the simmering situation with Barry Ferguson, a growing conflict that would eventually lead to the downfall of Monsieur Le Guen.

The press had picked up on the tension between player and manager, and probed for an angle. Le Guen was mischievously asked at a press conference for his opinion on the role of the team captain in modern football. Given the example of John Greig in the past, did Barry Ferguson carry out his duties in a similar way? The manager pondered, took the bait, and stated that he didn't believe that the football captain was as important as some people thought. It was pretty innocuous stuff, but he then added.

'We had a chat about that and Barry knows my way of thinking'.

Barry, it transpired, didn't know his way of thinking. In fact he vehemently disagreed with that statement, but held his council for a few weeks. Then, on the eve of December's Old Firm game, seemingly for maximum effect, he let rip. In front of the national press he rounded on Le Guen and very publically dismissed his thoughts on the club captain's role. When asked about his apparent discussion with Le Guen, Ferguson retorted:

'He didn't say anything to me!'

Barry Ferguson had, dramatically, thrown a hand grenade into the mix. He'd effectively called his manager a liar! This was no longer a general disagreement about the role of the team captain, this was a very public rebellion. The gauntlet had well and truly been thrown down.

Saturday 30th December was the day that my eyes were opened to the scale of the problems down Ibrox way. Watching the game against St Mirren, I became puzzled by a seemingly recurring theme, Barry Ferguson would receive the ball; he'd look up, see wide runs by Sasa Papac and Libor Sionko; then turn away and quite deliberately pass the ball in the other direction. Time after time this happened. Thinking it was my imagination; I nudged Graeme and asked him to watch out. Sure enough Graeme spotted it as well. Ferguson was consistently passing in one direction ... away from Le Guen's men! That's the kind of thing that occurs in a primary school playground – I'm not passing to you because you're not in my gang, it really shouldn't be happening at a professional football club! Something was very badly wrong!

Almost as worrying was the reaction of the fans at the end of the game. Normally a result such as this, a disappointing 1–1 draw, would have been met with disapproval, possibly a jeer or two. Today, the crowd meekly got up and left. There was resignation in the air; the passion, the excitement, the optimism ... it had all gone. No one seemed to care. It was sad, so sad – still it would soon be Hogmanay, a few drinks would signal the New Year and hopefully ring in a change of fortune.

On Tuesday 2nd January 2007, I strolled down to the local shop for a newspaper and was met by banner headlines proclaiming a crisis at Ibrox.

'A seething Barry Ferguson stormed out of Murray Park yesterday, refusing to take part in training after manager Paul Le Guen told him he was dropped for today's trip to Motherwell. The Daily Record understands that Le Guen took the drastic action because Ferguson refused to follow his tactical orders during the second half of Rangers 1–1 draw with St Mirren.'

I rushed home and had the news, along with other lurid details confirmed by the sports reports on both Radio Clyde and Scotland. I desperately wanted to be at Fir Park, but the previous evenings drinking, plus a can of beer for breakfast precluded that. So I had to stick to the radio broadcasts. The news got progressively worse; Ferguson had been stripped of the captaincy. Gavin Rae, a man who had only started three games all season, was now club captain! I didn't know whether to laugh or cry! What was going on?

Listening to the match commentary it quickly became clear that by far the majority of the travelling support were vocally backing the ex-captain over the manager – as were at least some of the players. When Kris Boyd scored the only goal of the game, he ran to the away fans and held up six fingers. It was an open show of defiance, quite blatantly displaying his solidarity with the deposed #6. This was civil war! Crisis talks were urgently required.

Le Guen met with David Murray and accused Ferguson of undermining him; the player had far too much influence. Le Guen told Murray that he was struggling to cope with the mentality and drinking habits of Scottish players. Ferguson, he said, had to be transfer listed.

It wasn't a one-way discussion though. Le Guen had previously told the press that Murray had been kept informed of the ongoing crisis, but apparently the Chairman had been blissfully unaware, enjoying a winter break in the South of France. Murray was furious that he hadn't been consulted. It was a mess, and a few days later it was all over. Paul Le Guen left – by mutual consent, though it was hard not to conclude the Frenchman had been persuaded to leave.

It was, in all honesty, the correct and only decision that could have been made. Le Guen had clearly lost the dressing room; he'd lost the support and the trust of the chairman. There was no way back. Speaking personally though, I feel that David Murray stopped too soon in his disciplinary actions. He should have called the ex-captain to his office and shown him the door as well. Good player or not, Ferguson was equally culpable for the shambles that had engulfed the club. Ferguson may or may not have liked Le Guen. He may or may not have agreed with the tactics employed. But in any line of work, the boss is the boss and his instructions have to be followed. If they aren't then the whole structure of the organisation will fall apart – I give you Rangers circa 2006!

The appointment of Le Guen had been a bold and imaginative move, and given time and different circumstances it might have worked. He may have taken the club onto a new plateau. But it hadn't worked. However, in one of his final interviews, Le Guen showed, if nothing else, he had learned just a little. He uttered words that Barry Ferguson would do well to reflect upon.

'Rangers are more important than Paul Le Guen, even than Barry Ferguson. Rangers will be there after me, but after Barry Ferguson too!'

Rangers were in total and utter disarray and needed a firm hand on the tiller, someone who could steady the ship and guide it back on course. There was really only one man for the job; the supporters knew it, the media knew it, and David Murray certainly knew it. Taking decisive action, the chairman got on the telephone, called Walter Smith, and asked the current Scotland boss if he would come home. Walter had no qualms and he returned, bringing his assistant Ally McCoist. If anyone could sort out the mess, it was this pair.

On Saturday 21st January 2007 I received a phone call that put all minor football inconveniencies completely into context. Gloria, the Uphall Diamonds match secretary, broke the news that one of our players, Reece Anderson, had been killed in a road accident. It was one of those *what can you say* moments, I was stunned. One minute he was a full of life fourteen year old, enjoying himself, his whole future in front of him, and the next he was gone, snatched away. Life just isn't fair sometimes.

Our game that weekend was cancelled as players, coaches and friends tried to come to terms with the tragic events. A week or so later we all gathered in a Broxburn church to pay our respects. The average age of the congregation that morning was little more than sixteen or seventeen years of age, something that just reinforced the tragedy. Whilst solemn, it was also a colourful occasion, with the majority of the teenagers present sporting bright and cheerful clothes. Football colours were also worn, with the green and white of Hibernian FC very prominent, all in tribute to Reece who was a dedicated Hibee. As his coffin was slowly carried into the church, a haunting tune broke the silence. It was a song familiar to all football fans.

When you walk through the storm,
Hold your head up high,
And don't be afraid of the dark.
Walk on, walk on, with hope in your heart,
And you'll never walk alone,
You'll never walk alone.

You would have a heart of stone, not to have shed a tear at that moment, and I don't have a heart of stone.

The following Saturday, Uphall Diamonds returned to the football field and played Whitburn in the first round of the League Cup. At kick-off both teams linked arms for a very poignant minute's silence – then got down to business. A charged-up Diamonds won by seven goals to one, every player fully committed and determined to give one hundred percent for Reece. This competition, a trophy for second division sides, then hit the top of our priority list. We desperately wanted to win it for our friend.

Back at Ibrox, Rangers were ticking over quite nicely; Walter Smith had picked up sixteen league points from a possible eighteen, and guided his team into the next round of the UEFA cup. The aftershock of the Le Guen era still rumbled on though, with some damaging stories filtering through, one example being a comment from Bernard Lacombe. He'd been the director of football at Lyon, when Le

Guen was winning league titles at the club, as reported in The Mirror:

'I think it was difficult for Paul to accept certain things that went on at Rangers ... players would turn up for training in the mornings in states that are inconceivable for professional footballers to be in ... I think the time came when he felt these excesses had become intolerable.'

He was of course alluding to alcohol abuse. A heavy drinking culture had been well established in Scottish football for many decades, one just had to recall the demise of the late great Jim Baxter to appreciate that. What I didn't realise, though, was the depths to which alcohol had filtered into the game, into Scottish culture – I was soon to find out!

Uphall Diamonds were by now in the League Cup semi-final, playing BFC Linlithgow away from home. Top of the table Uphall verses third-placed BFC. This was a tough game, but winnable if everyone was focused and well prepared. At our final training session the players were sent away with a request that they get an early night, and keep fresh for this vitally important cup-tie.

The game was as tough and competitive as we'd expected, no quarter asked and none given. Midway through the first half we had to make a change, as one of our players was looking a little jaded. On leaving the park, the substituted player spurned his tracksuit, shot past the assembled spectators and made a beeline for the nearby bushes. He then lurched forward and was violently sick. We were obviously concerned about the boy's welfare, but our fears were quickly allayed by his mother who laughed and announced:

'I'm surprised he lasted as long as he did. He was pished out his head last night!'

I was flabbergasted, on two counts. What on earth was the boy thinking, getting drunk the night before a big game? A semi-final for heaven's sake! But more seriously, was the mother happy that her son, fourteen years of age, was routinely getting 'pished out of his head'? I'm guessing here that it wasn't an unusual occurrence. Teenage drinking wasn't of course a new phenomenon; I'd started on Carlsberg Special Brew at fifteen years of age back in the 1970s, so why was I being so sanctimonious? The difference then was, we didn't get steaming drunk, and we hid ourselves away when indulging. We certainly didn't, or at least tried not to let our parents know what we were up to. My mother would have murdered me if she'd known! Today, younger and younger kids seemed to be drinking, and quite openly. Changed days!

Meanwhile back on the park, the rest of the Diamonds were fully fit and on top form. The game was won by a couple of goals to nil – we were in the final! Rangers, on the other hand, would not be competing for silverware. The last chance of a trophy disappeared with a UEFA Cup defeat to Osasuna. This was Rangers first trip to Spain, since that eventful night in Villarreal, and was unfortunately marred by off-the-park problems.

There had been some trouble inside the ground, and most of it perpetuated by a Spanish police force grimly intent on beating the vocal Rangers support into a pulp. I wasn't there, but from eyewitness accounts it appears that the overall organisation of the game was a shambles, the stewarding chaotic, and the policing barbaric. The fans inevitably came under heavy post-match criticism, getting tarred, I'm afraid, with the same old brush; drunken louts, blah, blah, blah. But was the blame solely with the travelling fans? A few weeks later Tottenham Hotspur played in Spain, and had a not dissimilar experience. As reported in The Independent:

'Tottenham yesterday accused the Spanish police of hitting a disabled fan and knocking him out of his wheelchair during Thursday night's chaotic UEFA Cup quarter-final here which erupted in violence.'

Later in the year Aberdeen had the misfortune to be drawn against a Spanish club. The Daily Record posted a similarly depressing report:

'Brutal Madrid riot cops were branded 'animals' last night after they went berserk and laid into innocent Aberdeen fans with their batons ... The club's security chief, former policeman John Morgan, witnessed the mayhem. It was disgusting and horrific. I saw a child of about ten being hit with a baton and women were also struck.'

Heavens above, even the self-styled 'greatest fans in the world' suffered at the hands of an extremely volatile Spanish police force. From the Irish Independent in 2003:

'An independent study found police guilty of 'gratuitous and unprovoked assault' ... A number of Celtic fans were pictured with blood streaming from head wounds after being attacked ... fans claimed a wheelchair-bound Celtic fan was attacked by Spanish riot police.'

The common denominator here was an overreaction from the Spanish police. They seemed unable, or unwilling, to deal sensibly with a boisterous travelling support. Everyone was fair game for their batons, including women, children and the disabled.

Regrettably, that wasn't the end of the Osasuna troubles, Rangers managed to become embroiled in yet another charge of 'discriminatory chanting'. And once again we were the architect of our own downfall. With little evidence to go on, UEFA were struggling to justify a charge ... then some idiot posted his souvenir video on YouTube. The clip showed him, and a section of the travelling support being rather unpleasant to a man from Rome. Within hours UEFA were bombarded with video clips, accompanied by helpful lyric sheets, all sent from outraged and offended computers in the west of Scotland. A Celtic support clued up on good PR had taken advantage of an outstandingly stupid own goal. Rangers were fined £8,000 and given another warning as to their future conduct.

A catastrophic season drew to a close on a semi-positive note with Rangers winning the final Old Firm game 2–0. The win at Ibrox was most welcome, even though the result was completely immaterial. The league title had of course long gone. Curiously the best moment and biggest cheer of the day was not for any of the goals, nor the sound of the final whistle, but for a common or garden substitution. Goalscorer Kris Boyd was replaced by Filip Šebo. Now, Šebo was a terrible player; we knew it, they knew it, everyone knew it. When the Slovakian came running onto the pitch, Ibrox rocked to a spontaneous and deliciously mocking chant.

'Šebo's on, we're taking the piss! Šebo's on, we're taking the piss!'

May brought the climax of the West Lothian youth football season, and an exciting time for Uphall Diamonds. We had two games left to play, both against Armadale, and both with trophies at stake. First up was the League Cup final, and then a Second Division title decider. The cup final was to be played at Volunteer Park, home of Armadale Thistle Juniors. So, hardly a neutral venue, but no matter; it was eleven verses eleven on a big patch of grass – may the best team win! What followed was one of the most epic games I'd ever seen, let alone been involved in.

We sent our players out with a message to relax, enjoy the game, get a few touches and keep it tight for the first five or ten minutes. Armadale kicked off, charged upfield, and fired a cross into the penalty box. Their centre-forward met the ball and volleyed it into the roof of our net. Great goal, it has to be said, though that's not exactly how I described it at the time! Ten seconds gone, 1–0 down, and game plan out the window! Undaunted, the Diamonds responded and scored three times to take a well deserved half time lead.

Play swung from one end to the other in a pulsating second period. Armadale pulled a goal back, the Diamonds scored again to restore their two-goal advantage, but almost immediately lost another. Going into the final minute, the game was finely, and nerve-wrackingly, balanced at 4–3. Armadale mounted a last gasp attack and won a free kick. Everyone pushed forward. A cross-ball was swung into a crowded six-yard box and bulleted home for a dramatic equaliser. For fuck's sake!

Utter despair; 4–4, extra time was looming with Armadale undoubtedly favourites. Then we saw the linesman's raised flag – we'd been reprieved, the goal disallowed for offside. Now in injury time, all the Diamonds had to do was clear their lines and the game would surely be over. Unfortunately possession was nervously and carelessly given away, Armadale charged forward, it was now or never for them. A pass was threaded into the penalty box, and a forward needlessly brought down, penalty awarded. For fuck's sake!

The Armadale dugout was naturally whooping it up. A few yards away, we watched in abject misery. The penalty was taken and saved, yet another escape. Our turn to celebrate, and how the Diamonds bench danced in delight. That delight was but momentary; the referee's whistle sounded, and to our horror, he pointed back to the penalty spot, indicating that encroachment had occurred. The kick was to be retaken. For fuck's sake!

With the Armadale side roaring their approval, I lost it, and angrily swung out a kick. Aimed at nothing in particular I managed to blooter the trackside wall, dislodging a brick completely from it. Whether that says more about the extent of my frustration, or the standard of the original brickie's workmanship, I don't know. All I do know is that there was an agonising crack as my big toe snapped. Hopping about in pain and anguish, I watched as the penalty was retaken, and unbelievably driven past the post.

Joy! Then unconfined joy as the final whistle sounded. Pandemonium ensued as the Diamonds' big support spilled onto the park to acclaim their heroes. Pleasingly, one of those spectators was Reece Anderson's mother, who was there to see the trophy lifted, the win dedicated to her son and our teammate.

If nothing else, that cup final gave me a little appreciation of the pressure that managers and coaches come under. If I was going mental at an Under 15s game, and I most certainly was, what must it be like for someone whose job and livelihood depends on the result of a game of football?

A long and hard football year drew to a close, with another game between Uphall and Armadale, a game that would decide the destination of the second division championship.

The Diamonds had gone top of the table on the opening day of the season with a victory over Mid Calder, and stayed in pole position for ten long months. They were still leading the way, until the final ten minutes of that very final game. At that moment, Armadale scored to take a 3–2 lead and claim the top slot. A fourth goal in stoppage time was purely academic and just sealed the deal – it was all over, Armadale had snatched the championship. To be honest we could have no complaints, the league table at the end of the day doesn't lie. Congratulations to them.

Looking back, a trophy had been won, and promotion to the first division was achieved. It hadn't been too bad a year for a team who eighteen months earlier had been the worst in West Lothian!

Chapter 23:
Mr. Smith Goes To Manchester

Walter Smith was now in charge for his first full season (part two). Seven straight wins followed by a 0–0 draw was a good start, and the goalless draw was hardly a failure, achieved, as it was in Belgrade against Crvena Zvezda (better known as Red Star to us old codgers), and meant entry into a Champions League group containing Barcelona, Lyon and Stuttgart. Exciting stuff!

Uphall Diamonds were also in with the 'big boys', now playing in the West Lothian Under 16s First Division. This was a big step up in class, with every game a real challenge, a team used to winning most weeks now had to graft for every single point. The local youth football scene was refreshing compared to the professionalism and cynicism of the SPL; it was football in its purest form. Teams were sent out to play, by and large, good attacking football. The players got on with the game, no diving, no simulation, and no feigning injury. Fair play was genuinely the watchword – though there was the odd exception to that rule.

In September we played a Scottish cup tie against a team from Central Region, I don't really want to name them in case I get into bother with the SYFA or West Lothian disciplinary beaks, but let's just say that they came from the same town that spawned the Cocteau Twins – a pretty decent clue for those of an Indie music persuasion. The match was delicately poised at 1–1, when it unexpectedly exploded into mayhem. A Diamonds player was rather cynically scythed down, a clear yellow card which quickly became red when the perpetrator of the foul argued fervently with the referee. Despatched from the field of play, he was serenaded by a chorus of 'cheerio, cheerio' from the home support, not it has to be said a particularly sporting, or in hindsight, clever thing to do. The opposition touchline took great umbrage at this ironic chant, and one of them bellowed over to the red-carded player,

'Are you going to take that?'

The player stopped, pondered for a millisecond and then turned. With his face contorted in rage, he stomped back across the park, heading directly for our technical area ... and he wasn't coming for an amicable chat! Sensing the impending confrontation, I bravely positioned myself as a buffer between our substitutes and their enraged player.

'Calm down son!' I told him.

Wise words that were sadly ignored. Denied of his primary target, the player chose his next best option and smacked me in the face! All Hell broke loose! The substitutes stepped in to protect their beleaguered coach, and the attacker was repelled. The opposition charged across the field to defend their man, and a mini brawl erupted in the centre circle! Fortunately it was over almost as quickly as it had started, helped in no small way by the father of one of our players. He used to run with the Rangers ICF, and used his experience in such matters to deter any of the adults on the other touchline from becoming too actively involved!

But, let's make it clear, other than this one isolated incident; youth football in West Lothian was a delight.

Rangers performed well in the Champions League but failed to qualify from their group. Third spot did mean continued European football though, with a slot in the UEFA Cup, and for a Scottish club, that's pretty much success.

The festive period brought tragedy to Scottish football when Phil O'Donnell, Motherwell's captain, collapsed during a game against Dundee United. The player was given instant medical help, but sadly failed to regain consciousness and died shortly afterwards. The cause of death diagnosed as heart failure. It was a huge shock to everyone in the football community, and served as a stark reminder of the fragility of life. My dad had died of a similar ailment at forty-four years of age. O'Donnell was even younger, a fit and seemingly healthy man of thirty-five. A message perhaps that we should all enjoy life to the full while we can. None of us, after all, know what lies round the corner.

Motherwell's next few games were cancelled, Fir Park becoming a shrine of floral tributes. A minute's silence was arranged for the remaining New Year SPL fixtures, which were all scheduled to go ahead as normal, but that soon changed when Celtic asked for their game to be cancelled, their opponents that day being Rangers. O'Donnell had of course been with Celtic for a couple of years. Did the postponement benefit a Celtic team who had won only three of their last eight games? Let's just say possibly, and leave it at that!

Normal service was resumed in the SPL when Artur Boruc, Celtic's increasingly eccentric goalkeeper, hit the headlines complaining bitterly about decisions going against his team. He whined – *there is one rule for everyone else and different treatment for us*. A Celtic player complaining about refereeing decisions, you'd almost think that they were trailing in the league race – oh, wait a minute, they were!

Ironically, were it not for favourable refereeing decisions the Parkhead men would have been even further adrift. Since the turn of the year Celtic had been given the benefit of a string of questionable calls. I'd hate to be accused of paranoia, but…

Sunday 27ᵗʰ January 2008: Falkirk 0 Celtic 1.

'The home supporters left aggrieved at the performance of referee John Underhill, who denied Falkirk two reasonable penalty claims and approved a winner that had a hint of offside.' (*The Herald*)

Sunday 24ᵗʰ February 2008: St Mirren 0 Celtic 1.

Celtic scored from a very late free kick, given when Nakamura mysteriously tumbled over. 'The sense of injustice felt by Gus MacPherson's men was intensified by the highly contentious nature of the free kick awarded by referee Eddie Smith.' (*The Scotsman*)

Wednesday 16ᵗʰ April 2008: Celtic 2 Rangers 1.

With less than thirty seconds gone, Celtic's Barry Robson viciously swung his elbow into Christian Daily's face. In any other game, at any other time, Robson would have been instantly red-carded, incredibly he wasn't even booked. Referee Kenny Clark just didn't have the courage to reduce the home side to ten men.

Saturday 19ᵗʰ April 2008: Celtic 1 Aberdeen 0.

'Referee Iain Brines today admitted he wrongly disallowed the goal which could have ended Celtic's title challenge.' (*Evening Times*)

Sunday 27ᵗʰ April 2008: Celtic 3 Rangers 2.

'They [Rangers] had already fallen behind to an early Scott McDonald strike which should not have stood … the stadium waited for the offside flag from assistant Tommy Murphy.' (*Evening Times*)

Saturday 3rd May 2008: Motherwell 1 Celtic 2.

'How did the referee do? Steve Conroy had a bit of a stinker. His poor decision led to Celtic's winning goal.' (*Evening Times*)

Six games with crucial and controversial decisions that all went in Celtic's favour, and all of them won by the narrowest of margins. Who knows how those games would have panned out had the decisions been different. Celtic may have won them all regardless, but the fact remains that a potential twelve points had been gifted to the Parkhead club by officialdom, by referees who supposedly favoured the other Glasgow team.

I wasn't, of course, becoming paranoid. I knew very well that decisions, both good and bad, balance themselves out over a period of time. Celtic had simply plundered a rich vein of good fortune. To be fair, Rangers had also benefitted from some dodgy calls, an example being their victory over Dundee United at Ibrox. The visitors were denied a cast-iron penalty and had a perfectly good goal disallowed. United thoroughly deserved to win that day, but lost 3–1. That's football for you!

Rangers were battling on all fronts. The League Cup had been won, the Scottish Cup was still up for grabs, and the SPL title race going to the wire – a domestic treble was on. But more than that, European glory also beckoned. Parachuted into the UEFA cup, Panathinaikos, Werden Bremen and Sporting Lisbon had all been overcome. Dogged defending, coupled with a smash and grab attack had taken the Ibrox men to the giddy heights of a European semi, only Fiorentina stood in the way of the UEFA cup final.

The first leg was at Ibrox and ended 0–0. The return game, live on TV, was a real backs-to-the-wall job, the ultimate nail-biting experience; goalless at half time, goalless after ninety minutes, and goalless after extra time. Penalties would be required.

I sat in my East Calder living room, frightened to watch ... but scared to look away. This was murder! Barry Ferguson assumed the captain's role, stepped up to take the first kick, and saw his shot dramatically saved. Being typically pessimistic I turned away in despair, muttering, 'that's it then, it's all over!' Graeme, sitting next to me, was just a little more pragmatic. 'Don't worry; they'll miss one as well!'

I just shook my head and admired the optimism of youth, but it wasn't going to happen. Minutes later I was eating my words and hugging Graeme in delight ... Neil Alexander had saved from Fabio Liveranti! The score in the shootout stood at two apiece. The tension was cranked up another notch. Brahim Hemdani scored, Christian Vieri missed, and suddenly, sensationally, unbelievably, Rangers were one kick away from a European final.

Nacho Novo made the long and solitary walk from the centre circle to the penalty spot. I don't know how he felt at that precise moment, but I was a quivering wreck, curled up in a ball, watching through a crack in the fingers that covered my eyes. Nacho stepped back, concentrated, and then ran forward – GOAL! – I leapt high into the air; by the time I landed I was pondering the chances of Graeme and me getting a ticket for the final, a game to be played in Manchester – we could only wait and hope that we would be lucky in the eventual ballot.

A week or so later, there was some good news. A letter dropped onto the doormat, in it was confirmation that I'd been allocated a ticket for Manchester, but no mention of Graeme. I wasn't worried though, his confirmation would come in a separate letter and was probably held up in the post ... but it wasn't. Someone had decreed that juveniles would not be allocated tickets. Graeme wasn't getting one, and that seemed dreadfully unfair. He'd paid his money like everyone else; he was a member of the continuous credit scheme with priority for cup ties and cup finals. He'd supported his team through thick and thin, and surely deserved at least the opportunity of a ticket, a shot in the lottery.

I had a ticket, Graeme didn't, and that put me in an awful position. In the post-match euphoria of the semi-final, I'd told Graeme that we'd go to Manchester together, or not at all. I thought we'd get a pair of tickets or nothing, so I'd promised that I wouldn't go without him.

What to do? To go, or not to go, that was the question.

I agonised for days, and then made the inevitable decision – I was going. Graeme had the chance of another final some time in the future, the chances of me living that long were remote in the extreme! I just had to go. Graeme put on a brave face when I told him. He said it was okay, he understood, but I could see he was hurt. It was a horrible, horrible moment, and I felt like a complete and utter bastard – Still went though!

Manchester started with a 6am departure from East Calder and with the car already loaded and prepared, there were no delays – other than to check, for about the tenth time, that I really did have my ticket with me! I drove a few hundred yards and was joined by another car, bedecked in Rangers colours, clearly heading in the same direction as me. Entering Mid Calder I slotted behind the Tap Shop Loyal. By West Calder, ten minutes into a two hundred and twenty-five mile journey, there were at least a dozen cars following that Mid Calder supporters' bus. At every junction, at every roundabout, the line of cars just grew and grew. With apologies to C.W. McCall and his catchy 1975 #1 hit single…

'Cause we got a brand new convoy,
Goin' south in the morning light,
Yeah, we got a growing convoy,
Ain't she a beautiful sight?
Come on and join our convoy,
Ain't nothing gonna get in our way,
Gonna roll this bluenose convoy,
Just to see the Rangers play,
Convoy!

The journey south was an absolute joy. Even at this early hour there were groups of well-wishers on street corners, waving as we drove past. Flags and banners hung from every motorway flyover. Crowds gathered on walkways, saluting the amazing armada of vehicles. It was an incredible feeling, being part of something that was so massive, so special, and so unique.

The dearth of hotel rooms in Greater Manchester meant that I'd be camping at a game once again, just like in the old days! The plan was to relax for a few hours at the camp site, have a can of beer, and then head into the city. But I was far too excited and set off immediately. I wandered through the sleepy village of Hollins Green, having a pint in both of its pubs, Ye Olde Red Lion and the Black Swan, then to Irlam and the train into Manchester.

The chances of getting a beer in any of the city centre bars was remote in the extreme, as all were filled to capacity and closed to new customers. In any case it wasn't a day to be cooped up in a pub; it was scorching hot, the sun splitting a gorgeously blue sky. The best place to be was in one of the fan zones, so I set off for Albert Square, but was unable to gain entry. Security staff had to push people away; there was just no room inside.

With time to kill, I started walking in the direction of Old Trafford, intending to do the stadium tour. It was too hot for walking though, so I gave up and settled instead for a beer in a surprisingly quiet canal side bar. Note, for those familiar with the alternative Manchester scene, not a Canal Street bar! I managed to get a bite to eat before heading back into the throng, where I'd arranged to meet up with Craig and Gloria from the Diamonds.

Late afternoon I finally forced my way into Albert Square. Earlier in the day stewards had tried to restrict entry and prevent bottles and cans being carried in, but they'd long since given up on that, the sheer weight of numbers rendering their job impossible. The square was packed solid, with thousands, tens of thousands, all squeezed in enjoying the atmosphere and drinking the Carlsberg lager that was being poured conveyer belt style by the hard worked ladies in the beer tent. Now, if I'm being honest, the amount of beer being consumed was just a little disconcerting. It seemed like drinking on an industrial scale! I was still trying to remain on the correct side of sobriety, but some in the square looked to be verging on paralytic. Not good with three or four hours 'til kickoff.

Eventually it was time for the football. Walking with Craig and Gloria, we decided to pick up a few refreshments. Looking for a couple of cans of lager, I jumped into a supermarket and emerged with a twelve pack, not through choice I hasten to add. The local shopkeepers had decided to maximise profit and were only selling in bulk. On the road to the stadium we passed Piccadilly Gardens, a place that would later become synonymous with the 2008 UEFA cup final. I'd thought Albert Square had been busy; that was nothing compared to Piccadilly, which resembled the packed terracing of the old Hampden Park. It was wall to wall bodies, all crammed in like sardines in a giant tin!

Then it was Eastlands, the City of Manchester Stadium, and the UEFA Cup Final. Nervous and apprehensive, optimistic yet fearful – so many emotions rolled into one.

Forty-five years since my first ever game, I was now watching my team in a European final, from East Stirling to Zenit St Petersburg, it was so hard to believe. I felt the emotions welling up inside of me, particularly when I spotted a few members of my old supporters' bus. We reminisced about our old friend John Niven and I don't mind admitting that I shed a tear or two, wishing that he could have been with us. And then to the game, which was over in an instant.

Walter Smith's men were set out in their now traditional 5-4-1 formation, and from the start it became clear that they were playing for a 1–0, or more likely, a result on penalties. The supporters, brought up on success, craved victory, and eighty percent of the stadium roared Rangers towards that vision. We believed it, but deep down I don't think the team did – where was big Marvin when you needed him! The dream of glory survived 'til the seventieth minute – then Zenit scored. It was a heartbreaking moment and one that seemed to knock the stuffing out of Rangers. It looked to be all over.

With ten minutes remaining, it was surely time to go for it, all or nothing. I'm loathed to criticise Walter Smith, but bringing on Lee McCulloch, was hardly the most adventurous of moves, highly unlikely to craft an equaliser. With four minutes remaining top goalscorer Kris Boyd came on, but it was too little too late.

In the closing minute we had to suffer the ignominy of ex-Ranger Fernando Ricksen warming up for the Russians. He jogged up and down the touchline, not good enough to get on the park, but clearly enjoying himself. Lingering at the corner flag, he turned to the Rangers support and gleefully indicated, using his fingers, that his team were leading 1–0. What a cock of a man! Frighteningly, there are still some who consider him to be an Ibrox legend!

On ninety minutes the inevitable happened, and Zenit scored a second – now it really was all over. The final whistle sounded soon after, with the Rangers fans in full voice, supporting their team to the bitter end. A post-match pitch invasion by a large group of Zenit supporters looked ominous, but despite being under severe provocation the Teddy Bears did not respond, preferring to cheer on their fallen heroes.

There have been two distinct moments when I've been intensely proud of being a Blue Nose, and curiously both have been in defeat. Firstly when our Champions League dreams died against CSKA Moscow, and then the day at Parkhead when the Scottish Cup was lost and the nine-in-a-row team broke up. The UEFA Cup Final became a third on that list. The team had given their all, and unfortunately come up short. The supporters, well, they were absolutely magnificent. Rangers were cheered to their runners up medals, Zenit St Petersburg warmly applauded as they lifted their prize. Rangers were acclaimed as they did a circuit of the ground, as were the Russians with their newly acquired European trophy.

Walking back into the city centre there was little to indicate that there had been any kind of bother, let alone a major disturbance. Sure there was the sound of police sirens in the distance, but that was far from uncommon after a big game. Even the sight of policemen in riot gear seemed unremarkable. What I didn't know was that there had been major disorder in Piccadilly Gardens when the big screen showing the football had, on public safety orders, been switched off – oh, sorry! I meant to say – when the big screen showing the football in Piccadilly Gardens had mysteriously broken down. The trouble, the violence, then spilled over into the city with a small minority of the Rangers support venting their fury and frustration onto the Greater Manchester Police. Blissfully unaware of the unfolding events, I made my way to Oxford Road to catch the train that would drop me off in Irlam. I waited on the platform, and waited some more. The train was ten minutes late, twenty minutes late, then half an hour late. Eventually there was an announcement – the Liverpool train had been cancelled. A replacement bus service would shortly be available and we were to leave the premises immediately. As if on cue, a van load of police turned up, and in full riot gear, they persuaded the disgruntled travellers to leave the confines of the station. Fifty of us, a mixture of supporters and civilians, were then decanted to an Oxford Road bus stop. Behind us, the station shutters clattered down.

As time passed the stranded passengers grew more and more restless, a good hour had now passed since the promise of replacement busses. Thoroughly hacked off, a group of lads from Liverpool decided to take matters into their own hands and organised a sit down protest, right in the middle of the busy road. In for a penny, in for a pound, I joined them. If we weren't going anywhere, then neither was anyone else! We were going to sit there 'til someone did something about those missing busses.

Our attempt at halting the traffic was most successful, and within minutes a long traffic jam formed, cars snaking all the way up and down Oxford Road. With tempers raised and horns tooting we sat there, causing major havoc. Though, in hindsight, blocking one of Manchester's major arteries was hardly going to aid the progress of any busses that may have been heading in our direction, but it did seem to be a damned good idea at the time!

Being rather gallant, we allowed a good looking lady driver to pass through our blockade; we weren't totally heartless after all! Spotting the opportunity, another vehicle attempted to follow her, but was immediately stopped, the driver being neither good looking, nor female! Seething, he argued for a few moments and then took unilateral action. He revved his engine, lifted the clutch, and spectacularly bounced his car onto the pavement. He accelerated at full tilt, scattering both protesters and pedestrians in all directions. As he swept past, I was sorely tempted to give his car a good kick, the madman certainly deserved it. Great minds think alike, and seconds later there was a loud thump as someone's boot came into contact with a BMW door.

The car screeched to a halt, and the driver leapt out to inspect the damage. Spotting a large dent in his pride and joy, he stormed towards us, demanding recompense, and worryingly his finger seemed to be angrily pointing in my direction. For some reason he was under the impression that I'd been the culprit – I wasn't – honest!

Thankfully, the Liverpool lads took charge and indicated that if the irate driver wanted to argue the point, then he was most welcome to do so. Sensing the odds weren't exactly stacked in his favour, he retreated, uttering a string of most unpleasant obscenities! Reacting to the commotion, the police were soon in attendance and they weren't messing about. We were abruptly informed:

'There are no busses coming. Disperse from here right now, or you'll all be arrested!'

This wasn't the time to argue, or play 'call my bluff', so we reluctantly dispersed, wandering into the chilly Manchester gloom, the warm afternoon sunshine now but distant memory. Apparently Piccadilly station was still open, so I headed that in that direction; at least I'd have a roof over my head. A last gasp chance of transport presented itself when a taxi drove past.

'Hollins Green, the camp site?' said the taxi driver. 'No problem, that'll be £150 ... cash up front!'

Eh! One hundred and fifty pounds, for a ten mile journey! I told him, in not so many words, that he could stick his taxi up his…!

So I ended up in Piccadilly Station, joining several hundred others littered across the station concourse, trying to get just a little shut eye. Not easy with an announcement booming out every few minutes, 'Would Inspector Sands please report to the operations room immediately.' I was heartily sick of that mythical inspector by the time morning broke. Cold, dirty, hungry and just a little hungover – I'd had better nights!

Driving back to East Calder, I had time to reflect on the previous twenty-four hours, and try to make some sense of it all, and hindsight is, of course, 20/20 vision. Manchester just hadn't been prepared. They'd banked on a Fiorentina vs Bayern Munich final, with sixty-odd thousand visitors, and got instead Rangers vs Zenit, with close to a quarter of a million. The fan zones were inadequate for the numbers involved; the city's infrastructure just couldn't cope. They'd simply underestimated the numbers attending, and reacted too late when the scale of the invasion became apparent. Although to be fair, I don't think they could ever have coped, the city was simply too small. Manchester had a population of approximately 500,000. Rangers had, in the space of twenty-four hours, added over 200,000 to that total, and all tightly squeezed into the city centre.

As for the disturbance in Piccadilly Gardens, I can't really comment as I wasn't there to witness it. But I did catch some of the scenes on television and can only condemn those involved in the violence, it shouldn't have happened. The sight of a policemen being kicked senseless by a baying mob was particularly sickening. Post-match, I was so proud of the Rangers support, and nothing will ever take that away. However, viewing that particular incident made me profoundly ashamed. No matter the frustration, no matter the provocation, there is never, ever, ever an excuse to behave like that. Those supporters – and let's not pretend that they weren't Rangers supporters – were an absolute disgrace, and hopefully all got the jail sentences they thoroughly deserved.

Three days later my team were in action again, drawing 1–1 at Motherwell. A win at St Mirren then took the season to a last day climax, but the dropped points at Fir Park meant that we now needed Celtic to slip up, and sadly it didn't happen – there was to be no repeat of Helicopter Sunday. Instead it was Rangers who faltered, losing 2–0 in a tired performance at Aberdeen. Celtic were SPL champions for the third year in a row.

The season ended with a trophy, Queen of the South beaten 3–2, but it was a flat and uninspiring afternoon, everyone associated with Rangers was physically and emotionally drained. The Queens certainly enjoyed their day, and came very close to causing an upset. At 2–0 down they rolled their sleeves up and gave it a right good go, managing to pull the scoreline back to 2–2 ... if only we had tried that in Manchester.

Relaxing on Sunday, a poem by the American Quaker and abolitionist John Greenleaf Wittier came to mind. A section of *Maud Muller*, written in 1856 read:

'*God pity them both, and pity us all,*
Who vainly the dreams of youth recall,
For of all sad words of tongue or pen,
The saddest are these: It might have been!'

Those words neatly encapsulated my feelings towards the UEFA Cup Final. I felt that on the night, Rangers were just happy to be there, that was their achievement. If only the Ibrox men had shown the spirit and bravery of Queen of the South. I know that they ultimately left Hampden with runners up medals, but I'm willing to bet that none of their supporters had any post-match regrets.

Rest assured, I hadn't suddenly become arty-farty, and I certainly wasn't a fan of 19th Century poetry. I did, however, enjoy the sitcom Frasier. The poem was used in season three, episode sixteen, 'Look before you leap'.

Chapter 25:
Nae Dough, Two in a Row!

A rip-roaring season had come and gone, and whilst the press, police and politicians chewed over the bones of Manchester, I got on with my standard close-season routine – doing all the domestic chores that I'd studiously avoided for the previous ten months! June moved into July, the grass was cut and the weeds pulled up, the garage was tidied and the bedrooms decorated.

Season 2008/2009 was about to start, and for Rangers it began with a crash, bang and a wallop. They drew 0–0 with minnows FBK Kaunas at Ibrox and then tumbled to a quite calamitous defeat in Lithuania. Out of the Champions League with no parachute into the UEFA cup – massively disappointing from a football perspective but absolutely catastrophic financially. Rangers were one week into the new season, and already £10m down in their potential earnings. Something had to be done to recoup the loss, and it was; player of the year Carlos Cuellar was sold to Aston Villa for £7.8m. Rangers claimed that the Spaniard had a clause in his contract allowing him to move when a suitable offer came in, and perhaps he did, but the more cynical amongst the support saw the timing of his departure as suspicious, nothing more than a fire-sale, and I have to say I had a great deal of sympathy with that viewpoint.

Kaunas had been a disaster just waiting to happen, the Scottish champions had gone into the tie with a severely depleted midfield, new signings were urgently required, but none were made – short term penny pinching in my opinion. Avoid paying transfer fees and wages for as long as possible, and then do the business when the Champions League money was secured. A good plan I suppose, if it had worked – but it hadn't, and the European pot of gold was gone.

The midfield was eventually strengthened; Steve Davis and Paulo Mendes signed. This was obviously good news, but not good enough to placate at least some in the Rangers support. Stunned by the Kaunas debacle and its aftermath, a demonstration was organised. Normally a very conservative bunch, the Teddy Bears were becoming just a little restless.

On Saturday 16th August 2008 a relatively small group gathered on Edmiston Drive to express their disapproval of the Cuellar sale. David Murray's stewardship of the club was also under attack, as was, to a lesser extent, Walter Smith's management style. The sting, however, was taken out of the protest when Sandy Jardine emerged from the main door of the stadium to introduce the club's latest signing target; Maurice Edu, another midfielder. The protestors could hardly boo and jeer in front of the new boy, and the demonstration inevitably fizzled out.

The Saturday afternoon radio pundits were almost orgasmic in their admiration of this diversionary manoeuvre. Declaring the introduction of Edu as a masterstroke, it was hard to disagree. David Murray, an undoubted expert in media manipulation had pulled a fast one on those uppity supporters. Well done, David, but just a thought; might it not have been a bigger masterstroke to sign Edu, Mendes and Davis *before* that Champions League qualifier?

The SPL had an encouraging start with two consecutive victories. Celtic had already slipped a couple of points adrift, and for once they weren't bitching about referees. I wonder why?

10th August 2008: Celtic 1, St Mirren 0.

'It's a conspiracy I tells ya! Well, actually its not. But try telling that to St Mirren and their manager Gus MacPherson who left Parkhead yesterday burning with injustice and convinced that they had just been turned over by referee Eddie Smith.' (*Daily Record*)

17th August 2008: Dundee United 1, Celtic 1.

'Charlie Richmond got it horribly wrong in not awarding Dundee United a penalty.' (*Daily Record*)

Decisions even themselves out over a period of time; every sensible and rational person knows that – but I must admit, even I was starting to have my doubts. Were Scottish officials possibly helping Celtic? On Monday 25th August 2008, the Daily Record reported on both the Rangers and Celtic matches.

At Pittodrie: 'The linesman ... chopped off a last minute strike by DaMarcus Beasley that would have clinched victory for Rangers ... even though Beasley had timed his run to perfection.'

At Parkhead: 'Raging Falkirk star Michael Higdon launched an amazing attack on referee Iain Brines and accused him of being a Celtic fan. The Bairns' striker said the referee bottled out disallowing the Hoops' opening goal.'

Over the years, I'd grown weary of Celtic's incessant complaints; the Parkhead persecution complex had become more than a little tiresome. Just how many advantageous decisions would it take to convince them that it was all a figment of their own overblown imagination? This isn't a tome about Celtic and their insecurities, so I'll desist from cataloguing their continuing good fortune. Well ... perhaps just a couple more.

17ᵗʰ November 2008: Hamilton 1, Celtic 2.

'Celtic were awarded a penalty ... for a foul that happened a yard outside the box.' (*Daily Record*)

22ⁿᵈ November 2008: St Mirren 1, Celtic 3.

'Celtic got lucky with a dodgy refereeing decision for the second week in a row ... the debate about ref Willie Collum's failure to send Artur Boruc packing for Pole-axing Craig Dargo will naturally rage into the week.' (*Sunday Mail*)

This year's AGM was a gloomy affair. The quite wonderful run to Manchester had resulted in a record club turnover of £64m, and a trading profit of £7.6m, yet the club debt had somehow increased by a whopping £5m. Shareholders were starkly informed that existing levels of expenditure could not be maintained. The inference was quite clear; don't expect any signings in the near future. A matter of months after what should have been their most lucrative season ever, Rangers were feeling the pinch!

Trying to lighten the mood, a bullish David Murray announced a spectacular development for the Ibrox area. On the assumption that suitable partners could be found, £350m was to be spent on a hotel, concert hall and retail outlet, all with underground parking. The club couldn't afford to invest in its playing staff, yet intended to become involved in a project costing over a third of a billion pounds. To coin a phrase – I'll believe it when I see it!

Of course, the chairman had previous for this sort of thing. Just ten months earlier, he'd mooted plans to revamp the entire stadium. One of those schemes envisaged Ibrox being razed to the ground and replaced by a brand new 70,000 all-seated arena, complete with a floating removable pitch and retractable roof – things that make you go hmmm!

New Year approached, with Rangers ready, and seemingly willing, to sell top goal-scorer Kris Boyd and team captain Barry Ferguson. The club's only hope of redressing their balance sheet problem was to win the SPL and qualify automatically for those Champions League millions, and the strategy to achieve that important goal was to hawk their best players. Curious!

The football continued and the Ibrox men travelled to Perth for a tricky Scottish Cup tie against St Johnstone. News of the financial strife had clearly spread, and proved too big a temptation for the McDiarmid Park DJ who took great delight in blasting out a string of themed songs, just for our delectation:

Abba: 'Money, money, money'

Dire Straits: 'Money for nothing'

Simply Red: 'Money's too tight to mention'

The windup tunes just kept on coming. It was hard to take, but I suppose, having lorded it financially over Scottish football for so long we deserved just a little come-uppance. Discontent was brewing though, as shown by a banner held aloft amongst the travelling support. It was quite explicit in its sentiment: MURRAY MUST GO.

Oh dear, I thought, *the chairman isn't going to like that!*

A few days later the Rangers Supporters Trust entered the fray with their 'We Deserve Better' campaign, and a well thought out document was issued. In it the Trust highlighted concerns over the way the football club was being run. To paraphrase – the fans understand the current situation will take time and a workable strategy to escape from, but the club must make the necessary changes, rather than conduct transfer window fire-sales and lurch from crisis to crisis with no discernable game plan.

It wasn't a confrontational document in any way, shape or form, but it brought an immediate rebuttal from the chairman. Mr Murray didn't like criticism, be it directly through the McDiarmid park banner, or indirectly through the RST statement. He blasted back...

'Those people who are doing all the shouting are in danger of ruining Rangers Football Club!'

Well excuse me! I was a member of the RST, was he referring to me? I'd been a Rangers supporter for nearly fifty years and attended over nineteen hundred games. I'd been a season ticket holder since 1988, I was a shareholder, and religiously bought the club newspaper and program. For many years I'd been a pools agent – and *I* was in danger of ruining Rangers? I know Mr Murray owned the club, but just who did he think he was!

David Murray then spoke to the press, and in an attempt to allay any fears for the future, he issued a firm and confident statement:

'Rangers are strong, even in the current position, and people are mischief making about the extent of our financial problem'

Those were encouraging words in troubling times. The warm feeling was of course fully dependant on the chairman telling us the whole story, and he was – wasn't he?

I was by now an avid user of the 'Follow Follow' website, a good source of unofficial news and gossip. Their message board was always entertaining with postings ranging from the incisive to the downright nutty! Browsing one evening in February I noticed a thread entitled 'Remember the Wink RIP'. Opening the link, I saw a picture of a familiar face, and read the attached message with growing dismay. Garry Lynch, an old friend, had suffered a sudden brain haemorrhage, and collapsed and died. It was so hard to fathom, a man so full of life, so vibrant, had been taken at the tragically early age of fifty-one.

A few days later I sat in Kirkhill Old Parish Church for Garry's moving memorial service, before heading to Daldowie Crematorium for his final send off. Over two thousand mourners attended, a measure of the status in which Gary was held within the Rangers family, and indeed the community at large. The biggest, and best tribute to the big man, would be for his team to lift this seasons SPL, and victories over Kilmarnock and Hamilton propelled them in that direction. They went top of the table – only on goal difference, but the top – then calamity.

Rangers were at home to their bogey team, Inverness. The game was drifting towards a disappointing and costly goalless draw, when the Highland side were dramatically awarded a last gasp penalty. Graeme and I stood and watched, as did the rest of the stadium, everyone bar the tiny band of away supporters praying that the spot kick would be missed. It wasn't, and a few seconds later the game was over: Rangers 0, Inverness 1. There was a stunned silence, 'til Graeme, in a mixture of fury and frustration lashed out and blootered the seat in front of him. As the seat rattled and shook, he exclaimed, 'FUCKING SHITE!' I really couldn't have put it any better myself!

Graeme was disappointed; he wanted the league title, and this defeat was a savage blow to those hopes. I was no less disappointed; I also wanted the title at Ibrox, but I was scared and desperately worried for the very future of my team. Losing this season's championship, with the subsequent loss of Champions League money could very well be a terminal blow to the club I loved – it was genuinely that serious!

Fortunately Rangers knuckled down and strung together an unbeaten run of nine games, picking up twenty-three points from a possible twenty-seven. During the same period Celtic only mustered eighteen. It meant that with one game remaining Walter Smith's men could win the title at Tannadice, and that's just what they did, beating Dundee United 3–0.

The RST took a bit of a post-season battering, belittled in the media, derided by other team's supporters, ridiculed even by some in the Rangers support as arrogant spoiled brats. SPL champions, Scottish Cup winners – *What on earth were the Trust complaining about? What more did they want?* Well, the RST concerns were still relevant. The football team may have been winning trophies, but the football club was in a downward spiral. Despite winning the championship, despite having guaranteed Champions League money there would be no further investment. The RST wanted a discernable strategic vision, and what Rangers FC was offering was no better than stagnation.

Rangers won their first three league games of 2009/2010, but all was not well. Walter Smith was clearly irked that there had been no money spent on his first team squad. He wanted some cash guarantees for the remainder of the season, but given the clubs recent financial history, that seemed highly unlikely. The man clearly had a lot on his mind, and in October it all boiled over. I was on the M8, driving home, tuned as always to Radio Scotland, listening to the day's football roundup. Over at Ibrox, Walter Smith was being interviewed by Chick Young, talking about the 1–1 draw with Hibs. It was the standard post-match stuff, decent performance, disappointing result, etc, etc. All very predictable, but in closing, Walter Smith casually dropped a bombshell into the mix:

'Life is difficult at the moment because the bank has taken over the running of the club!'

What did he say!? I took my eyes off the road and stared irrationally at the radio, waiting for Chic Young's follow up. It's not an action recommended in the Highway Code, especially whilst travelling at 70mph. I failed to notice the slowing traffic and very nearly smacked into the back of a nearby supporters bus!

'Thank you Walter' was the Radio Scotland man's incisive response!

Unbelievable! I wanted more, I needed more. Walter Smith had just made one of the most dramatic and important statements ever issued by a Scottish football manager. Chick Young had been presented with the sporting scoop of the century, and all he could utter was a (feeble) thank you. Is it any wonder I nearly crashed the car?

The Sunday papers took up the mantle, and a sorry tale emerged. The claim was repeated that Lloyds TSB was in financial control; contracts and conditions would now be negotiated by the bank, and on much more reduced terms. Knowing the mentality of the modern footballer, that could only mean one thing: players would soon be leaving. Transfers – well, there wouldn't be any, not incoming anyway. Walter Smith in the Sunday Mail made no attempt to paper over the cracks.

'Every member of the squad is up for sale and if anyone thinks that has a motivational effect on players then they live in a different world from me.'

Lloyds TSB denied they were running the club, and the Rangers board denied that Lloyds were running the club, yet Walter Smith said they were. So who was telling the truth? Tell you what – I believed the manager.

The situation was bleak, and wasn't about to get any better. Walter Smith's position was also in doubt, his contract was due to expire in January and no one at Ibrox, or at the bank, was in any particular rush to renew it. The men in charge of my club – whoever they might be – seemed to be clinging to the hope that Walter would continue in his current role for the remainder of the season, and work without the security of a contract. Well, would he? The Daily Record took the bull by the horns and asked the vital question. Walter Smith's reply just piled more pain onto my growing anguish:

'Would I work without a contract? Well if I'm asked. They would need to ask me first.'

There were ten short weeks 'til Walter's contract expired and no one had bothered to ask the most important man at the club what his plans or intentions were! Just what was going on?

And what of David Murray? He'd surrendered the chairman's role, and put the business up for sale, but still owned ninety percent of the club. Surely he would have something to say. I'm afraid not. It looked as though Murray had cut and run, or had he been pushed aside, squeezed out by the faceless men at Lloyds. No one knew. We were entering a period when the Rangers support, the heart and soul of the club, would be kept firmly in the dark.

Let's just reflect back for a moment, to January 2009, only ten months earlier, when we were told 'Rangers are strong, even in the current position, and people are mischief-making about the extent of our financial problem.'

Well, the club's financial position didn't look too clever now, in fact, for the first time the dreaded 'A' word was being bandied about: administration.

On Saturday 21st November, Walter Smith's men drew 0–0 with Kilmarnock. Twenty-four hours later Celtic lost at Dundee United. Rangers as a business was a complete and utter shambles, but as a football club they'd managed to go top of the league table. Just how successful could they be if they were run properly?

Everyone at Ibrox was given a welcome boost when Walter Smith announced that he would continue as manager for the remainder of the season. It was an act of faith that seemed to inspire the team and they embarked on a terrific run of form, five successive games were won, twenty-three goals scored with only three conceded.

The transfer window opened with the financial contrast between the Glasgow giants looking glaringly obvious. Celtic splurged into the market and totally transformed their squad with five players moving out, seven coming in. Rangers, in contrast, did nothing, that is 'til the final few days when two players were offloaded. The talented and important Paulo Mendes was sold to Sporting Lisbon, the useless and superfluous Jerome Rothen despatched back to Paris St Germain.

The window closed with no additions to the Rangers squad. Two players down, Walter Smith would just have to manufacture another league championship miracle with what he had. Meanwhile, on the other side of Glasgow, car park hysteria was breaking out. Celtic were still wheeling and dealing, and at midnight they dramatically introduced their latest recruit, Robbie Keane. Three thousand exultant Tim Malloys gathered outside Parkhead to welcome the Irishman to his temporary home. The signing universally acclaimed as the season's defining moment. This was the night Celtic won the league title – well, that's what the faithful bhoys and ghirls thought.

Twenty-four hours later: Kilmarnock 1, Robbie Keane's Celtic 0.

Putting monetary problems to one side, Walter Smith and his men concentrated on what they did best, winning games of football. St Johnstone were beaten in a Hampden snow storm to propel Rangers into the League Cup final. The euphoria of the victory was only temporary, quickly dampened by Walter Smith's post-match interview. When asked if this made the future a little brighter, he replied, rather matter of factly:

'The crisis isn't going away, even if the treble is won.'

Walter wasn't painting a pretty picture, but at least he was keeping the fans updated. No one else, not Rangers FC, or Lloyds TSB, or, for that matter, David Murray, seemed remotely interested in passing on any information. It was profoundly depressing.

Rangers FC had been on the market for some time now, with no serious or credible bids received. Then, out of the blue, the unknown Andrew Ellis burst onto the scene. Takeover talks were allegedly at an advanced stage; the club would have a new owner by May – or so the newspapers would have us believe! But who was this mystery man?

Ellis was an estate agent and property developer who had previous involvement with two other football clubs; Northampton Town and QPR, though neither of those associations had been particularly fruitful. His attempt to buy Rangers was shrouded in secrecy. Did he have the necessary finance? Was he possibly the frontman for a mystery consortium? Unfortunately, no one really knew!

With their league title hopes slipping, Celtic turned to an aspect of the game where they excel: moaning about injustice! A dossier of dodgy refereeing decisions was submitted to the SFA. Included was a bizarre observation that Scottish referees and linesmen were just not fast enough to keep up with whizz-kid Robbie Keane! Rangers in the meantime just got on with winning matches, and stretched their SPL advantage to thirteen points.

The first trophy of the season came wrapped in red, white and blue ribbons, Rangers beating St Mirren in the League Cup. The following Wednesday, the men in blue travelled to Tannadice for a Scottish cup quarter-final replay.

Knowing the critical importance of the league championship, Walter Smith played it safe and rested a number of his first team regulars. The game was lost to a last-minute goal and as a consequence the prospect of a glorious treble was gone. A lot of supporters took the result very badly, and Smith was openly criticised for his overly defensive approach. I was disappointed, of course, but I also recognised that the SPL title was the more important prize, and absolutely vital to my team's long-term survival. Anyway, Wattie being cautious? Surely we were all used to that by now!

Playing that night for Dundee United was Keith Watson, the son of my old Livi Star colleague Derek. Having overcome some serious injury problems, it was good to see Keith doing well, even if it was at our expense! He'd been a dedicated footballer, from Soccer Sevens at Livi Star all the way through the Dundee United youth set-up. Keith would go on to win a Scottish Cup winner's medal and should be an inspiration to all young players in West Lothian, demonstrating what hard work and dedication can achieve.

The disappointment of the Scottish Cup defeat was tempered by a very cheery score line filtering through from Paisley: St Mirren 4, Celtic 0. It was a result that pretty much clinched the SPL title for a Rangers team who only required a maximum of nine points from eight games. Celtic's defeat did of course give more ammunition to the Walter Smith critics who were still mourning the loss of the treble – but it's easy to be wise after the event.

Rangers didn't slip up, and the title was clinched on Sunday 25th April, with three games to spare. The much maligned Kyle Lafferty scoring the only goal in a 1–0 victory over Hibs.

Isaac Newton, way back in the seventeenth century, published his famous third law of motion: 'to every action there is an equal and opposite re-action.' Rangers in 2010 seemed to have modified that rule, in their case it read 'for every piece of good news there is an equal and opposite dollop of bad news.' The SPL had been retained, Champions League millions assured. What could possible go wrong now? Well, the title hangover had barely subsided when some devastating news broke.

'Rangers have confirmed that the Scottish Premier League club is under investigation by Her Majesty's Revenue and Customs (HMRC) over a tax issue. BBC Scotland has learned that the investigation relates to payments made into offshore accounts.' (*BBC Scotland website*)

A spokesman for the club responded and denied they'd done anything wrong; they were simply exploiting a loophole in the tax laws, a loophole that many others had used. The club would be robustly defending the matter.

One could only hope that the defence would be successful because the amount of unpaid tax was looking to be astronomical. A cursory glance at the club accounts showed an expense in the 'Staff Costs' section. This item, 'Contributions to Employee Benefit Trust' first appeared in 2001 with a figure of £1.01m, and peaked in 2006 at a massive £9.19m. By 2009 it had reduced to £2.36m. In total, over £46m had been diverted to the trust. If tax was now due on that amount, plus interest, plus penalties, then the club would be in very serious financial trouble, possibly terminal financial trouble. I couldn't help but recall the words of Hugh Adam, way back in 2002:

'If Rangers continue on their present track, their ultimate destination will be bankruptcy.'

Had David Murray, as club chairman and owner, approved this method of player payment? Had he gambled the club's future on the premise that the Employee Benefit Trust was efficient tax management and not illegal tax evasion? Was this to be David Murray's legacy to Rangers – bankruptcy?

There were so many unanswered questions regarding the future, one of which regarded the position of the manager, Walter Smith had of course agreed to fulfil the final six months of the season without a contract, but would he continue into 2010/2011? Who would blame him if he took a well-deserved retirement and walked away with a league and cup double?

The football year was over and it was season ticket renewal time. Was I going to renew? Of course I was, hoping that at least some of my hard-earned £440 would help the club, and not just flow into the coffers of Lloyds TSB. Driving over to Ibrox, I passed La Fiorentina in Kinning Park, a long established and well respected restaurant, and a place used by countless Rangers players over the generations. I'd always fancied having a meal there, so, with time to spare, I nipped in for a late lunch.

Perusing the menu, my attention was captured by an American accent. Looking over at an adjoining table, I was astonished to see the Rangers chairman Alastair Johnston, accompanied by CEO Martin Bain and financial director Donald McIntyre. I ordered some lasagne and casually glanced back, a double-take was now required as the three men had become a quartet, Walter Smith had joined them! I tried to discreetly shuffle a little closer, hoping to pick up some juicy gossip, but my earwigging was sadly and abruptly thwarted by the introduction of Luciano Pavarotti over the restaurant sound system – most frustrating!

The Rangers party were having a quiet meeting, no doubt discussing crucial club business, what they didn't need was an interruption from a well-meaning supporter, but that's what they got. On leaving the restaurant I introduced myself and shook Walter's hand, thanking him for all he'd done. I then politely advised Johnston and Bain to get the manager re-signed as soon as possible. The advice was unwanted and unneeded, and shouldn't have been given – but I just couldn't help myself. A few weeks later Walter Smith signed a contract to remain at the club for one final year – perhaps my advice had been heeded after all.

One document not being signed was the sale missive for Ibrox. The Andrew Ellis takeover bid, imminent in May, had pretty well fizzled out. On the 16th of June, Murray International Holdings announced that it was no longer actively marketing its controlling stake in Rangers FC, the MIH statement was signed by David Murray. The Ellis deal was dead in the water, and we were regrettably back at square one, and at the mercy of Lloyds TSB.

The close-season saw the Ibrox revolving door rotate in one direction and one direction only, and sadly that was outwards. Player after player departed. At the start of 2009–2010, Rangers had a first team squad of twenty-two players; as the new season approached that was down to a mere fourteen.

Was this any way to run a football club?

Chapter 26:
It's the Final Countdown!

2010/2011 kicked off with Rangers in a relaxed mood, playing some low-key friendlies down under in Australia. Celtic, on the other hand, had no such luxury; they were eleven thousand miles away in Portugal, competing in what was possibly their most important game of the year, a Champions League qualifier. They lost 3–0 to SC Braga, and their manager Neil Lennon, setting the tone for a turbulent season, unleashed a blisteringly critical attack on Belgian referee Serge Gumienny. It was, rather predictably, a case of new manager; same old Celtic!

Meanwhile, back at Ibrox, the chequebook had been rediscovered and put to good use. Four new players arrived at the club, the pick of the bunch being Nikica Jelavić. Jelavić was without doubt a highly rated striker, but with such a depleted squad, would his £4m transfer fee have been better spent on quantity rather than quality? Only time would tell.

The league campaign had an excellent start with nine wins in a row, and with Kenny Miller in blistering form, scoring thirteen times. Unfortunately, party poopers Inverness then came to Ibrox and did their traditional smash-and-grab routine, pinching a point and spoiling the 100% record. Season 2010/2011 then went ever so slightly mad…

A new phrase entered the football lexicon, *we want clarification,* and it was uttered by the Celtic manager every time a decision went against his side.

Rangers won a penalty at Parkhead – we want clarification!

Celtic denied a penalty at Tannadice – we want clarification!

Celtic denied a penalty at Tynecastle – we want clarification!

Curiously, Lennon did not want clarification on the very lenient yellow card issued to his player Anthony Stokes, who quite brutally lunged studs up into Rangers fullback Saša Papac. I wonder why?

Wednesday 10th November brought an unusual occurrence; both sides of the Old Firm played on the same day, at the same time, and simultaneously lost, Rangers 3–0 at home to Hibs, Celtic 2–1 away to Hearts. The respective team managers did their routine post-match interviews. Walter Smith calmly congratulated Hibs on their victory; he praised their performance and wished them well. Neil Lennon, conversely, was in a snarling rage. He demanded the inevitable clarification, and openly questioned the integrity of the match officials. The contrast between the two men could not have been more apparent.

News then broke that Scottish referees were considering strike action; they'd clearly had enough of the petty criticism and wanted to express their collective disapproval. After a meeting it was announced:

'The incessant and adverse nature of recent comments on referees has placed intolerable pressures on personal and professional lives. Statements questioning honesty and integrity have been aimed across refereeing in general and have led to an unprecedented level of abuse and genuine concerns for safety.'

This was serious stuff, Scottish football was starting to spiral out of control, and it was surely time for clubs – *all clubs* – to take a step back and accept that referees make genuine and honest decisions, and sometimes they make genuine and honest mistakes!

Most commentators and punters thought the referees were bluffing, but they weren't, and on the weekend of 27th November they carried out their threat and withdrew their labour. Industrial action or not, the show must go on, and in response, the football authorities shipped in referees and linesmen from all over the continent. At Parkhead, a team of Luxembourg officials were warmly applauded onto the field of play. Normally left wing and vehemently anti-establishment, the Celtic support enthusiastically endorsed a trio of strikebreakers – these were perplexing times! Rangers, as it transpired, were unaffected; their game at Tannadice fell foul of the weekend weather. The strike lasted but a single week, and the referees returned to work with nothing seemingly resolved. Though they had, I suppose, made their point. Hopefully football could take centre stage again.

The majority of football fans buy their newspaper and immediately turn to the sports section. For the Teddy Bears, the front page was becoming just as important as the back, a case in point coming in November when the Daily Record headlined the name of Craig Whyte. This mystery man was revealed to be the latest *prospective* buyer of Rangers FC. A deal was *apparently* at an advanced stage, Rangers, it was proclaimed, *could* have a new owned by Christmas. I read the article, and wearily thought, let's just wait and see – we had, of course, been down this road before. Encouragingly though, the Record then reported that the Whyte deal had entered its endgame, an announcement was apparently imminent.

November moved into December, and then January with absolutely nothing resolved. In fact, the only deal to be concluded was Kenny Miller's departure from Ibrox. The striker had turned down the offer of a new contract, preferring to sample the Turkish delights of Bursaspor, and a reported salary of £50k per week! Rangers could have retained the player 'til the end of the season and taken advantage of his goal-scoring prowess. Instead, they offloaded him for £400k. Or, had Lloyds TSB sold him? No one was really sure who was pulling the purse strings any more. As he departed for pastures new, Kenny gave us one last entertaining moment, in a farewell interview he announced 'I'm going to Bursaspor to win medals, not for the money.' Sure thing Kenny. I'll believe you – thousands wouldn't!

In the space of six months, my team had lost three strikers, Novo, Boyd and Miller, a fifty-goal partnership, and in return received a paltry £400k. In the coming transfer window, Celtic flogged their dodgy defender Stephen McManus to Middlesbrough for £1.5m. It was difficult not to conclude that one half of the Old Firm had an astute business plan, and it most certainly wasn't the blue half.

The season continued apace, with the two Glasgow giants going neck and neck for the championship. Old Firm games were, as always, important, and unfortunately for Rangers they were becoming problematic. The next two league encounters were lost 2–0 and 3–0, results that propelled Celtic to the top of the table – and then there was the Scottish Cup calamity. The men in blue couldn't overcome a ten-man Celtic, and were, to be honest, fortunate to escape with a draw. The replay didn't go well, and would have been instantly forgettable, were it not for its chaotic climax.

An injury-ravaged Rangers were a man down and a goal down, going into the final minute, their prospects bleak. A desperate cause then became mission impossible when Madjid Bougerra was dismissed, further reducing the away side to nine. The referee's final whistle signalled the end of the game, the cup run was over – but not the drama.

El Hadji Diouf, no stranger to controversy, managed to snag his team's third red card of the evening when he collectively upset the Celtic dugout, the referee, and Strathclyde police. Not to mention ninety-nine percent of the Parkhead support. They really didn't like him, did they!

Meanwhile, the respective team officials were having their own little spat; sporting handshakes were exchanged, but only momentarily. Ally McCoist leant in, and made a private comment to Neil Lennon, something that clearly irked the Celtic man, and, spitting feathers, he lunged at the bold Alistair. The incident was over in a few seconds, and was nothing more than a storm in a teacup, but its aftermath lingered for weeks. We had, wouldn't you know it, another Old Firm shame game!

In a complete over-reaction, the media went into a feeding frenzy. 'Mayhem' declared the Daily Record. Both sets of supporters were inevitably castigated, despite the fact that they were generally well-behaved. Alex Salmond and his cronies in the Scottish Government then splashed in and organised a summit – to investigate those dreadful scenes. Goodness, you'd almost think there was an election on the horizon!

Walter Smith in the meantime had re-discovered his golden touch, or should it be his silver streak, and guided Rangers to a League Cup triumph, at last getting one over on the old enemy. One man who still hadn't achieved his goal was Craig Whyte. His bid to buy the football club was ongoing, but numerous deadlines has come and gone with no apparent progress. Was it going to happen? Both David Murray and Lloyds TSB had given their seal of approval, so it was surely just a matter of time – surely!

April started with a couple of devastating blows. A £2.8m tax bill from HMRC dropped on the Ibrox doorstep, and nothing to do with the well-publicised EBT investigation, this unexpected invoice was for some other indiscretion. Once again the club's finances were under the spotlight, and once again questions were asked of those in charge. Just how many more nasty little surprises were lurking round the corner? One could only hope, that for his sake, Craig Whyte's due diligence process was exceedingly diligent!

Reeling from that financial blow, Rangers were nearly KO'd by Dundee United. The Taysiders came to Ibrox and won a critical league game, a game that succinctly demonstrated the fine line between football success and failure. The clock registered ninety minutes, the score stood at 2–2 when a Stephen Whitaker header crashed off the crossbar. The ball was cleared, Dundee United made a lightning breakaway and unbelievably scored at the other end. In the blink of an eye the points had been hijacked.

The magnitude of the task facing Rangers was amply demonstrated by this fixture. Rangers had a substitutes' bench consisting of an experienced goalie, three teenagers and Salim Kerkar, a man who'd yet to make his first-team debut. Four days later Celtic played and beat Hibs at Parkhead. On that evening they put their best eleven onto the field. They had seven full internationalists on the bench, and a further three clicking their heels in the stand. The fact that Rangers were even mounting a title challenge was nothing less than a minor miracle, and testament to Walter Smith's managerial and motivational skills. Yet there were some in the Rangers support who wanted him dismissed for a perceived lack of ambition! Most peculiar!

An increasingly bizarre season then managed to turn sinister with Neil Lennon receiving death threats. Live bullets were posted to him, and packages described as viably explosive were intercepted. This was frankly absurd and beggared belief. I wasn't a great fan of the man, that's for sure. At times he acted like an irritating little nyaff, but, at the end of the day, Neil Lennon wasn't Robert Mugabe, leading a despotic and oppressive regime, he wasn't Colonel Gaddafi, slaughtering his own people, and he certainly wasn't Osama Bin Laden, directing world terrorism. He was simply a football manager and most certainly didn't deserve this kind of attention.

I've said it before, and I'll say it again, football isn't more important than life and death. It never has been and never will be. Whoever was issuing these threats, sending these devices and packages really ought to grow up and join the real world.

April ended with a potentially title-deciding Old Firm clash. Both teams battled out an entertaining but goalless game until the eightieth minute when Celtic were awarded a somewhat dubious penalty – the league race was about to end. This was the goal that would clinch the championship, well that's what the Celtic support thought, and, if the truth be told, so did I. Georgios Samaras, in front of an exultant Broomloan Road Stand, struck the penalty goalwards only to be thwarted by a magnificent Alan McGregor save. Stunned silence from the green and white hordes, delirium everywhere else. The game ended 0–0, a result that undoubtedly favoured the Parkhead side who were just five wins away from the league title.

A feeling of gloom started to descend upon a weary Rangers support. Dundee United, a team who had played so well at Ibrox, went to Parkhead and capitulated. Celtic were only four wins from the league title. The SPL was slipping away, and, by the looks of it, so was the Craig Whyte takeover. On the cusp of a deal, an independent committee on the Rangers board voted ... no. A new consortium emerged from the shadows, led by an existing director Paul Murray. It was truly a mess, then suddenly, and unexpectedly, the sun came out, and in the space of a few days the season was turned on its head.

Inverness 3, Celtic 2 – God bless those party pooping Highlanders!

The championship was now in Rangers' hands. They were only three wins away from three in a row! And then, even more unexpectedly, the takeover happened! In a complete turnaround the independent committee gave its full backing to Craig Whyte – my team were under new ownership!

It was the end of a twenty-two year dynasty, David Murray had finally gone and we were left to assess his time at the helm of the club. For some, Murray was the great saviour, a man who brought nothing but success and good times. For others, he was the great Satan, someone who used the club to his own advantage. The truth, as always, lies somewhere in-between those two extremes.

When discussing David Murray, it's always helpful to establish a few basic facts. Despite what many think, he didn't completely re-build Ibrox, he didn't appoint Graeme Souness as manager, and he didn't bring in players like Terry Butcher, Chris Woods and Richard Gough. So, was David Murray a good chairman and owner?

He most certainly gave us some wonderful years, trophies galore and a string of magnificent players, but he also presided over, and authorised, an outrageous and crippling level of debt. For many years he was hands-on and enthusiastic, though latterly he'd appeared lacklustre and disinterested.

Personally, I'd give Mr Murray a critical pass mark, were it not for one crucially important factor. Many years ago he'd stated that he wasn't the owner of Rangers FC – he was its custodian, keeping the club safe and secure for the generations to come; a noble and generous statement. However, and unforgivably in my opinion, as custodian he led Rangers into a reckless form of tax avoidance – a scheme that has resulted in the football club, like a common criminal, being taken to the highest court in the land.

The very future of Rangers FC depends on the outcome of this court case. They may emerge triumphant – let's hope so – but many legal experts expect the judgement to go the other way, and if it does, and the full and worst case penalties are imposed, then the team I love could flounder, bypass administration and head directly to liquidation. So, has David Murray been a good owner? I'm going to leave my options open, but can't help but worry when I recall the punchline from a very old joke.

Yes doctor, the operation was a huge success – unfortunately the patient died!

But enough of retrospection, there was still football to be played. Three games left; three games to win a championship.

Rangers 4, Hearts 0 – two games away from the title.

Rangers 2, Dundee United 0 – one game away from the title.

Normally the subway loyal slip away early from the match, generally from the eighty-minute mark, but tonight the old stadium was still packed to the rafters on the final whistle, and rightly so. This was Walter Smith's final game at Ibrox, and everyone wanted to salute a genuine legend. Ten league titles, six league cups and five Scottish cups wasn't a bad haul, but more importantly Walter Smith had been the cement that had held Rangers together in these financially troubled times, and for that alone, every Blue Nose should be eternally grateful.

The emotional evening had one unexpected bonus. Way back in 1994, Deacon Blue's song 'Dignity' had been lost to me, celebrating Dundee United fans at Hampden had tainted the tune, seemingly for ever more. The Ibrox tannoy that evening changed all that, the old song was blasted out, this time in tribute to the Rangers manager. In an instant, 'Dignity' had been reclaimed; it was Walter Smith's song now.

One game to go, we were one game away from the title. Could we do it? A blitzkrieg start in Ayrshire provided the answer; a resounding yes – Rangers were three goals up inside seven minutes. No helicopter would be required this year – there was time to deliver the trophy by bicycle!

The professionals season may have been over, but that didn't signal the end of the football year, far from it. I was still involved in the West Lothian Youth football scene, and still with Uphall Diamonds, concentrating now on a team I'd formed from our Soccer School way back in 2006. This team, the Diamonds '98, had progressed well and worked their way though Soccer Sevens, from the lowest league at Under 9s, to the top division at Under 12s. In season 2010/2011 they made the big step up to eleven a side football, playing in the West Lothian Under 13s First Division.

In a difficult year, we won some and lost some, though in truth it was more like we won a few and lost a lot! Bottom of the table for a spell, the young Diamonds battled, scrapped, and hauled themselves out of the relegation zone – a great effort. Our season ended with the chance of a trophy, the Presidents' Cup, a competition for the bottom four teams in the league. Okay, it was a consolation cup, but we still wanted to win it, and to do that we had to overcome Pumpherston United.

It was a horrible evening for football with a howling wind blowing down the pitch, a game where you really wanted to win the toss and take advantage of the conditions. We lost the toss, and quickly found ourselves three goals down. Undaunted, the Diamonds fought back in the second half, 3–1, 3–2 and then 3–3. The Pumpherston keeper made a magnificent save to keep the scores level, a shot was cleared off the line, the keeper made another great save. There looked to be only one winner, then disaster. The visitors broke free and delivered the classic sucker punch, scoring with their only shot of the second half.

Down but not out the young Diamonds rolled their sleeves up and pounded Pumpherston. The keeper made another sensational save, another shot was cleared off the line, and then in the final minutes a shot crashed off the inside of the post. It just wasn't our day, and the final whistle sounded to end our dreams.

There were tears. My players were devastated, yet still had the courage to pick themselves up and shake the hands of their victorious opponents. I was immensely proud of my little team that evening, and I'll tell you what – at that moment I'd have swapped the SPL title for the Presidents' Cup, and I really mean that! What I saw that evening was a group of boys with real commitment and passion for football, players with a desire and love of the game. With youngsters like this, the future of Scottish football is undoubtedly safe.

I was in the twilight of my football journey. For these lads, it was just the beginning. Hopefully they'll all be successful in the game – good grief, even if they turn out for Celtic!

But back to the Rangers, what did the future hold for them? At present, little is really known of Craig Whyte's plans and aspirations. We can only give him time, and hope he guides the club to football success and calmer financial waters. But so much depends on the outcome of that HMRC investigation. It's the great unknown. I like to think Rangers will win the tax case, go from strength to strength and eventually parade the Champions League trophy round Glasgow on an open-topped bus, and whilst part of that dream is somewhat unlikely – we can always hope!

But what of the other side of the coin, what if Rangers lose the tax case and are hit with unpayable penalties? What if the unthinkable happens and the club is liquidated? Well, I'll take a ball down to Fleshers Haugh on Glasgow Green, put some jumpers down for goalposts and invoke the memory of Moses and Peter McNeil, Peter Campbell and William

McBeath, those gallant pioneers who founded my football club.

And I'll tell you what. If that dreadful day ever happens, I'll bet I'm not alone!

I'm Rangers 'til I die,
I'm Rangers 'til I die,
I know I am.
I'm sure I am,
I'm Rangers 'til I die.